THE PRIME MOVERS

Traits of the Great Wealth Creators

EDWIN A. LOCKE

AMACOM

American Management Association

New York • Atlanta • Boston • Chicago • Kansas City • San Francisco • Washington, D. C.
Brussels • Mexico City • Tokyo • Toronto

Special discounts on bulk quantities of AMACOM books are available to corporations, professional associations, and other organizations. For details, contact Special Sales Department, AMACOM, a division of American Management Association, 1601 Broadway, New York, NY 10019.
Tel.: 212-903-8316. Fax: 212-903-8083.
Web site: www.amanet.org

This publication is designed to provide accurate and authoritative information in regard to the subject matter covered. It is sold with the understanding that the publisher is not engaged in rendering legal, accounting, or other professional service. If legal advice or other expert assistance is required, the services of a competent professional person should be sought.

Library of Congress Cataloging-in-Publication Data

Locke, Edwin A.
    The prime movers : traits of the great wealth creators / Edwin A. Locke.
      p. cm.
    Includes bibliographical references (p.) and index.
    ISBN 0-8144-0570-3
    1. Entrepreneurship—Psychological aspects. 2. Success in business—Psychological aspects. I. Title.
    HB615.L63   2000
    338'.04—dc21   99–089272

Printing number

10 9 8 7 6 5 4 3 2 1

BK
$20.12

Contents

Foreword

Over the last 250 years, the quality of life throughout the world has been transformed. Life expectancy has increased from nineteen years in 1750 to seventy years today, and practically everyone today lives better than a king in the 1700s. There has been more progress during this period than in the preceding 25,000 years.

What kind of environment has made this incredible progress possible? Dr. Edwin A. Locke's answer is one based on reason, individual rights, and free markets.

Who made this great leap in productivity possible? Dr. Locke is unequivocally clear that productive geniuses from Thomas Edison to Bill Gates are the Prime Movers of human progress. While these men amassed great fortunes, they raised the standard of living for all of us. Tragically, despite their enormous contributions to human well being, they have been unjustly branded as "robber barons" and "greedy capitalists."

What characteristics enabled these men to make such a significant contribution? These great creators have the capacity to see the big picture trends others cannot foresee: vision. They have active and independent minds with an undying commitment to action, the capacity to make rational decisions based on the facts, the ability to judge ability in others, and the willingness to reward superior contributions by others. These attributes produce a level of confidence and competence that leads to success.

Dr. Locke's view is radically different from the common belief that progress more or less happens automatically or is the result of some undefined collective effort. Dr. Locke sees a relatively small number of outstanding individuals who make a disproportionate contribution to human well-being.

My experience as a banker and CEO of a successful S&P 500 company supports this conclusion. Over the years, I have learned from making loans to many types of businesses that when a company fails, it is practically never true that the average employee of the failed company is intrinsically less competent than the average employee of a successful company. It is almost always true that the reason for failure is poor leadership at the top of the organization. Sometimes, unknowable and uncontrollable economic factors cause companies to fail, but 90 percent of the time, the failure is the result of irrational decisions made by the leaders. Success is the flip side of failure in this context. Occasionally people get lucky, but 90 percent of the time, successful companies are created by powerful leaders.

I have often seen mediocre-performing operations transformed into high-performing units by changing leadership. While it is true that to be successful in the long term, a business must have excellent performance from all its employees, exceptional leaders have the capacity to enable others to achieve more. Oftentimes, this change in performance is created simply (but profoundly) by being sure that everyone is headed in the right direction.

It is interesting to reflect on the implications of Dr. Locke's thesis. If Dr. Locke is correct, we owe a huge debt to these Prime Movers, and we have a moral obligation to recognize that debt. The term "robber barons" should be driven from our vocabulary.

If the characteristics that Dr. Locke discusses have contributed to these individuals' success, we should teach these attributes to our children. Clearly, the foundation attribute is an unwavering commitment to make independent, rational decisions based on the facts—which is the ultimate form of honesty.

We must avoid the temptation to use government to put "balls and chains" on great people. "Balls and chains" are created by excessive taxation and mind-numbing government rules and regulations.

Every person alive today has a far better quality of life thanks to Thomas Edison. Edison's list of life-enhancing inventions is incredible, including the invention of the research laboratory itself. When we put "balls and chains" on great people like Thomas Edison (or Bill Gates), we reduce the quality of life for the rest of us.

The same concept can be applied to industries. There have been gigantic leaps in productivity in the financial services, telecommunications, and transportation industries as these businesses have been deregulated. What industry is making the greatest progress? Technology. What industry is the least regulated? Technology. Government interference in free markets inevitably reduces productivity.

It is interesting that (so-called) "intellectuals" on our college campuses still defend communism and socialism even after the unbelievable human misery created by communist governments has been exposed. They use the "robber barons" myth as an example of the evil of socialism's alternative: capitalism. These "intellectuals" say that communism is good in principle, but difficult to practice because human nature is flawed. The "flaw" is that people tend to do what they are rewarded to do. They believe that people should be self-sacrificial. They must also believe that Mother Nature herself is flawed or they fail to recognize an immutable fact of nature, which is that everything that is alive must act in its self-interest or die. A lion must hunt or starve. A deer must run from the hunter or be eaten. Man must obtain food or perish. Our choice is to act in our self-interest or die (or barely survive in abject poverty, e.g., North Korea).

The underlining ethics of communism is: From each according to his ability, to each according to his need. In other words, the more incompetent and less productive you are (i.e., the more needy), the more you receive. The more competent and productive you are, the harder you get to work. No wonder there are many needy people in such a system, and not many producers.

The morality of capitalism is exactly the opposite: From each according to his ability; to each according to his productivity. The more you produce, the more you receive. This is justice. No wonder there are many productive people in a capitalist system, and a higher standard of living for everybody.

Capitalism is the system that allows Prime Movers to make their *maximum* contribution. It provides the innovators and creators the freedom they need to use their independent judgment, often to do things that the crowd cannot see or understand. Prime Movers are the driving force of human progress, making our lives longer and happier.

—John Allison, CEO, BB&T, Inc.

Preface

The process of wealth creation has long been of interest to economists, historians, philosophers, and statesmen. However, their focus has been on the conditions such as geography, demographics, traditions, laws, ideas, etc., that make possible or facilitate wealth creation. Although many factors set the stage for the creation of wealth (especially economic freedom), in the end, the wealth has to be created by the specific actions of specific individuals—and some are much better at it than others. I call those who are very good at wealth creation "Prime Movers," borrowing a term used by Ayn Rand in *The Fountainhead* to characterize great creators, and also used by Aristotle in a different context.

My fascination with prime movers was first kindled by Ayn Rand's epic novel *Atlas Shrugged* (rated in a Library of Congress survey to be second only to the *Bible* in its influence on people's lives), in which she showed businessmen to be heroic and moral achievers without whom the whole world would collapse into stagnation and poverty.

Some years ago, I started teaching an MBA elective on "Business Heroes." My own research on wealth creators began with late nineteenth and early twentieth century heroes (who were falsely labeled as "robber barons") such as Andrew Carnegie, Pierre DuPont, Henry Ford, James J. Hill, J. P. Morgan, John D. Rockefeller, and Thomas J. Watson, Sr. I continued my research through the rest of the twentieth century, and my MBA students studied many dozens more. It became clear very early on that these wealth creators, despite many nonessential differences, had a great deal in common. Every time I taught the class, we would make up lists of traits (usually about twenty) based on our reading, and then, through combining similar ones, we would reduce them to a core list of about ten or twelve. For this book, through further integration, I have cut the list to seven (although some are combinations).

Many inspiring books have been written about great businessmen and -women, but these have virtually always focused on one person at a time. After reading any such book, one cannot readily conclude whether the wealth creator was simply idiosyncratic or whether he or she shared important traits in common with other wealth creators. In other words, what was needed was integration. One book, *Profiles of Genius* by Gene Landrum, focused on multiple wealth creators, but even these were discussed one at a time. Although he attempted to identify some core traits, I consider many of these to be nonessential (e.g., being first born, being slow learners as children, being charismatic). I also believe that many essential traits (e.g., egoism, virtue) were omitted.

I concluded that a book was needed that focused primarily on traits rather than on people. To be more precise, I organized the book around traits, using specific people as examples in each case. I identified the traits through induction. The traits are based on the study of more than seventy wealth creators.

This book is directed, first, to anyone who wants to become a wealth creator. Not everyone can do it, and not everyone should try. If you want to try it, see if you have "the right stuff." Second, it is directed to venture capitalists who want to know with whom to invest their money. They like to focus on how good the business plans are, but maybe they should focus equally on the characteristics of the person who made the plans. Third, the book is directed to search firms and companies who are looking in the upper, middle, and lower ranks for future leaders. Fourth, it is directed to business students who want to know what kind of people create wealth. Fifth, it is directed to Prime Movers themselves; I hope this book will help them see their own value. And finally, it is directed to anyone who loves heroes. As I demonstrate, great wealth creators are not low-level "grubby materialists," but men of intelligence, vision, morality, and passion. They are the men who move the world; they are Prime Movers.

I am indebted to a number of people who helped make this a better book. I want to acknowledge first and foremost Dr. Gary Hull, whose detailed and penetrating editorial comments improved every chapter of the book. Of course, I take ultimate responsibility for the final decisions made with respect to content.

I also want to thank Dr. Rajshree Agarwal of the University of Central Florida for her very able economic research, and Donna Montrezza for her outstanding job of copyediting.

Finally, I owe a major debt to the many able Maryland MBA students whose research projects in my "Business Heroes" class provided a considerable amount of material for the book. The students whose research I used were: Clifford Barney, Greg Blough, Kent Churchill, Salvatore DiPaola, Todd Fine, Lawrence Ford, Christopher Gleason, Candida Kirkpatrick, Jonda Langford, Tara Long, Jo Ann Loos, Frederick Martin, Robert McKinnon, Margaret Naab, Alexander Novak, Elvis Pellumbi, Kathleen Pruette, Gary Richardson, Michael Ross, Patrick Seburn, Michael Stadler, Mark Stavrou, Richard Ste. Marie, Don Tannenbaum, Debra Vanderhoven, and Eve Zimmerman.

It should be noted that there are many great wealth creators who are not mentioned in this book. This is because: (a) I have not studied all of them, and (b) only so much material can be included in one book. The failure to be mentioned does not imply a deliberate lack of recognition.

—Edwin A. Locke,
College Park, Maryland,
August 1999

1

The Creation of Wealth

If then everything that is in motion is moved by something, and the [prime] mover is moved but not by anything else, it must be moved by itself.[1]

—Aristotle

In the latter part of the nineteenth century, wealth was created in the United States of America at a rate rarely surpassed in world history. In a little over half a century, the country evolved from an agrarian society of small farmers into the world's leading industrial power. The growth rate for each ten-year period from 1879 to 1988 is shown in Figure 1-1. From 1879 to 1898, the U.S. growth rate exceeded that of Japan, Germany, the United Kingdom, France, Italy, and Canada. This country has retained its position of economic leadership through the end of the twentieth century (but note the steady decline in growth rate since the turn of the century, paralleling the relentless increase in government controls). What made such an achievement possible?

Reason

Most fundamentally, the cause of this wealth creation was philosophical. The United States was the country of the Enlightenment[2]; the eighteenth century, the period of the Enlightenment, made the nineteenth century possible. The Enlightenment represented the culmination of more than twenty centuries of Western thought. The core idea of the Enlightenment was the belief that

Figure 1-1. Average annual growth rate (U.S.: 1879–1988).

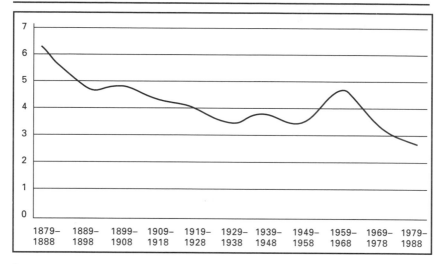

Data:

Decade	Average Annual Growth Rate
1879–1888	6.3%
1889–1898	4.9%
1899–1908	4.8%
1909–1918	4.4%
1919–1928	3.9%
1929–1938	3.4%
1939–1948	3.7%
1949–1958	3.6%
1959–1968	4.6%
1969–1978	3.2%
1979–1988	2.7%

Source: For 1869–1958 data on Gross National Product: *Historical Statistics of the United States,* U.S. Department of Commerce, Bureau of the Census.
For 1959–1988 data on Gross National Product: *Survey of Current Business,* August 1996, U.S. Department of Commerce, Bureau of Economic Analysis.

reason (using the material provided by the senses) was efficacious—that by using it, man could understand the universe. The triumph of reason was the culmination of a terrible struggle. The original spark was Greek philosophy; it was the Greeks, especially Aristotle, who (philosophically) discovered reason and identified its nature. The spark was nearly extinguished by the medieval assault on reason in the name of faith but was rekindled by St. Thomas Aquinas, who helped rediscover Aristotle and paved the way for the Renaissance. Gradually, the dominance of faith, superstition, tradition, revelation, and dogma was supplanted by confidence in the power of man's rational faculties. In America, "For the first time in modern history, an authentic respect for reason became the hallmark of an entire culture."[3]

The development of modern science was one practical outcome—as well as a further cause—of the Enlightenment outlook. Isaac Newton, for example, demonstrated that through induction man could grasp the most basic laws of nature. With the aid of observation and mathematics, one could understand gravitational force, planetary motion, acceleration, and even the nature of light. Thanks to Renaissance and post-Renaissance scientists such as Bacon, Galileo, Kepler, and Newton, progress in every field of science accelerated. Now that nature could be grasped by the human mind, divine revelation was no longer relevant.

Rights

The political expression of the Enlightenment was the discovery of the concept of individual rights. Philosopher John Locke, the leading advocate of rights, demonstrated for the first time that men do not exist to serve governments, but rather governments exist to serve men. Rights limited the power of government; the individual, not the government, was sovereign. Rights protected man's choice to think and to act using his own rational judgment; this concept freed him for the first time from the tyranny of other men. The concept of rights declared that individuals were ends in themselves and could pursue life, liberty, property, and personal happiness without anyone's permission.

Technology

The earliest economic consequence of the Enlightenment was the Industrial Revolution and modern capitalism. With reason as his guide, modern science as his tool, and rights as his protection, man was free to discover and implement new technology:

The steam engine began to replace muscle power; iron and steel superseded wood; textile factories supplanted home weaving; the cotton gin and the reaper displaced field labor; railroads replaced oxcarts; automobiles supplanted the horse and buggy; and electric lights took the place of candles. At last, after millennia of struggle, man was acquiring the power to master his environment. Just as the concept of rights had begun to free him from the vicissitudes of other men, so technology had begun to free him from the vicissitudes of nature.

Thanks to technology (including mass production) and property rights, by the late nineteenth century, wealth—the production of material goods—could be created on a scale undreamed of in the history of the world. Men were free not only to build but also to keep the profits of their efforts, which served as an inducement to invest further, which in turn allowed more wealth to be created. Each discovery created more wealth; each infusion of wealth allowed more investment.

For the first time, people began to understand what making money really meant. To quote Ayn Rand:

> If you ask me to name the proudest distinction of Americans, I would choose—because it contains all the others—the fact that they were the people who created the phrase "to make money." No other language or nation had ever used these words before; men had always thought of wealth as a static quantity—to be seized, begged, inherited, shared, looted or obtained as a favor. Americans were the first to understand that wealth has to be created.[4]

The Relationship between Freedom and Wealth

It is not an original observation to claim that freedom is a precondition of wealth creation. Everyone seems to understand it—except for some modern economists who claim not to know what causes material progress.[5] The latter's attitude is very puzzling. In broad terms, the relationship between freedom and wealth is virtually self-evident and needs no statistical validation. How many prosperous socialist countries (that is, countries in which the government owns all property and totally manages the economy) exist in the world? None. How many have ever existed? None. Socialism is not a method of production at all but a method of enslavement, a method of forcibly crushing the mind's ability to function. The only results socialism has ever achieved and ever will achieve are mass poverty and stagnation.

Perhaps what actually puzzles economists is that among those countries that allow some freedom accompanied by some controls (that is, all mixed economies), they cannot predict which particular Rube-Goldberg conglomeration of taxes, regulations, subsidies, favors, and prohibitions is better than which other Rube-Goldberg conglomeration. Is an income tax rate of 28 percent plus 150,000 regulations of types A and B better than a 38 percent tax rate plus 137,500 regulations of types C and D or a tax rate of 48 percent and 106,000 regulations of types E and F? Since each regulation has repercussions way beyond its intent and every market distortion in one sphere causes distortions in other spheres, it is doubtful if any supercomputer could figure out which mixed economy contraption is best over the long term. It is enough to say that the higher the tax rate, the greater the government's share of the gross domestic product (GDP), and the greater the number and severity of regulations, the more the rate of growth is slowed.[6] Steve Forbes has noted, quite correctly, that economic growth also requires sound money (which means no government-caused inflation) and a firm recognition of property rights.[7] Any country that abolished the income tax and all economic controls, practiced sound money, and consistently protected property rights would become so wealthy that even modern economists would be able to figure out the cause-and-effect relationship involved.

Economic and Political Freedom

Much confusion has been generated over the issue of economic versus political freedom. On the one hand, it is clear that without economic freedom there can be no political freedom. If the state owns or totally regulates the means of production, then every wage earner is its slave. Those who speak out against the regime or opt for a competing political party are easily bankrupted or forced into starvation.

On the other hand, what about economic freedom without political freedom, as in modern-day countries such as Singapore, Indonesia, or China? Of course, these countries allow only limited economic freedom; businesspeople in these countries operate by permission, not by right; the permission can be withdrawn at any time. Furthermore, private business may have to compete with subsidized state enterprises and use bribes and political connections to function on a daily basis; they may also have restricted access to capital markets. Nevertheless, even half-baked capitalism promotes far more wealth creation than would be possible under socialism.

Politically, this makes for a potentially explosive situation for dictators. By allowing wealth creation, they raise hopes and get people used to a higher standard of living. The greater the wealth creation, the more dangerous it becomes for the leaders to crack down on the aspiring capitalists. And if they try to manage the economy, such as by deciding which businesses should be encouraged, they will inevitably make wrong decisions. Dictators do not make good capitalists.

At the same time, the more freedom dictators allow, the more freedom people will demand. The rational mind does not function under coercion. When some people are allowed to function freely, others will demand the same privilege. And it does not take long for people to extend their desire for freedom from the economic into the political realm (e.g., if we can choose how to invest, why can't we choose our leaders, too?). Thus, any country that allows economic freedom without political freedom is in a state of politically unstable equilibrium. Eventually, either political freedom has to evolve or economic freedom has to be curtailed.

Of course, there are no countries today with full economic and political freedom. The universal pattern, outside the socialist bloc, is the mixed economy. Most mixed economies have a relatively high degree of political freedom but only partial economic freedom. This, too, is an unstable situation. The typical pattern is for controls to breed more controls until the economy stagnates; then there is a swing to the right (freedom), only to be followed by a swing to the left (controls). The cause of this pendulum pattern is a conflict between two moral philosophies: egoism and altruism.[8]

Prime Movers

A respect for reason, scientific knowledge, and economic freedom are essential prerequisites for the creation of wealth but are not sufficient. Freedom does not create wealth automatically. It would be neo-Marxist thinking to assume that cultural and social circumstances (that is, the environment) condition people to engage in a process of production; the environment simply sets the stage for it. The stage metaphor is an apt one. You can build the theater, train the actors, buy the costumes, and sell the tickets, but there is no show until someone writes and produces the play.

For wealth to be created, individuals must create it, and they must do it by choice. Thinking is done by choice, and action is done by choice, based on one's thinking. History shows very clearly that some people are much better at the process of wealth creation than others. I will use the term *Prime Movers* to refer to those businessmen (until the late twentieth century, they were virtually all men) who moved society forward by the force of their own creative imagination, their own energy, and their own productive capacity. There are, of course, degrees of any human trait. A small shopkeeper is a Mover—a creator of wealth—on a small scale. In this book, however, I will focus on those who created wealth on a large scale. (All Prime Movers were not entrepreneurs; many grew existing businesses.) I will reserve the term *Prime Mover* for them. Many people I mention in this book have created a billion dollars or more of wealth.

Prime Movers are a rare commodity in any culture, even in a free economy. This is one reason why they are able to earn so much money—they stand out markedly from the rest. Even among small businesses, only 3 percent of them do most of the growing.[9] The number of small businesses that grow to be dominant is minuscule. It takes a remarkable person to achieve and sustain large-scale, long-term growth.

Throughout recent history (since the beginning of modern capitalism), Prime Movers have been denounced, caricatured, belittled, smeared, and denied in every possible way. For example, it is argued that they were lucky because there was a brief window of opportunity, and they happened to be there in time to step through it. It is never explained why hundreds of thousands of other people who were at the same place at the same time failed to step through the same window. As one intelligent business writer put it, "There is no such thing as an accidental billionaire."[10]

It is claimed, by Matthew Josephson and others, that great wealth creators did not earn their money but in some way stole it—they were not creators but "robber barons." For example, read what one minister said about John D. Rockefeller, upon being told that the oil magnate (who was quite religious) had donated $100,000 to the Board of Foreign Missions:

> Is this clean money? Can any man, can any institution, knowing its origins, touch it without being defiled? [This money was accumulated] by methods as heartless, as cynically iniquitous as any that were employed by the Roman plunderers or robber barons of the Dark Ages. In the cool brutality with which properties are wrecked, securities destroyed, and people by the hundreds robbed of their little, all to build up the fortunes of the multi-millionaires, we have an appalling revelation of the kind of monster that a human being may become.[11]

Rockefeller's sin? It was being the most efficient refiner, transporter, and marketer of oil in the United States and, in the process, making the United States a world power in the oil business. Like any successful capitalist, he put less efficient producers out of business and ended up dominating the industry. In other words, he earned the money—and the Board of Foreign Missions kept the donation!

Other Prime Movers have been attacked because they did

not personally invent the products that made them rich. For example, Steve Jobs, it is claimed, did not deserve what he made because Steve Wozniak and others actually did the key technical work on the first Apple PC. What the critics miss is the fact that Jobs saw the value of the PC when no one else did and carried the project through to fruition when no one else thought it could be done or that it was worth doing. This is why he got rich, and deservedly so.

The Marxists deny the value of all work except physical labor, making all Prime Movers exploiters by definition. But what Marx and his followers (who today exist mainly in the United States and Cuba) evade is the fact that wealth at its deepest root is the product not of physical labor but of intelligence, of creative vision. Action is required to actualize the vision, but physical labor not guided by human intelligence is virtually worthless. For proof, look at countries where physical labor is nearly all there is (e.g., China before semi-capitalism). How much wealth does an unexploited manual laborer (or a billion of them) produce?

Another common means of disparaging Prime Movers is to accuse them of being "materialistic," in order words, spiritually flawed. This criticism is usually made by religionists whose views derive from the philosophy of Plato. Plato asserted that there were two parts to man's soul: the higher rational part and the lower irrational part. Moneymaking was, to Plato, a product of the lower soul. In this view, wealth creators are a lower type of person—greedy, money-grubbing, lizard-like, soulless, and unethical.

What this book will demonstrate, however, is that *earning money* (as contrasted to taking or stealing money or getting it through government favors or handouts) *is a spiritual achievement*. By *spiritual*, I mean that money is earned through virtue—the cardinal virtue being the relentless use of one's rational faculty. Moneymaking does require action in the material world, but it has to be action guided by thought. Man's mind is his basic means of survival, which means it is his means of creating the conditions, including the goods and services, on which his survival depends.

Those who begrudgingly admit that there were some great

wealth creators in the past sneer that the day of the great leaders or the dominant individualists is now over and that, today, wealth is created by participative groups. To "prove" their point, they use the following straw man argument: If the individual were really important, he would create the wealth all by himself; however, since business leaders have to depend on others, the leader's role is not that important. This is a dangerously wrong-headed view, as well as a non sequitur. The leader needs to select the followers and make sure they work together toward a common vision. There has to be someone, a single mind, to set the course of a company. Companies can glide along on the energy and vision of a past leader using group consensus, but only for a while. In the end, there can be no great companies without great leaders. This has always been true and will always be true.

Some leadership gurus disparage the importance of Prime Movers by claiming that such people cannot produce enduring greatness, since at some point they must retire. Rather, they claim, enduring greatness is ensured by the company's culture and core purpose as well as by the mechanisms that support them. I disagree. *To ensure enduring greatness, companies need a succession of great leaders.* Tom Watson, Jr., set up a great culture, a clear core purpose, and many key mechanisms at IBM, but the leaders who followed him (until Lou Gerstner) were not of his caliber, and the vaunted IBM culture was completely unable to cope with the radical changes in technology that occurred in the 1980s. What IBM needed in the 1980s, and never got during that period, was a new Prime Mover! Compare Coca-Cola, which got two great leaders (Woodruff and Goizueta) in a row.

It is often claimed that the reason that Prime Movers have been viewed with suspicion at best and hatred at worst is envy—envy felt by the nonproducers or small producers toward the big producers. Such envy is the egalitarian protest against the alleged metaphysical unfairness of the existence of individual differences in ability and achievement and the resulting rewards. As one rabid college professor I knew put it to me, "No one has a right to a house unless everyone has one." Metaphysical differences between people are not unfair; they just are. The concept of fairness does not apply to genes any more than it applies to the weather; genes are simply a fact of life. Moral principles apply only to actions about which one has a choice. Fairness only applies to how people evaluate and treat each other.

Envy, the desire for and resentment of things of value created by others, is not an entirely corrupt emotion. At least the envious person values what the other person has: Mr. A has X, and I would really like to have it, too. However, the desire for another person's creations is not the most fundamental motive behind the pervasive assaults on Prime Movers. The most basic motive—which is always hidden under plausible-sounding rationalizations (such as those mentioned above)—is much worse. It is "hatred of the good for being the good"[12]—it is hatred of the Prime Movers because they are intelligent, successful, and competent, because they are better at what they do than others are. The ultimate goal of the haters of the good is not to bring others up to the level of the most able (which is impossible) but to bring down the able to the level of the less able—to obliterate their achievement, to destroy their reward, to make them unable to function above the level of mediocrity, to punish them, and, above all, to make them feel unearned guilt for their own virtues.

To a considerable extent, the haters of the good have been successful in furthering their viewpoint. In the nineteenth century, great wealth creators were damned as sinners by the clergy; later (as now) they were stopped, slowed, or penalized by antitrust laws, taxes, and regulations. Always they were vilified by the press. But above all, they were damned by everyone for the greatest sin of all: the sin of egoism, that is, the sin of working for their own selfish interest. Against this charge, the Prime Movers have had no defense except the apologetic claim that they were not working for themselves at all but for the public interest. It is true that if that catch phrase has any rational meaning at all, the public was better off as a result of the actions of wealth creators. But this was not their prime motive; they knew it and everyone else knew it, too. Their prime motive was that they loved doing it—for their own selfish pleasure.

Until the publication of Ayn Rand's epic novel *Atlas Shrugged* in 1957, no one had ever provided a full philosophical defense of egoism as a moral ideal. To quote from Galt's speech:

I have called out on strike the kind of martyrs who had never deserted you before. I have given them the weapon they had lacked: the knowledge of their own moral value. I have taught them that the world is ours, whenever we choose to claim it, by virtue and grace of the fact that ours is the Morality of Life. They, the great victims who had produced all of the wonders of humanity's brief summer, they, the industrialists, the conquerors of matter, had not discovered the nature of their right. They had known that theirs was the power. I taught them that theirs was the glory.[13]

Now, there is no need to find a way to defend Prime Movers on moral grounds. This has already been accomplished (although it is true—and sad—that most modern businesspeople have not taken advantage of the priceless philosophical gift they have been given in *Atlas Shrugged*). What is needed now is to identify the qualities or traits that made their great achievements possible.

When I talk about traits, I do not necessarily refer to the Prime Movers' consciously espoused philosophy of life. People's conscious philosophies are typically a mass of contradictions and random ideas and are often quite different from (and even contradictory to) the premises that regulate their everyday actions. Most Prime Movers did not and do not have consistently rational convictions about every subject. On subjects outside the realm of their own business activities, they tend to be no more rational than anyone else. Henry Ford, for example, was an automotive genius, but he was also totally ignorant of history and virulently anti-Semitic (and at the same time had many Jewish employees). J. P. Morgan was anti-Semitic and a social snob. Andrew Carnegie was a naïve follower of intellectual fashions. George Soros's attempts at philosophy have been soundly trashed by numerous commentators. Only a few, such as T. J. Rodgers of Cypress Semiconductor, are philosophically rational and consistent. However, in this book I will focus only on the business achievements of Prime Movers and what made those achievements possible. Thus, I am deliberately not dealing with the whole person but with only those attributes that caused wealth creation.

Another point that must be made clear about Prime Movers is that their great achievements in business were not always accompanied by excellence or happiness in their personal (i.e., family) lives. Some were devoted husbands and fathers; some were very poor at both roles.

I will offer one hypothesis about the latter: It is my strong impression that the worst family men among the Prime Movers (and this may also be true of non–Prime Movers) were those who had very unhappy childhoods (e.g., cruel, tyrannical, or neglectful parents). It is not that one's childhood seals one's fate forever, but when children are deeply hurt, they can develop many wrong conclusions about themselves, other people, and the world (e.g., others are not to be trusted, emotional closeness is inevitably painful, the world is a treacherous place). Great businessmen, being men of action, are characteristically quite unskilled at introspection and, being men of great strength in dealing with the outside world, are not willing candidates for psychological counseling. Thus, they are rarely able to identify or change the wrong premises they acquired as children.

A case in point is the late oil billionaire John Paul Getty. His mother had been traumatized by the previous loss of a daughter and Getty's own serious illness, and she was both overprotective and cold. His father was cold, stern, and puritanical. Getty revolted against the moral puritanism but retained his parents' cold indifference toward other people. He became a lifelong womanizer and treated his various wives and children as if they did not exist.

J. P. Morgan's case is a bit different and resembles in certain respects a tragic grand opera. His childhood was not particularly happy, though much better than Getty's. His father was stern and demanding, and Morgan suffered from constant illnesses and an embarrassing skin problem. At age 24, he fell passionately in love with Amelia Sturges, who was already dying of tuberculosis. At the wedding, he carried the weakened Mimi down the stairs of her parents' house and held her up during the ceremony. She died four months later. Excepting the lack of poverty, in spirit it was a scene right out of Puccini's *La Bohème,* even down to the bride's name. Shattered by this loss, Morgan evidently never had a close romantic relationship again. His second marriage was unhappy, and he had a string of mistresses.

Let me make it clear that I am not going to assert, as some self-proclaimed experts in psychology or psychiatry do, that all great business achievements are compensations for feelings of childhood inferiority. I consider this to be a totally absurd explanation of wealth creation. In the first place, millions of people feel inadequate in one way or another as children; in fact, probably most people do to some extent. But only an infinitesimal number of these become great wealth creators. Second, feeling inadequate does not produce wealth. If anything, it would undermine one's ability to take and sustain the grand scale of actions required to start and grow a large business enterprise. Third, some wealth creators, such as Thomas Edison and Michael Milken (whom, as we shall see later, I do not consider a criminal but a victim), had relatively happy childhoods.

I believe that those Prime Movers who had unhappy childhoods made their fortunes not because of but in spite of their difficult early years. Their achievements required the same qualities as were required of the Prime Movers with happy childhoods. It is also worth noting, in this age of victimhood, that those with unhappy home lives did not wallow in self-pity; become alcoholics, drug addicts, or criminals; demand special treatment from the government due to emotional disability; or give up on life. Like Walt Disney, they moved ahead as best they could and did not let their suffering stand in their way. In this respect, they are a good object lesson to the moderns who are urged to weep and demand special treatment as a compensation for every painful emotion they might feel. Furthermore, the sternness of many of their parents (which means, in part, that the parents held their child to standards of conduct), while sometimes taken to extremes, would be a healthy antidote to today's culture of emotional indulgence.

It may be asked why those with unhappy childhoods were successful in business but not so successful in their family lives. The reason, I think, is that in business you need an underlying passion to succeed to act as your driver, and reason is paramount as a guide to your actions. However, in family life, although reason is essential for understanding your spouse and raising your children, emotional communication is also critical. This is the sphere in which an unhappy childhood, if the wrong conclusions and premises are not identified and corrected, can be crippling. People with unhappy childhoods often conclude that, in contrast to the world of things, the concept of reason does not apply in the realm of people. People, they decide, are incomprehensible and irrational and are best ignored.

It is not surprising that people who are unable to develop good relationships with others are not usually very much fun to work for, although they may attract some loyal followers through the force of their genius and energy.

The Traits

Making a list of traits pertaining to success in any profession is difficult. The usual procedure is to just make a list, combine it with other people's lists, and publish the total. The problem with this procedure is that the lists become very long—too long to even hold in one's mind. Furthermore, the traits usually show substantial overlap, and no distinction is made between the more and less fundamental ones. Finally, there is no attempt to show why such traits are important.

The list I have formulated was derived from three main sources: my own reading of business history; research done by students in my MBA course, "Business Heroes in Fact and Fiction"; and Ayn Rand's novel, *Atlas Shrugged*. This last one may seem surprising since it is a work of fiction, but my students and I have repeatedly found that real-life Prime Movers possess the same traits as the business heroes portrayed in that novel.

In most classes, we start from scratch and usually accumulate a list of twenty or so traits. By combining similar qualities and dropping those that are less essential, we usually pare the list down to a dozen or so. For the purpose of this book, I have further combined and condensed so that my final list comprises seven traits, although in several cases I have combined some that go together. (At the end, I will briefly note a few less fundamental traits.)

Even though the categories (and traits) are not, in reality, independent since each reinforces the others, I have grouped these traits into four categories:

1. Thinking
   - Independent vision (Chapter 2)
   - Active mind (Chapter 3)
   - Competence and confidence (Chapter 4)

2. Motivation
   - Drive to action (Chapter 5)
   - Egoistic passion (Chapter 6)

3. Attitude Toward Employees
   - Love of ability in others (Chapter 7)

4. Character
   - Virtue (Chapter 8)

These traits will be the subject of the next seven chapters. Chapter 9 is a summary and conclusion.

Some caveats. First, no claim is made that this list of traits is exhaustive. One can always come up with more. I do believe, however, that the list is fundamental. Second, in this book I do not deal with business strategies except as a side issue. If a Prime Mover does not come up with the right strategies, he will not make a profit. Some Prime Movers, such as Henry Ford, used good business strategies early in their careers and poor ones later. I will discuss later why I think this happens. Third, I do not address the issue of specific skills (e.g., how to market, how to finance ventures, how to deal with employee conflict) in this book. Prime Movers either develop such skills because they view them as necessary for their own success or hire other people who have them (e.g., Walt Disney hired his brother Roy to oversee financial matters).

Conclusion

The study of Prime Movers can be useful for two reasons. First, we can learn something about the process of wealth creation by observing them and understanding what made their achievements possible. Second, they can serve as a source of inspiration to all of us, even those of us who are not capable of creating huge amounts of wealth. In Prime Movers, we can see efficacious people at work, people who use their own independent judgment and who—through passion, tenacity, and ability—succeed against all odds.

The Prime Movers discussed in this book are mainly (although not exclusively) white American males who lived after 1850. This is because most Prime Movers have been male and because I am most familiar with the American businessman. However, I consider the traits I will be discussing to be necessary for wealth creation regardless of person, time, or place. The task of large-scale wealth creation is always difficult, and it takes a special type of person to do it successfully.

My analysis does not apply to what Ayn Rand called "Money-Appropriators" and Burton Folsom called "political entrepreneurs"—men who get rich primarily through government favors such as state-sponsored monopolies and handouts. Such men have more in common with politicians than with wealth creators.[14]

Notes

1. Aristotle, *Physics,* bk. 8, in J. Barnes, ed., *The Complete Works of Aristotle,* vol. 1 (Princeton, N.J.: Princeton University Press, 1984, p. 428). Aristotle's conception of the prime (first, unmoved) mover has mystical overtones. I am using his term here to refer to great wealth creators. Although this is not Aristotle's actual meaning, it is consistent in spirit with Aristotle's essentially pro-this-earth philosophy.
2. L. Piekoff, *The Ominous Parallels* (New York: Stein & Day, 1982), Chapter 5.
3. Ibid., p. 102.
4. A. Rand, *Atlas Shrugged* (New York: Signet, 1992), p. 386.
5. B. Wysocki, Jr., "For the Economist, Long Term Prosperity Hangs on Good Ideas," *The Wall Street Journal,* January 21, 1991, pp. 1ff.
6. P. Brimelow, "Freedom Pays," *Forbes,* June 16, 1997, pp. 142–143. See also K. Holmes, B. Johnson, and M. Kirkpatrick, eds., *1997 Index*

of Economic Freedom (Washington, DC: Heritage Foundation, 1997). And J. Gwartney, "Less Government, More Growth." *The Wall Street Journal*, April 10, 1998, p. A-10.

7. S. Forbes, "Fact and Comment," *Forbes*, July 29, 1996, p. 25.

8. See L. Peikoff, op. cit.

9. M. Hopkins, "Help Wanted," *Inc.*, May 20, 1997, pp. 35ff.

10. A. Serwer, "Michael Dell Turns the PC World Inside Out," *Fortune*, September 8, 1997, pp. 76ff.

11. P. Collier and D. Horowitz, *The Rockefellers* (New York: Holt, Rinehart and Winston, 1976), p. 3.

12. A. Rand, "The Age of Envy," in *The New Left: The Anti-Industrial Revolution* (New York: Meridian [Penguin], 1993), pp. 152–186.

13. A. Rand, op. cit., p. 967.

14. A. Rand, "The Money-Making Personality." *The Objectivist Forum*, vol. 4, no. 1, 1983, p. 4. (This article was originally published in *Cosmopolitan* magazine, April 1963.)

2

Independent Vision

The great creators—the thinkers, the artists, the scientists, the inventors—stood alone against the men of their time. . . . Every great new invention was denounced. . . . But the men of unborrowed vision went ahead. They fought, they suffered and they paid. But they won. . . .

Men have been taught that it is a virtue to agree with others. But the creator is the man who disagrees. Men have been taught that it is a virtue to swim with the current. But the creator is the man who goes against the current. Men have been taught that it is a virtue to stand together. But the creator is the man who stands alone. . . .

The creator—denied, opposed, persecuted, exploited—went on, moved forward and carried all humanity along on his energy.[1]

—Howard Roark in *The Fountainhead*

All business, contrary to Marx, is fundamentally about brain power, not muscle power. Physical action powered by human labor is required in order to bring any idea into reality, but without the guidance of the idea, action is just mindless motion without direction, purpose, or value. Thought comes first, action second. The creation of wealth starts with vision.

No concept in the leadership and business literature has been more popular in recent years than that of vision. The term is not really new even in a business context, but its increasingly wide use reveals a growing recognition of its importance. Unfortunately, the more the term is used, the greater is the confusion about what it actually means.

What Is Vision?

James Collins and Jerry Porras treat vision broadly to include the organization's core values, its core purpose (its reason for being), and its envisioned future focused around a long-range goal.[2] While I regard all of the foregoing as important to an organization's success, my view of the essence of vision is somewhat different, although it is closest in meaning to Collins and Porras's third element.

Vision is fundamentally foresight—not foresight focused around what you want to do but rather around what will work in the future. It is seeing the potential of some product or service or technology or market: Henry Ford saw the potential of a low-priced automobile; Bill Gates foresaw the value of computer software; Howard Schultz (Starbucks) saw that people would buy coffee that was made as if it were a type of gourmet cooking; John D. Rockefeller saw the potential of the oil refining industry. John Archbold (later to become president of Standard Oil) said of Rockefeller, "In business we all try to look ahead as far as possible. Some of us think we are pretty able. But Rockefeller always sees a little further ahead than any of us—and then he sees around the corner."[3]

I consider formulating a vision to be the single most important (but by no means the only) task of a business leader. Furthermore, I believe that it has to be fundamentally the work of a single mind. Gulf War Logistics Chief Gus Pagonis agrees: "Vision must be defined by the leader."[4] General Pagonis stresses that the vision must be clear before specific goals are set. Other people (e.g., the top management team, consultants) can be consulted, but in the end there has to be one coherent vision, not a mushy democratic conglomeration of the ideas of scores or hundreds of people reduced to their lowest common denominator. This applies to both Prime Movers and less-than-Prime Movers; the only difference is that the visions of Prime Movers are more original, more audacious, and more ambitious than those of others. Joe Doaks might envision a new door handle for the car while Henry Ford would see a whole new type of car. Bill Smith might picture a local neighborhood store while Sam Walton would foresee a nationwide chain.

Myopic Visions

Seeing ahead (and being right) is a rare quality—and not only in business. Most new ideas, especially radical new ideas, are disparaged by experts (the airplane), mocked by the press (the electric light), belittled by consultants (xerography), ignored by the higher-ups in one's own company (the minivan), and often refused initial funding by most investors (Federal Express).

Consider the following examples of myopic visions[5]:

- "Computers in the future may weigh as little as 1.5 tons." (*Popular Mechanics*, 1949)
- "I think there is a world market for maybe five computers." (IBM, 1943)
- "I have traveled the length and breadth of this country and talked with the best people, and I can assure you that data processing is a fad that won't last out the year." (editor in charge of business books for a major publisher, 1957)
- "But what . . . is it good for?" (IBM engineer commenting on the microchip, 1968)
- "There is no reason anyone would want a computer in their home." (chairman of a major computer company, 1977)
- "This 'telephone' has too many shortcomings to be seriously considered as a means of communication. The device is inherently of no value to us." (Western Union internal memo, 1876. *Note:* Alexander Graham Bell's telephone did have many shortcomings, but a man named Thomas Edison found a way to eliminate them.)
- "The wireless music box [radio] has no imaginable commercial value. Who would pay for a message sent to no-

body in particular?" (David Sarnoff's associates in response to his suggestion for investment in the radio, 1920s)

- "The concept is interesting and well-formed, but in order to earn better than a 'C,' the idea must be feasible." (Yale management professor's evaluation of Fred Smith's paper proposing an overnight delivery service)
- "Who the hell wants to hear actors talk?" (Warner Brothers, 1927)
- "A cookie store is a bad idea. Besides, the market research reports say America likes crispy cookies, not soft and chewy cookies like you make." (expert's response to Debbie Fields's idea for Mrs. Fields Cookies)
- "We don't like their sounds, and guitar music is on the way out." (Decca Recording Co. rejecting the Beatles, 1962)
- "Heavier-than-air flying machines are impossible." (Lord Kelvin, president, Royal Society, 1895)
- "If I had thought about it, I wouldn't have done the experiment. The literature was full of examples that said you couldn't do this." (Spencer Silver on the work that led to Post-It notepads)
- "So we went to Atari [and asked for funding] and they said 'No.' So we went to [another major electronics company] and they said 'Hey, we don't need you. You haven't gotten through college.' " (Steve Jobs on the PC)
- "Professor Goddard does not know the relation between action and reaction and the need to have something better than a vacuum against which to react. He seems to lack the basic knowledge ladled out daily in high schools." (*New York Times* on Robert Goddard's pioneering rocket work, 1921)
- "You want to have consistent and uniform muscle development across all of your muscles? It can't be done." (response to Arthur Jones, developer of Nautilus weight-training equipment)
- "Drill for oil? You mean drill into the ground to try to find oil? You're crazy." (driller's response to Edwin Drake, who drilled the first oil well, 1859)

- "Stocks have reached what looks like a permanently high plateau." (Yale University professor, 1929)
- "Airplanes are interesting toys but are of no military value." (leading French general)
- "Everything that can be invented has been invented." (U.S. commissioner of patents, 1899)
- "Louis Pasteur's theory of germs is ridiculous fiction." (French professor of physiology, 1872)
- "The abdomen, the chest and the brain will forever be shut from the intrusion of the wise and humane surgeon." (surgeon-extraordinary to Queen Victoria, 1873)

It is easy to be smug about quotes like these from our modern perspective, but we should not be too hard on these poor souls. They did not really know any better. It takes a rare genius to see past the status quo, and geniuses in any society are always in short supply. How many of us, even those of us who are experts, can foresee the developments of the next century?

The Danger of Experts

The reason why experts are so often wrong is that what they are expert at is what is already known, what has been discovered in the past. Although it is critical to learn from the past, it is all too easy to go from "that's never been done" to "that can't be done." Consider the example of the airplane in the quote from Lord Kelvin above. It is a fact, based on Newton's laws, that unsupported objects above the ground naturally fall to earth. But the context here is critical: Things fall to earth unless something keeps them up, that is, unless another force counteracts the force of gravity. If Lord Kelvin had considered the full context of the knowledge available to him, he would have considered that birds—which are heavier than air—can stay up in the air, thanks to (1) wings and (2) forward motion. Thus, the two issues for man would be: (1) Can we develop something that works like a bird's wings? (2) Can we invent a means of gaining sufficient forward motion to make the wings work? Kelvin, of course, would have no way of knowing what might be invented or discovered in the future, but it is never valid to claim that something will never be discovered unless that discovery would be a contradiction of the facts of reality. [An example of such a contradiction would be time travel, which is based on the premises that that which happened in the past has not yet happened and that which has not yet happened (the future) has already happened.] Many ideas that superficially appear to be contradictions (e.g., heavier-than-air flying machines) are seen, upon closer inspection, to be things that no one has thought of before or no one has yet figured out how to do. No one can predict what human genius will discover in the future. [This is why, incidentally, doom-preaching environmentalists who scream that we will run out of raw materials (e.g., oil) in the near future always end up looking like fools.]

The suspicion heaped on experts has the same root as the suspicion many entrepreneurs have of higher education. Educators are, one hopes, experts. They teach everything (within the time allowed) that is known or that has been done as well as the best known ways of doing everything. This is very useful knowledge. Thomas Edison was a voracious reader of reports of what other people had discovered. He wanted to save time by not reinventing what had already been invented or repeating mistakes that other people had made. But educators, including MBA instructors, cannot teach what is not known or how to do what has never been done before. This is not a problem so long as such instructors do not discourage creative thinking. It is one thing to teach "Here is what people have done" and quite another to teach "And don't you dare try to do something different." When teachers do the latter, they become millstones around the neck of progress.

Let us consider the same issue in the field of business. No one had built a minivan before Chrysler built it, and no customer had ever asked for one. Hal Sperlich championed the idea at Ford and got fired for it. People who had championed similar ideas at GM and at Chrysler (before Lee Iacocca) had been squashed. Experts might naturally conclude from this that there was no market for such a vehicle. Visionaries like Sperlich and Iacocca, however, knew better. They saw that there was a potential market for a minivan because it fulfilled an unmet and unarticulated, though real, consumer need: the need for the roominess of a small bus with the comfort and handling of a car. Once the minivan began to sell, Iacocca pushed for a second plant to manufacture the vehicle. Everyone opposed him, but he built it anyway.

Similarly, an expert might conclude that we got along just fine for millennia without Xerox copiers, that no one ever asked for such a copier, and that the potential market for such a machine must be very small. A visionary, however, might see that people like to copy things, that the information explosion would vastly increase the need for copying, and that the availability of a copy machine would itself promote new uses.

Henry Ford, in his early years, developed a brilliant antidote to naysaying experts: "Our new operations are always directed by men who have no previous knowledge of the subject and therefore have not had a chance to get on really familiar terms with the impossible."[6]

I do not want to make being visionary sound easier than it is. Plenty of visionary people are wrong in one or more of their predictions—even those who are right on the major issues. Visions must constantly be questioned and checked against reality. Fred Smith, for example, correctly envisioned the widespread use of fax machines, but his particular vision (Zap Mail) came too soon for the market (as they say, timing is everything!), and the form in which he conceived it (faxes sent from a service center) turned out to be off target. This error cost the company hundreds of millions of dollars. But his basic FedEx vision was right on target and made the company billions of dollars.

It is important to recognize that customers can rarely be relied on to identify as yet unarticulated or future needs. Strategy experts Gary Hamel and C. K. Prahalad state: "Customers are notoriously lacking in foresight. Ten or fifteen years ago, how many of us were asking for cellular telephones, fax machines, and copiers at home, twenty-four-hour discount brokerage accounts, multivalve automobile engines, compact disc players, cars with on-board navigation systems?"[7] Prime Movers are able to discover, through their own creative imagination, what customers will want once it is offered.

Visions as Evolutionary

Business visions do not spring full-blown from the head of Minerva. No business leader (or anyone else) is omniscient. It is impossible to predict the future—including future business developments and technological discoveries—with certainty, insofar as they are a result of human choice.

Furthermore, I believe it is critical that business visions not be too ambitious or too all-encompassing at the beginning even if, through imagination, they could be so formulated. A grand vision at the outset will tempt one to move too fast and to not deviate from one's original plan. Thousands of businesses have foundered because the leader could not manage growth, because he or she did not learn enough as the company grew. It is virtually impossible to envision the ultimate end at the beginning. Most Prime Movers took many years (sometimes twenty years or more—though today it can happen much faster) to go from their first success to a billion-dollar enterprise. It is best if ambition manifests itself not through grandiosity but rather through constant learning and constant striving to do better.

Usually business visions begin with one core idea. This core idea Professor Ian C. MacMillan of the Wharton School calls "the entrepreneurial insight." Without this, the aspiring Prime Mover can go nowhere. The core idea or insight is then developed incrementally, with new elements being added as more knowledge and experience are acquired. Consider Rockefeller as a case in point. His first vision was to go into the oil refining business. He foresaw, at age 26, that it had much greater potential for growth than the business (marketing grain) he was in. He had to buy out his grain marketing partner Maurice Clark, who jointly owned a refinery with Rockefeller and a third party. Clark thought he got a great bargain—but then Clark was not a visionary.

Next, Rockefeller saw that by keeping his costs very low, he could outcompete other refineries. As he began to buy up his competitors, he saw that he could use his size to get rebates from the railroads that shipped the oil, giving him a further advantage. Later he got into the marketing and transportation of oil both in the United States and abroad. He fitted the pieces together so well that at one point he controlled 90 percent of the U.S. oil market. He actually made the price of a barrel of oil cheaper than that of a barrel of water. As Archbold said, Rockefeller was always one step ahead of everyone else. Note that Rockefeller did not discover oil, invent refining, discover rebates, or originate the idea of pipelines or international marketing. In the end, what he did was to envision the oil industry and to make the United States a world power in it.

Bill Gates's vision also had to evolve. It started with the value of software as such. Then it encompassed the values of specific operating systems (e.g., Windows) and the integration of software with the Web. Prime Movers who do not update their visions (e.g., Ken Olson, Ray Noorda) can go downhill very fast, especially in today's fast-paced, global economy, but even the old-timers (e.g., Henry Ford) were not immune from the failure to keep facing forward.

Most Prime Movers have one business vision (following early business experience), and they stick with that and modify it throughout their careers. James J. Hill, builder of the Great Northern Railroad, held many jobs before getting into the railroad business. His grand vision was to build a transcontinental system, and he spent the remainder of his life doing it.

A few very restless, creative Prime Movers, however, have pursued several visions in sequence. For Steve Jobs it was Apple first, Next second, and then Pixar. For Wayne Huizenga it was Waste Management, then Blockbuster Entertainment, and then Republic Industries (focused around used-car supercenters). In neither case were all three visions pursued with equal success (although both men are still hard at it), but the motive power represented by their efforts was remarkable and many of their achievements spectacular. Not to be outdone, McCaw Cellular founder Craig McCaw has founded *five* new companies: Nextel, Nextlink, Nextband, Internext, and Teledesic.

Vision Communication

Prime Movers need to communicate their visions to their followers in some form. There are two primary reasons for this:

1. *To ensure a sense of common purpose.* There is nothing so frustrating and unmotivating as a blurred vision. If it is blurred in the minds of employees, this usually means that it is blurred in the mind of the leader, which means it will lead to blurred results (including organizational anarchy). Every organization needs an integrating idea to focus its actions.

2. *To excite followers.* People need to get rewarded with money, of course (an issue I will address in a later chapter), but it is even better when they believe that what they are doing to earn the money is significant, important, and thrilling. This turns willingness into enthusiasm, obedience into initiative, contentment into joy.

Visions are often communicated in words, including brief vision statements or slogans, but ultimately they are expressed in everyday actions. Without the commensurate actions, words are just moving air. There are many very articulate businesspeople around who can mesmerize people with the eloquence of their words, but listeners should be very cautious in appraising these charismatic personalities until they see whether the words are being translated into action—and especially into results. On the other side of the coin, many very successful businesspeople are not good verbal communicators at all (e.g., Craig McCaw) yet still manage to attract passionately loyal followers.

Now let us consider in more detail some specific examples of the independent visions of Prime Movers.

Independent Visions

Ayn Rand writes, "[T]he essential characteristic of the Money-Maker [Prime Mover] is his *independent judgment.* . . . A man of independent judgment is a man of profound self-esteem: he trusts the competence of his own mind. . . . He looks at the world, wondering, 'What can be done?' or 'How can things be improved?' "[8] The visions of Prime Movers are independent visions, but they are not created solely in someone's head— nothing is created that way—but rather from the Prime Movers' firsthand observations of reality, their own integrations of the facts they observe, and their own projections of what might be and ought to be as well as what they learn from others. Craig McCaw's vision of an international communications network using hundreds of satellites, a "celestial Internet," has not yet come to fruition, but the audacious scale of the idea staggers the imagination.[9]

W. Chan Kim and Renée Mauborgne found that companies around the world that showed the highest rate of growth in revenues and profits were companies that engaged in value innovations, that is, innovations that defied conventional approaches (e.g., movie complexes with twenty-five screens, plush seats, unobstructed views, and ample leg room; hotels with clean quiet rooms and few amenities; airlines with first-class services and economy prices).[10]

Visionaries and Their Companies

Airlines

One of the value-innovative companies, Virgin Atlantic Airways, was founded by a rebel, British entrepreneur Richard Branson, who took on an airline hundreds of times larger (British Air), and came away with a lot of its profits.

Branson did not originally conceive of the idea for Virgin Atlantic Airways, but he did see the potential of Randolph Fields's plan. Branson asked his managers for their opinion of the plan, and they were dead set against it. Branson invested in it anyway. He saw value where others saw danger—specifically, he saw the opportunities inherent in the coming airline deregulation in the United States and the United Kingdom. His low-cost, high-service strategy paid off handsomely.

Computers and Electronics

Thomas J. Watson, Jr., was not the first person to see the business potential of electronic computers, but few saw it more clearly. He took an enormous risk by making the decision to totally reorient IBM when it was making record profits from punched-card machines. He was so successful in dominating the market that the government trustbusters, with their usual lack of wisdom, came after him.

When he was developing the personal computer, Steve Jobs was told by a number of eminent scientists and businessmen (including those from Hewlett-Packard, Intel, and IBM) that his product would fail.[11] It was claimed that there was no mass market for the Apple and that it would be used only by hobbyists. Fortunately, Jobs was too independent to listen to the experts and made the Apple anyway.

Bill Gates observed early in his career that computer software was going to become more valuable than hardware, but his vision extended way beyond this. He grasped the potential of MS-DOS and of Windows (both initially developed by other companies) when IBM did not; more fundamentally, he saw the significance of the whole information revolution and its tie to software systems, the Internet, and PCs. He made the choice to forge ahead with Windows, even in the face of delays, cost over-runs, legal problems, technical difficulties, and his own executives' opposition.

Ross Perot, like Gates, saw value in computers other than their hardware. His vision was to sell the services that make the hardware work. Feeling stifled at IBM, he left and started his own company, Electronic Data Systems (EDS), which became the dominant player in the field of computer services. Beginning with a contract with Blue Cross-Blue Shield of Texas, the company expanded so rapidly that Perot became a billionaire.

Michael Dell envisioned the idea of low-cost, high-quality computers marketed directly to customers. His idea was scoffed at by the big boys, and he was dismissed as too young by older and wiser experts when the company lost money. Nobody is dismissing him now that he is worth many billions, has made thousands of stockholders rich, and is approaching number one in the world in market share.

Joseph Liemandt knew that he wanted to start his own company as soon as he got to college. Through painstaking research, he discovered that manufacturing companies had never developed sophisticated software to help them process orders. Using programming approaches that had never been used before in the field of sales configuration, he and his colleagues developed a software program that did the job. His Trilogy Corp. is now worth about $1 billion.[12]

German Prime Movers Hasso Plattner and Dietmar Hopp have made SAP into a global powerhouse with a vision even bigger than Liemandt's. Rather than developing software for a single area, such as manufacturing or sales, they decided to tie every part of a company's operations, including foreign operations, together. The R/3 system has been a stunning success and has propelled sales above the $3 billion mark. (Lately, the company's growth rate has slowed as it struggles to meet new competitive threats.)

Consumer Products

Mary Kay Ash is one of America's greatest female entrepreneurs, but her success did not come easily. She spent many years in the retail business and was often blocked from advancement or promotion because of being a woman. In the course of her work, she came across a skin product that she—but no one else—believed held great promise. Ash decided to open her own cosmetics company, but her second husband died just before the opening. Her lawyer and accountant told her to abandon her plans because there was no way she could succeed on her own. She opened the company anyway. It now has over $1 billion in sales, and she herself is worth more than $300 million. Not bad for a woman who started as a housewife at age 17 and raised three children!

Coca-Cola CEO Robert Woodruff's genius was to see the value of advertising and marketing, both domestically and internationally. He pursued the international market against the express wishes of his own board of directors. He, more than anyone, helped make Coca-Cola a household name.

When Roberto Goizueta took over the helm in 1981, it was widely believed that Coke was a slow-growth industry, which meant that stockholder value could only increase gradually. Goizueta proved the experts wrong. By stressing the importance of return on capital and the cost of debt, by taking more control over the bottlers, by rapidly expanding international sales, by introducing a slew of new products (and quickly recovering from failures like New Coke), by clearly differentiating his products from competing products, and even by (temporarily) entering other businesses, Giozueta jump-started Coke's growth. What he understood better than anyone was the value of Coke's brand name and how it could be used to sell other products. Goizueta created more than $100 billion in stockholder value—clearly one of the greatest achievements in business history.

Phil Knight's first core idea was to sell quality running shoes on the West Coast. When his relationship with a Japanese manufacturer went sour, he started Nike and enlarged his vision exponentially. Nike designed its own high-quality shoes, found its own manufacturers, and went from running shoes to athletic shoes and from the West Coast to the world. Later Knight enlarged the vision further by making heavy use of celebrity endorsements.

Knight's reward for achieving market dominance in the athletic shoe industry and becoming a multimillionaire was to be pilloried by the press for the alleged sin of using sweatshop labor in foreign countries. The critics are careful never to define the term *sweatshop* too precisely, but the implied definition is "pay that is lower than in the United States"—which means that they expect Nike to destroy its competitive advantage and profits by ignoring a basic tenet of economics: Pay close to the market price. (There was evidence that some supervisors were mistreating employees in some foreign plants).

Edwin Land decided that he would develop a camera that would take and develop a picture in seconds. Experts, including camera dealers and experienced photographers, said it was impossible. Wall Street derided him. The problems involved in such an invention seemed insurmountable. He surmounted them in six months and eventually earned a multimillion-dollar fortune.

Before Henry Ford built the Model T, it was generally believed, even by his own partner Alex Malcomson, that automobiles were luxury products that should only be sold at high prices to wealthy people. Ford's vision was different: He foresaw a cheap ($450–$650), reliable car that could dominate the mass market. His first sight of a self-propelled vehicle (a farm wagon with a steam engine and chain drive) thrilled him, and the root of his life vision may have started there. Ford expressed this vision in 1907 as follows:

> I will build a motor car for the great multitude. It will be large enough for the family, but small enough for the individual to run and care for. It will be constructed of the best materials, by the best men to be hired, after the simplest designs that modern engineering can devise. But it will be so low in price that no man making a good salary will be unable to own one.[13]

Over the next nineteen years, the Model T would sell 15 million units and would make Ford Motor Co. (for a while) the number one automobile manufacturer in the world.

Entertainment

Few Prime Movers have been more at home in the world of the imagination than Walt Disney. He and his studio pioneered animation techniques, synchronized sound, Technicolor, feature-length animated films (*Snow White*), many cartoon characters (Mickey Mouse, Donald Duck), and theme parks (Disneyland). He also helped promote color programming on TV. Both *Snow White* and his first Mickey Mouse film, *Steamboat Willie*, were considered even by some of his own colleagues to be foolish, money-losing ventures. His idea for Disneyland aroused such skepticism that he had to start a new company and get his own financing to see it through.

Finance

John Bogle, founder of the Vanguard Group of Mutual Funds, introduced (although he did not in every case invent) many new ideas in the mutual funds business (e.g., mutual fund families, bond funds, no-load funds, market index funds, foreign funds). Bogle pioneered methods of reducing the costs of fund management to consumers that gave these funds a clear competitive advantage in the marketplace and led to Vanguard being repeatedly ranked first among mutual fund families in terms of the value offered investors.

Another Prime Mover in the investment business is Warren Buffett. Buffett persistently ignored experts, conventions, fads, trends, public opinion, and decision-via-consensus when making decisions; instead he used his own judgment to determine the real (objective) value of stocks. Time after time he would buy stocks that everyone else had written off (e.g., Geico, American Express) or whose competitive advantage no one else had seen (e.g., dominant newspapers).

Billionaire Michael Bloomberg's business information empire started with the Bloomberg terminal, which provides reams of information on securities in a very user-friendly manner using the most advanced technology available. Bloomberg did not invent the business computer terminal, but he jumped way past his competitors with respect to quantity, quality, timeliness, and ease of use of information provided. The terminal was the start of what is now a business media empire that encompasses radio, TV, and magazines. Never one to follow the lead of his competitors, Bloomberg is constantly innovating with respect to products, services, and customers.

Michael Milken is the most tragically victimized Prime Mover in U.S. history—a victim of those who hated the good for being good.[14] A financial genius—arguably the greatest financial genius since J. P. Morgan—Milken grasped what no one else in the industry grasped: High-risk or so-called junk bonds (i.e., bonds that were not given investment-grade ratings) had a value that could be calculated and could be sold to investors at a premium. Later these bonds were used to finance hostile takeovers of inefficiently run companies. Milken's vision was to use these bonds to get funding for other companies, such as MCI, McCaw Cellular, Turner Broadcasting, Time Warner, Safeway, Chrysler, Barnes & Noble, and Macy's, that might be shut out from conventional sources of funding and allow them to grow and expand—and through this to restructure the whole U.S. economy.

Milken's company, Drexel Burnham, achieved market dominance, and he and the company got very rich. This led to their downfall: Takeover targets were resentful; tradition-bound bankers were envious; dishonest journalists smelled blood; federal agencies saw the "need" to protect the establishment; ambitious politicians saw a way to get elected (by scapegoating the rich); and fearful conservatives backed away from Milken or became his worst critics. A helpless Milken decided he had no choice but to confess to technical violations (some of which never actually occurred) that had virtually never been crimes until now and was sent to prison where he developed prostate cancer. Robbed of its brain, Drexel Burnham collapsed. Like Phil Knight would do later, Milken committed the sin of being too competent at what he did. It wasn't his soaring vision itself that was unforgivable to his enemies but the fact that he made it come true.

Marketing

Cyrus McCormick, a Prime Mover from an earlier age, fared better. His vision helped win the Civil War as well as make him very wealthy. The evidence suggests that he did not invent the reaper, but he did improve it enough to make it sell. McCormick was a true visionary in marketing. He saw the immense potential of the reaper, given the enormous size of the Midwestern wheat fields and the fact that that grain was normally harvested by hand. He used public demonstrations, competitions with other reapers, and testimonials by farmers who had bought one to call attention to his machine. He also introduced the idea of a money-back guarantee, mass production with standardized parts (though not invented by him), consumer credit, sales commissions, and regional sales agents. By the time of the Civil War, so many reapers were in use in the North that not only could men be released from the fields to fight but enough grain could be harvested to feed its population, including its Army; moreover, enough surplus was produced to export to foreign nations where the North needed credit.

A man with a similar name, Mark McCormack, also showed a visionary flair in the field of marketing, this time in sports. His was the other side of the Phil Knight coin. Rather than making a product and getting people to endorse it, McCormack, founder of International Management Group (IMG), conceived the idea of getting the sports figure under contract and then finding things for the athlete to endorse. Like Knight, his vision was global, and this vision soon expanded into event management. McCormack was quite explicit about the need to envision new ways of doing things (e.g., extending the Olympics through three weekends, playing Wimbledon both weekend days, made-for-TV events, appearance fees for professionals). Not even slowing down at age 65, McCormack is now working to represent and market musicians.

Retailing magnate Sam Walton was written off time after time by the experts as a small-town hick who would never be a major player in the discount business, but this did not discourage him in the slightest. He was confident that he understood how to make money in discount retailing. A Wal-Mart vice chairman said that Walton "is always his own person, totally independent in his thinking."[15]

Services

United Parcel Service (UPS) began in 1907 in Seattle as a local messenger service company, which soon began to deliver packages as well. Cofounder James Casey steadily pushed for geographic expansion, but the turning point was the idea to go nationwide after World War II, at first on the ground and later in the air as well. This was an audacious vision, not just in its scope but in the fact that it meant going head-to-head with the subsidized U.S. Postal Service—which even then had government-granted monopoly powers. Casey also saw the value both of technology as a means of reducing costs (e.g., conveyor belts, sorting machines) and of time study as a way of increasing efficiency. The result was a $22 billion empire that dominated the market.

Fred Smith may have miscalculated on the fax revolution, but he was brilliantly visionary with respect to overnight package delivery. The vision was especially audacious in that it was to be nationwide from the start and thus required enormous amounts of capital. He even foresaw the value of the hub-and-spoke system for routing cargo. There was enormous risk because implementing the vision required Smith to convince the government to make numerous changes in its regulations that were severely limiting his freedom of action. Furthermore, there would be indirect competition from UPS and the U.S. Postal Service and more direct competition later. Despite legal problems (some of his own making) and near bankruptcy, FedEx was a stunning success and made Smith and his stockholders rich.

Steel and Oil

Andrew Carnegie came to the United States from Scotland at age 13 with his pockets empty but his spirit full. He loved America because, like him, it was young, vigorous, and bursting with energy. Carnegie made several abortive starts: the oil business, the Pullman car business, the telegraph business, the iron business—all without a great deal of success. But he was not to be denied. He had recognized that steel was much better than iron, especially for building railroad tracks, but steel was expensive and hard to make. He saw that the Bessemer process was a fundamental breakthrough in steelmaking technology, and he built the first large steel plant designed around this process. His modern, efficient, and constantly improving plants, combined with skillful vertical integration, allowed Carnegie to undersell all competitors. He was America's first steel titan; his company became U.S. Steel after Carnegie sold it for a fortune of almost half a billion dollars.

Carnegie had made the United States the dominant global power in the steelmaking business, a position held until after World War II. Then began a staggering thirty-year decline caused by management ineptitude and union shortsightedness. Midway through this decline, a new steel titan rose from the ashes; his name was Ken Iverson. Named CEO of a failing, inept company whose only profitable line of business was manufacturing steel joists, Iverson decided that big steel prices were too high and that his company, renamed Nucor, would make its own steel bar, the material from which it made joists. In 1969 he built a small new factory—called a minimill—using the latest technology, melted scrap steel for raw material, incentive pay, and nonunion labor. The result was near bankruptcy because the company could not get the new technology to work. But eventually it worked, and Nucor became so successful and profitable that it kept building minimills and is still building them. Nucor is now one of the most powerful steel companies in the world and has made its stockholders, including Iverson, rich.

I have already mentioned John D. Rockefeller. John Paul Getty, despite a deservedly unsavory personal reputation, was forward-looking enough to use geology to spot promising locations for oil drilling. During economic downturns, he bought valuable oil properties that no one else wanted and also saw the value of Middle East oil ventures.

Transportation

Cornelius Vanderbilt was described by one biographer as "absolutely unconciliatory; he didn't care what people thought about him."[16] However, he grasped two business principles very thoroughly: cost control and technology. He started by putting the government-protected Robert Fulton out of the steamboat business by designing more technologically advanced ships and running them at lower cost than anyone else. He then saw an even greater opportunity in transatlantic shipping and competed successfully even with government-subsidized shippers. He was so feared as a competitor that, time after time, other businesses offered him subsidies in return for *not* competing with them.

At age 70, he sold all his ships and pursued what he considered an even better opportunity in the railroad business. Naturally, everyone thought he was crazy. Everyone was wrong. By age 76, he had consolidated a number of inefficient, competing railroads into the New York Central system, which became one of the most efficiently run and profitable railroads in the world. Vanderbilt has been criticized for engaging in bribery of various legislators in order to protect his business, but, in fact, it was the only way to survive under what was even then a mixed economy in which government had almost unlimited arbitrary power in economic matters. (Today, these bribes probably would be called "political contributions to support special interests.")

Conclusion

Vision is a necessary condition for the creation of great wealth, but it is far from a sufficient condition. We have to ask, What makes it possible for people to formulate productive visions and to grasp how they can be actualized? This is the subject of the next two chapters.

Notes

1. A. Rand, *The Fountainhead* (New York: Signet, 1993), pp. 678, 680–682.
2. J. Collins and J. Porras, "Building Your Company's Vision," *Harvard Business Review*, September/October 1996, pp. 65–77.
3. Quoted in B. Folsom, *The Myth of the Robber Barons* (Herndon, Va.: Young America's Foundation, 1991), p. 93.
4. W. G. Pagonis, "The Work of the Leader," *Harvard Business Review*, November/December 1992, p. 124.
5. These examples were taken from a posting on the Internet. I have no source for them.
6. Quoted in B. Folsom, *Empire Builders: How Michigan Entrepreneurs Helped Make America Great* (Traverse City, Mich.: Rhodes and Easton, 1998), p. 150.
7. G. Hamel and C. K. Prahalad, "Seeing the Future First," *Fortune*, September 5, 1994, p. 67.
8. A. Rand, "The Money-Making Personality," *The Objectivist Forum*, vol. 4, no. 1, 1983, p. 3. (This article was originally published in *Cosmopolitan* magazine, April 1963.)
9. A. Kupfer, "Craig McCaw Sees an Internet in the Sky," *Fortune*, May 27, 1996, pp. 62ff.
10. W. Kim and R. Mauborgne, "Value Innovation: The Strategic Logic of High Growth," *Harvard Business Review*, January/February 1997, pp. 103–112.
11. G. Landrum, *Profiles in Genius* (Buffalo, N.Y.: Prometheus Books, 1993), Chapter 6.
12. J. McHugh, "Holy Cow, No One's Done This!" *Forbes*, June 3, 1996, pp. 122ff.
13. Quoted in R. Lacey, *Ford, the Men and the Machine* (Boston: Little, Brown & Co., 1986), p. 87.
14. For an analysis of the flimsy legal case against Milken, see D.

Fischel, *Payback*. New York: Harper Business, 1995. See also a mock
trial I conducted based on the evidence against Milken in E. Locke,
"The Trial of Michael Milken," available on cassette tape from Second Renaissance Books, New Milford, Conn.

15. S. Walton and J. Huey, *Made in America* (New York: Doubleday, 1992), p. 117.

16. A. D. H. Smith, *Commodore Vanderbilt: An Epic of American Achievement* (New York: R. M. McBride, 1927), p. 34.

3

An Active Mind

A process of thought is not automatic nor "instinctive" nor involuntary—nor infallible. Man has to initiate it, to sustain it and to bear responsibility for its results.[1]

Ayn Rand

As I noted previously, business is fundamentally not about physical labor but about brain power or, more precisely, mind power. The most important tool of the Prime Mover (or any businessperson) is an active mind. But what is an active mind? It is not the same as an open mind. The term *open mind* connotes passivity, like an open door. Leave it open and see what wanders through or falls in. Anyone with an open mind will soon find it filled with an uninterpretable jumble of opinions, beliefs, evaluations, prejudices, impressions, emotions, facts, hypotheses, conclusions, and fantasies all mixed together at random. The result will not be knowledge but chaos. (For proof, visit any college campus.)

Thinking

An *active mind* does not wait for someone or something to feed it knowledge (or what passes for knowledge) but actively seeks to know, to learn, to figure out; it constantly asks questions and questions assumptions, and it looks for patterns among the facts it observes and identifies the implications of those facts. Based on what it knows, it makes new connections, projects the future, and imagines possibilities. An active mind is a mind that is constantly thinking, which means it is functioning at the human (i.e., conceptual) level.

Ayn Rand describes thinking as follows:

> Man's sense organs function automatically; man's brain integrates his sense data into percepts automatically; but the process of integrating percepts into concepts—the process of abstraction and of concept formation—is *not* automatic.
>
> The process of concept formation does not consist merely of grasping a few simple abstractions. . . . It is not a passive state of registering random impressions. It is an actively sustained process of identifying one's impressions in conceptual terms, of integrating every event and every observation into a conceptual context, of grasping relationships, differences, similarities in one's perceptual material and of abstracting them into new concepts, of drawing inferences, of making deductions, of reaching conclusions, of asking new questions and discovering new answers and expanding one's knowledge into an ever-growing sum. The faculty that directs this process . . . is: *reason*. The process is *thinking*.[2]

Consider an example. Businessman A observes evergreens growing along the roadside and observes that they look pretty, especially when partly covered with snow. At this point, his thinking stops. Businessman B observes the same trees and thinks, These trees would look good in people's living rooms at Christmas. I wonder what people would pay for them. How hard is it to grow them? What investment is required? How big should they be before being cut? How difficult would it be to cut and transport them? How much would it cost? How long would they keep before losing their needles? Where would they be sold? What would the competition be like? Could I make other, related products (e.g., wreaths)? Can I make money in such a seasonal business? Where? How much?

With respect to the subject of Christmas trees, Businessman

A is passive, whereas Businessman B is active. Businessman B has a chance of creating wealth; Businessman A does not—at least not in the Christmas tree business.

Volition

It is critical to note that thinking is a volitional process, which means it is done by choice.[3] Man's most basic choice is the choice to think or not to think, which means to focus on reality or not.[4] It is not forced on one by either heredity or environment. Even if a person has developed good thinking habits through repeated practice, they never become totally automatic. (The same is true of bad habits.)

It is obvious that some people choose to do a lot more thinking than others do. Of course, nobody thinks about everything; everyone is selective in what they choose to think about. What people think about is very much governed by their personal interests—if they have any interests. Many Prime Movers, for example, were indifferent students in school or college (e.g., Bill Gates). It was not that they were lazy, but they had more important (to them) things to think about than their studies.

Reality

To think, as I noted, means to focus on reality, not on wishes divorced from reality. A person engaged in self-deception is not thinking but evading. Even projections of the future, made for the purpose of developing a vision, must be grounded in facts. Consider the idea of a copy machine. Before putting such a copier on the market, the entrepreneur would have to consider the following: Does it work? Is the requisite technology available? What is the quality of the copies? Can the machine be readily and reliably manufactured? How reliable is the copier after continued use? What service will be required? What is the cost of the product in relation to other alternative products? How much will copies cost? How will it be marketed and sold?

To whom (what is the market)? What specifically would it be used for? Evading any of these questions could be fatal.

Many business disasters have occurred because someone did not want to see reality as it was—especially when it was different from the past. IBM, General Motors Corp., Apple, Kodak, and many other companies have suffered terrible losses in past years because they did not see reality objectively. In contrast, consider General Electric (GE). Unlike many business behemoths, GE has prospered mightily—over $200 billion in shareholder value—since the early 1980s under the leadership of CEO Jack Welch. I am convinced that one reason was the consistent application of one of his six core principles: "Face reality as it is, not as it was or as you wish . . . facing reality is crucial in life, not just in business. You have to see the world in the purest, clearest way possible, or you can't make decisions on a rational basis."[5]

According to a *Business Week* report, the reality principle was not followed by a recent Macy's CEO, Edward Finkelstein, whose main agenda seemed to entail denying problems, intimidating subordinates, and spending freely on perks for himself—while waiting for a nonexistent economic upturn to bail the company out of its troubles.[6] Instead of making billions like GE, Macy's went into bankruptcy.

Nor did Harry Merlo of Louisiana Pacific Corp. follow this principle when a new type of siding his company developed was found to deteriorate when exposed to the elements. Rather than fixing the siding, he kept selling more of it. The resulting legal claims cost Merlo his job and the company millions of dollars.[7]

Peter Drucker's insight is important here. He says that great business leaders "did not start with the question, 'What do I want?' They started out asking, 'What needs to be done?' "[8]

Author Martin Puris agrees. In a fascinating study of seven CEOs who successfully turned around troubled companies such as Continental Airlines, UPS, Honeywell, and Chrysler, he concludes that the single most important factor in these successful turnarounds was the CEO's determination to "pursue the truth. . . . They display a doggedness, even a kind of compulsion to dig beneath appearances and uncover the true state of affairs in the area of their enterprise."[9]

One of the most striking examples of this in the book was U.S. Surgical, which had been founded by dynamic entrepreneur Leon Hirsch and had grown rapidly until a sudden downturn in 1992 almost led to bankruptcy. After a period of self-delusion, Hirsch, at age 67, faced reality and totally changed the way the company did business, including the way he managed and the way the company dealt with customers.

Intuition

What is the role of intuition in relation to thinking? To expand on my earlier comments, intuition is not, as often believed, a mysterious power residing mainly in women. It is neither causeless nor incomprehensible. Intuition refers to ideas or hunches or feelings fed to the conscious mind by the subconscious, based on past experience and thinking. The subconscious plays a critical role in every person's thinking. In fact, 99.999 percent of our knowledge is stored in the subconscious and is pulled out by association when needed, based on our conscious purposes. In some people, the flow of ideas between the conscious and the subconscious is copious, whereas in others it is meager. The former are more likely to be creative.

Those who have the most active minds are the ones most likely to be endowed with intuition or, more precisely, to come up with useful (as opposed to nonsensical) intuitions. The reason is simple. People with active minds are constantly bombarding their subconscious with new ideas and new connections (integrations). The subconscious stores these ideas and—if the input is not too chaotic—integrates them further and feeds them back to the conscious mind. To name the other side of the garbage in, garbage out (GIGO) coin, call it gourmet in, gourmet out.

Sam Walton is a case in point. When Wal-Mart decided to buy Big K, Kuhn's 112-store chain, in 1981, it was on the basis of Walton's tiebreaking vote in the executive committee. He said of this decision, "It's generally my gut that makes the final decision.''[10] But this decision was made after *two years of thought and debate*. An enormous amount of conscious thought and discussion had preceded the final, intuitive decision.

It must be stressed that intuitive insights never emerge fully developed or fully validated from the subconscious any more than business visions do. There is a constant process of thinking, often followed by an intuitive insight, followed by thinking, followed by another insight. Ultimately, the intuition must be consciously validated. Consider, for example, the idea of having sensors planted in cars and in the roadbed so that highway traffic is controlled automatically by computers. This is clearly imaginative and some of the technology required to do this already exists, but implementing the idea on a wide scale would cost billions of dollars and require decades of developmental work (not to mention the nightmare of legal issues involved). Thus, it is not practical as a short-term vision (five to ten years). Long term, there are many unknowns (e.g., satellite control might replace road sensors), and new discoveries might totally change the concept. Thus it is not an idea that could be pursued or implemented on intuition alone.

Now let us examine the specific thinking processes of some Prime Movers.

Active Minds at Work

Having an Active Focus

Thomas Edison is a good place to begin. Few people in history have had such an active mind. He was well aware that in this respect he was very different from most other men. One of his favorite quotes (from Joshua Reynolds) was, ''There is no expedient to which a man will not resort to avoid the real labor of thinking.''[11] Edison himself was a virtual thinking machine. Almost until the day he died, his mind poured forth a torrent of ideas, and he might track as many as sixty experiments at a time in his laboratory.

Consider also Henry J. Kaiser (a magnate in steel, aluminum, shipbuilding, and other industries), who was sharing a room with executive Joe Reis on a train. In the middle of the night, Reis was awakened by Kaiser asking in a progressively louder voice. "Reis, are you awake?" There followed a long discussion of what to do at the next day's meeting. Reis reported that this happened frequently; Kaiser's mind would simply not rest.[12]

When he was at Apple, Steve Jobs would bombard people with his ideas, including investors, his board of directors, his customers, his subordinates, and his CEO John Scully. Scully describes him as follows: "You could almost hear his brain thinking out an idea. Then he'd leap from his seat, pick up a marker, and begin sketching diagrams and arrows on a whiteboard to explain a notion visually. His whole body would speak. His hands would come together as if he was holding a product in them. He would make you see what didn't exist yet."[13] Jobs's ability to communicate his ideas enabled him to inspire his employees to spend inhuman hours on the Mac and other projects.

Projecting the Future

All visionary thinking is directed toward the future, as the examples in the previous chapter reveal. In one respect, Edison's invention of the phonograph was even more remarkable than his invention of the electric lightbulb (see below) because no one had ever thought of the idea of a phonograph (recording sound) before. Even his own laboratory staff couldn't figure out why he was wasting his time on it, especially since he was half-deaf himself. But Edison not only invented it but foresaw its future uses, including the Dictaphone (which he also invented), books for the blind, elocution training, music, toys, and education.

Intel CEO Andy Grove says, "I have a rule in my business: to see what can happen in the next ten years."[14] Right now Grove is pushing Intel to create its own demand by inventing a new, upgraded bus, and by inventing or investing in new software that will increase the flexibility and usefulness of PCs.

It is important to note that an active, future-oriented mind is not a guarantee of omniscience. Edison was an inventive genius, but he made his share of mistakes, including the failure to see the value of AC current for transmitting electrical power, the appeal of disk records, and the potential of radio. However, his 1,093 patents and his $12 million fortune reveal a very active, reality-focused mind at work.

Seeing the Whole

Edison is most remembered for his invention of the electric light-bulb. The first commercially practical lightbulb, which he developed in 1879, was an astounding achievement, given that inventors had been trying to make the idea practical since about 1820. But it is not generally known that Edison's thought process did not stop with the bulb. He envisioned an entire electrical system to go with the bulb. In addition to lightbulbs, this system would include a central power station, an insulated wiring network, individually controlled lights wired in parallel, meters to measure electrical consumption, and a total cost competitive with natural gas lighting. Edison had to invent, in addition to the lightbulb, the dynamos that would power the stations, the method of wiring and insulation, meters, light fixtures, and fuses. These inventions were made in his laboratory in conjunction with the research on lightbulbs. Thus, it took only three years to get from a viable lightbulb to the first power station, which opened in New York in 1882. Edison's light business, of course, evolved into General Electric—and changed the world.

Seeing the Whole and Part Together

A striking fact about Prime Movers is that even though they can see the big picture, they can also see the small picture—the details that affect the success of the big picture. For example, Sam Walton would go over weekly sales reports in minute detail and analyze what they meant and what action they implied even as he envisioned a nationwide retail chain. John D. Rockefeller could see the future of the oil industry and could also size up at a glance the accuracy of a balance sheet for a particular plant. Harold Geneen of International Telephone and Telegraph Corp. (ITT) had the ability to constantly go back and forth between the big picture and the financial details of his many companies. John Huey, an experienced business writer, reports in relation to Roberto Goizueta, "There's the question of whether Goizueta was a hands-on detail man or an above-the-fray, clean-hands CEO. And the answer is clearly both."[15] Michael Malone says the same about James J. Hill, the builder of the Great Northern Railroad: "His genius lay precisely in his ability to master detail while fashioning broad vision and strategy."[16] Finally, consider Robert Lacey's description of Henry Ford:

> He threw himself into every detail, insisting on getting small things absolutely right. . . . [But] he never lost sight of the ultimate, overall objective. He had a vision of what his new car [the Model T] should look like. From all the improvisation, hard thought, and hard work came a machine that was at once the simplest and the most sophisticated automobile built to date anywhere in the world.[17]

This constant movement between the concrete (details) and the abstract (vision) is critical to business success because one has to know not only where one is going but how to get there.

Asking Questions and Seeking Information

Prime Movers are relentless question askers. A colleague describes James Casey of UPS as follows:

> I have never come in contact with a man with such an incisive mind. His questions were not superficial but to the point. He began knowing nothing about it [the issue in question], but proceeded directly toward the underlying causes. With his ability for questioning, which enables him to get to the root of a problem and gives him an overall view of the problem, I can easily see why he has been successful in business.[18]

The ability to get to the root of a problem reflects the ability to search for and think in terms of essentials, that is, in terms of a hierarchy of importance or fundamentality. Consider the executive of a major wood products company who was informed that employees were stealing tools and supplies from one of the plants. The superficial solution would have been to improve security (e.g., install video cameras, search employees as they left the plant), but the executive decided to get to the root of the problem by having a consultant ask the employees why they were stealing. Employees reported that they were doing it to get even with the managers, who were engaging in dishonest practices themselves. When these practices were stopped, the employees stopped stealing. The executive discovered that what seemed like random dishonesty was, in fact, a deliberate search for justice.

Disney's Michael Eisner "came into the company with an enormous curiosity, an incredible thirst for knowledge. He was smart enough to realize how much he didn't know. . . . He was like a sponge. . . . He was interested. . . . [He] would ask questions and let other people do a lot of the talking. He would grab good ideas from anyone he could. His own mind is a wellspring of creative ideas, some brilliant, some dumb. His subordinates protect him from implementing the dumb ones."[19]

Coca-Cola's Roberto Goizueta was so unyielding in his quest for knowledge that planning sessions with him came to be known as the "Spanish Inquisition." He also traveled incessantly to get information firsthand. One topic he wanted to learn about was finance, and he discovered the basic idea of economic value added (EVA) even before it became popular. He reduced the idea to this principle: "You borrow money at a certain rate and invest it at a higher rate and pocket the difference. It is simple."[20] Of course, it is not simple at all or else everyone would be a millionaire, but the genius of Prime Movers is their ability to reduce complexity to a few basic principles so that everyone can understand them and act on them.

Sam Walton was as big a pest as Goizueta. Retailing consultant Kurt Bernard writes of him: "When he meets you . . . he proceeds to extract every piece of information in your possession. He always makes little notes. And he pushes on and on. After two and a half hours, he left, and I was totally drained. I wasn't sure what I had just met, but I was sure we would hear more from him."[21] We did. Walton had the gall to insist that Abe Marks, president of the National Mass Retailer's Institute, look at his accounting sheets and tell Walton what he was doing wrong. (Conventionally, people would describe this type of behavior as revealing a small, as opposed to a big, ego. I will show in Chapter 6 that the truth is exactly the reverse.)

Harold Geneen, however, may have put even the most rabid information seekers to shame. In seventeen years as CEO of ITT, he increased sales from $765 million to $16.7 billion and earnings from $14 million (excluding nonoperating income) to $562 million. He did this despite having to keep track of 250 different profit centers and using a management technique that may never be duplicated. It was centered around numbers, frequent mind-numbing meetings, and the search for "unshakable facts." Geneen hired special staff people (a no-no in today's business climate) to track every detail of the performance of every business and then met with the business managers for one week each month to go over every facet of every business. Nothing escaped his ominvorous mind. Goals were set for every quarter; those who did not meet them had to have both a good reason and a plan to do better in the future. Geneen's training must have been good because more than a hundred of his managers became top executives in other corporations. Geneen's successor at ITT did not do as well. Some Prime Movers, I believe, are simply one of a kind and cannot be replaced.

It is worth noting that the other side of the question-asking coin is inhabited by what could be called the Prime Stagnators. Some simply do not want to exert the effort that sustained thinking requires. Others are people who feel too insecure to admit that they do not know everything and who spend their greatest efforts protecting the illusion that they are so brilliant that they do not need to learn anything new. Ignorance for them is not an opportunity but a threat. Such a deluded basis for self-esteem guarantees eventual failure. When reality becomes your enemy, reality always has the last laugh.

Improving Constantly

Edison-worshipper Henry Ford had a mind as active as Edison's, at least in the early part of his career in the realm of automobiles. He even took a job at the Edison Illuminating Company in Detroit so that he could learn about electricity. He worked ceaselessly to develop and then improve his first quadricycle, which led to the Model A Ford and a continuous series of new models down through the alphabet. He worked on improving the internal combustion engine in his own kitchen, with his wife as helper. He and his engineers developed a vertical cyclinder engine, a new (one-piece) cylinder block, a new carburetor, new steel alloys, new transmissions and electrical systems (including a new magneto), new paints, a radically innovative production process (the moving assembly line), vertical integration, and hundreds of other improvements. This torrent of creative ideas produced a torrent of high-quality, low-cost automobiles that dominated the market for close to two decades.

Sam Walton was one of the great active minds of the twentieth century. He built a small country store into the largest, most profitable retail chain in the country. One of the reasons for Walton's success, I believe, was that he was a thinking dynamo—as if powered by one of Edison's inventions. Here are some excerpts from his autobiography[22]:

> I never could leave well enough alone, and, in fact, I think my constant fiddling and meddling with the status quo may have been one of my biggest contributions to the later success of Wal-Mart.

> [I]n business, I have always been driven to buck the system, to innovate, to take things beyond where they've been.

> It's almost embarrassing to admit this, but it's true: there hasn't been a day in my adult life when I haven't spent some time thinking about merchandising.

Walton was not afraid to learn from competitors. His wife, Helen, claimed that he never went by a Kmart that he didn't stop and check out. His brother Bud said of him, "His mind is just so inquisitive when it comes to this business."[23] His motive, of course, was to steal any good ideas he could find. Call Walton obsessed if you will, but most Prime Movers *are* obsessed (I do not mean this in the clinical or neurotic sense) with their businesses, which is one of the reasons they are successful.

John Browne, CEO of British Petroleum, makes it clear that active minds are not confined to North America. His philosophy is, "Every time we do something again, we should do it better than the last time. . . . By asking every time we drilled a deep-water well, what did we learn the last time and how do we apply it the next time, [we reduced the time needed to drill such wells from 100 days to 42 days]."[24]

Browne's mind did not suddenly become active after he became CEO. When he headed BP Exploration and Production, he decided that he would attack the impossible task of developing some oil fields that seemingly could not be developed profitably. The estimated price for development was $675 million—way too high. So, Browne brought the best minds (including the contractors) he could find together, scoured the world for other good ideas, and used a radically new approach to bring the project in (profitably) at below $444 million.

Andrew Carnegie developed advanced accounting techniques, fostered research in the chemistry of steelmaking, kept up with and used the latest technology, developed new marketing techniques, discovered how to make money from waste products, mastered vertical integration, and made cost cutting an obsession. Thanks primarily to Carnegie, by 1890 the United States had overtaken Great Britain as the world's largest steel producer.

Like Carnegie, Jack Welch never sat on his laurels. Even as he nears retirement, he is looking for ways to improve GE. Recent initiatives have included a massive quality-improvement program, an increased push into services, and continuing acquisitions to give GE technological leadership in key industries. Welch was never one to simply solve existing problems. GE was quite profitable when he took it over in the early 1980s, so there were not many obvious problems. But Welch grasped that what they were doing then could lead to irreparable problems in the future, so he proceeded to turn the whole company on its head. Prime Movers are not just problem solvers; they are *problem finders*.

Reading Outside the Square

Many Prime Movers are avid seekers of knowledge outside the realm of their work. John Bogle was an avid reader. His son reported that he would walk by his father's study thousands of times and observe him constantly reading books that were scattered all over the desk, the floor, and his lap.

Fred Smith, the founder of FedEx, is also a voracious reader with interests in biography, history, science, and technology. His ability to see trends and the implications of new discoveries has enabled him to introduce innovation after innovation (e.g., package tracking, bar-code scanning, automated customer service, software tracking) and even to win the Malcolm Baldrige National Quality Award.

Active minds do not just receive information; they integrate and evaluate and disseminate it. Bill Gates can be described as an information-gathering, information-integrating, superpowered vacuum. His idea of a vacation is to study physics, history, literature, biology, and biotechnology. He also reads widely in the field of software technology, goes through hundreds of e-mail messages daily, reads business magazines, talks with the best minds in his company and many outside it, and pushes Microsoft relentlessly to develop new products and to improve the ones it already has.

For an active, integrative mind, knowledge acquired from outside one's own business domain can have application inside the business if one thinks in conceptual, not concrete-bound, terms. Imagine, for example, a case study of a new type of incentive system at a bank. A concrete-bound steel man might say, "Well, that's banking and I am in steel, so it has no relevance to me." But a conceptual steel man would say, "Well, I would have to adapt it to my business, but the principle used in the banking case looks quite promising." All this may sound obvious, but twenty-five years of teaching executives and MBA students has convinced me that thinking outside of one's own narrow frame is, for most, very difficult and very rare. This is another reason why Prime Movers themselves are rare.

Many Prime Movers confine their thinking primarily to their business, and many have few, if any, outside interests.

There is no great harm done unless something outside the business that can have a major impact goes unnoticed. In the case of Andrew Carnegie, active attempts to delve into philosophy, although well-intended, led him down many blind alleys and even to the moral subversion of his own half-billion-dollar fortune. In declaring that he was just a trustee for the poor, he admitted by implication that his wealth was not his by right.[25]

Bucking the System

When people with active minds are not in charge, they are often called troublemakers. Michael Bloomberg was a troublemaker when he worked for Salomon Bros. Not one to blindly follow the leaders, he kept telling them that they were going in the wrong direction. So they fired him—a common fate of those whose minds are more active than those of their bosses. That was no problem for Bloomberg, who then started his own company. No more able to leave well enough alone than Sam Walton, Bloomberg spent several years constantly improving his Bloomberg terminal until it became the best product in the industry. Bloomberg did not rest with just a terminal. His media empire now introduces a new media product or service every six months, in addition to a constant stream of new services on his terminal, and shows no signs of slowing down.

How Do Active Minds Go "Bad"?

Being an active thinker at one time, or even during one decade, does not guarantee that one will continue to make good decisions indefinitely. Henry Ford, Ken Olson, An Wang, Steve Jobs, and many other brilliant visionaries have made critical errors that threatened or severely damaged their companies. Of course, one reason for error is simply that one makes an honest mistake (e.g., misreads the market or future technological developments). Since no one is omniscient, this can happen to anyone.

But certain thinking processes can cause mistakes to happen. One cause of error is that visionary leaders may assume that what they did in the past will continue to work indefinitely. Their intuition, feeding back their stored memories of success, tells them—not necessarily in the form of explicit words but in the form of an emotion—something like this: I was right in the past so whatever I feel will work, will work. In the short run, such a mistake usually causes no irreparable damage. Anyone can become overconfident, see that they made an error, and correct it.

But then another, more fatal thinking error sometimes follows. Having embraced the status quo or having decided that an old idea is good or that a new idea is bad, based largely on emotion, they fail to continue checking their conclusions against reality. Introspection (looking inward at their own intuitions) permanently replaces extrospection (looking outward) as a means of gaining knowledge. Thus, they become passive rather than active thinkers in relation to reality. When new information becomes available that could modify their original decision, they do not consider it, or consider it perfunctorily, and then dismiss it out of hand. This perpetuates the error and makes correcting it impossible.

In support of this interpretation, Professor Pino Audia of the London Business School, in a study using a simulated management game, found that a consistent series of past successes led CEOs to assume that their successful business strategies would continue to work in the future even when there was clear evidence of changes in the market. They also were more likely than CEOs who had experienced less success to seek out positive information about the company and to avoid dissenting viewpoints. This led them to maintain their past strategy when the market changed, which led to huge declines in financial outcomes.

There is good reason to think that this simulation study applies to the real world. Edwin Land, after brilliant early success with Polaroid, failed to take seriously evidence that price was a critical factor in sales, causing the introduction of his SX-70 camera to be an expensive fiasco. Ken Olson saw the potential of the minicomputer and was brilliantly successful in this market for many years, but he never saw the potential of the PC. An Wang was also very successful (in the office word-processing business), but he failed to see the risks involved in proprietary software. Contrast these three to Bill Gates, who almost let the Internet revolution pass Microsoft by; through continually listening to conflicting evidence and dissenting views, he changed his mind and made the switch before it was too late.

Another case in point is McDonald's, whose stock along with operating profits and earnings had been lagging in recent years. CEO Michael Quinlan claimed, "We don't have to change. We have the most successful brand in the world." Most ominous is the fact that McDonald's executives were refusing to listen to critics, including their own franchisees. All negative press coverage was attributed to misperception and distortion rather than to real company problems. With such an attitude, one could predict more rough times ahead for Quinlan.[26] (In fact, Quinlan was soon replaced as CEO by Jack Greenberg, who has turned the company around.)

Disney's Michael Eisner is under no such delusion about past success. He recognizes that "today's hottest company is tomorrow's struggling, helpless giant."[27] Right now, Disney itself is struggling, and it remains to be seen if Eisner can restart the profit engine.

It is easy to be a Monday morning quarterback, of course. But the issue is not one of never making mistakes but rather of never turning off one's critical faculties even after important decisions have been made. There can be a fine line between proper changes, of course, and debilitating vacillation, resulting in total lack of direction. Vacillation usually occurs when bits of evidence are acted on but when the leader never puts enough of the pieces together to see, at least in rough outline, the whole picture. The Prime Mover somehow is able see enough of the picture to decide when to push on despite setbacks and when to switch gears. In Figure 3-1, I summarize the main differences between the active and the passive mind.

Conclusion

Prime Movers develop visions through relentless mental activity (i.e., thinking). However, not everyone is equally good at thinking, nor do they get equally good results from it. Thinking does increase one's knowledge and skill, but it does so more in some people than in others. Thus, it is impossible to explain the success of Prime Movers without addressing their ability as well as their confidence in their ability. This is the subject of the next chapter.

Figure 3-1. Main differences between the active and passive mind.

Active	*Passive*
• Conceptualizes.	• Relies on sense perception only.
• Thinks in principles.	• Remains concrete-bound.
• Acts rationally (is reality-focused).	• Acts emotionally (is wish-focused).
• Focuses on the present and future.	• Focuses on the past and present.
• Stays proactive and anticipates.	• Reacts.
• Integrates.	• Compartmentalizes.
• Sees whole plus parts.	• Sees parts only.
• Embraces new ideas.	• Coasts on past learning.
• Finds problems and solves problems.	• Solves problems only.
• Asks questions.	• Does not ask questions.
• Focuses on improvement.	• Accepts status quo.
• Thinks outside own business.	• Focuses on own business only.

Notes

1. A. Rand, *The Virtue of Selfishness* (New York: Signet, 1964), p. 23.
2. Ibid., pp. 21–22.
3. For a further discussion of volition or free will, see H. Binswanger, "Volition as Cognitive Self-Regulation," in *Organizational Behavior and Human Decision Processes*. 1991, Vol. 50, pp. 154–178. Also see L. Peikoff, *Objectivism: The Philosophy of Ayn Rand* (New York: Dutton [Penguin], 1991.) My discussion of virtue is based on Chapters 7 and 8 of the latter book.
4. A. Rand, op cit.
5. N. Tichy and S. Sherman, *Control Your Own Destiny or Someone Else Will* (New York: Doubleday, 1993), pp. 12–13.

6. L. Zinn, in review of *The Rain on Macy's Parade* by J. Trachtenberg, *Business Week,* December 9, 1996, pp. 18, 20.
7. E. Schine and A. Marks, "The Fall of a Timber Baron," *Business Week,* October 2, 1995, pp. 85ff.
8. P. Drucker, "Not Enough Generals Were Killed," *Forbes ASAP,* April 8, 1996, p. 104.
9. M. Puris, *Comeback: How Seven Straight-Shooting CEOs Turned Around Troubled Companies* (New York: Random House [Times Business], 1999), p. 11.
10. S. Walton and J. Huey, *Made in America* (New York: Doubleday, 1992), p. 198.
11. Quoted in A. Runes, ed., *The Diary and Sundry Observations of Thomas Alva Edison* (New York: Philosophical Library, 1948), p. 166.
12. A. Heiner, *Henry J. Kaiser: Western Colossus* (San Francisco: Halo Books, 1991), p. 48.
13. J. Sculley, *Odyssey: Pepsi to Apple* (New York: Harper & Row, 1987), p. 156.
14. D. Kirkpatrick, "Intel's Amazing Profit Machine," *Fortune,* February 17, 1997, p. 72.
15. J. Huey, "In Search of Roberto's Secret Formula," *Fortune,* December 29, 1997, p. 232.
16. M. Malone, *James J. Hill, Empire Builder of the Northwest* (Norman, Okla.: University of Oklahoma Press, 1996), p. 80.
17. R. Lacey, *Ford, The Men and the Machine* (Boston: Little, Brown, 1986), p. 93.
18. J. E. Casey, "Our Partnership Legacy," in *United Parcel Service of America,* (UPS, 1985), p. 120.
19. Quoted in J. Flower, *Prince of the Magic Kingdom* (New York: Wiley, 1991), pp. 157–158.
20. B. Morris, "Roberto Goizueta and Jack Welch: The Wealth Builders," *Fortune,* December 11, 1995, p. 88.
21. S. Walton and J. Huey, op. cit., p. 82.
22. Ibid., pp. 27, 47, 56.
23. Ibid., p. 190.
24. S. Prokesch, "Unleashing the Power of Learning: An Interview with British Petroleum's John Browne," *Harvard Business Review,* September/October 1997, pp. 149–150.
25. There are two reasons that most businesspeople are as helpless as children in dealing with political-philosophical issues: (1) Most of what they read is wrong because America's intellectuals have betrayed most of what America stands for; (2) businesspeople do not exhibit the same independence of thought in reading about philos-

ophy and politics that they exhibit with respect to their business activities.

26. D. Leonhardt, "McDonald's, Can It Retain Its Golden Touch?" *Business Week*, March 9, 1998, p. 71.
27. J. Flower, op. cit., p. 233.

4

Competence and Confidence

Studying mathematics, she felt, quite simply and at once, "How great that men have done this" and "How wonderful that I am good at it."[1]

—Dagny Taggart in *Atlas Shrugged*

Nothing is more obvious than the fact that people differ in their competence. One can observe that, even at a very young age, some children understand and learn things more readily than others even when they have the same degree of encouragement and opportunity. (This is also true at the physical level. Some children are naturally quicker, faster, and more coordinated than others.)

Competence and Learning

All this does not deny the obvious fact that most normal people can learn and can improve their skills, even if not at the same rate. I have no intention of getting into the nature versus nurture controversy here. First, we simply do not know enough to reach any firm scientific conclusions about this kind of issue. We probably know more about intelligence than any other cognitive trait. The evidence here is quite consistent in showing that intelligence is about 50 percent (or more) hereditary. Smarter parents will, on the average, produce smarter children. That leaves the other 50 percent to be explained by other causes.

Second, the nature-nurture issue is partly misconstrued because there are actually three, not two, causes of intelligence, human learning, and achievement. The third one is volition, which I mentioned in the previous chapter in relation to thinking. Volition pertains to what you choose to make of what is given to you by heredity and the opportunities provided by your environment. There are plenty of people with average intelligence and limited opportunities who are great achievers, and plenty more with high innate intelligence and great opportunities who accomplish nothing.

Actual knowledge and skill, whatever one's native endowments, are always acquired through effort and choice. Learning above the level of the simplest concepts always requires mental effort, and the more complex the skill involved, the greater is the effort required. Whatever the relative importance of the three causes of competence, however, competence is critical to business success.

All this aside, it must be stressed that competence is not infinitely malleable. No matter how hard some people study, they will never be math geniuses or nuclear physicists. Nor can just anyone run a billion-dollar corporation. One of the characteristics of people with higher intelligence is that they can grasp abstractions more rapidly and integrate greater amounts of information than people with lower intelligence. In our increasingly complex, high-tech world, intellectual ability will play an increasingly important role in business success.

One critical aspect of intelligence is inductive reasoning (i.e., the formulation of general principles or conclusions from particular facts). A great mind can take hundreds or thousands of facts or observations and tie them together into a meaningful whole, while a lesser mind only sees the parts. A great mind can find order where others see only chaos. It can separate what's essential from what's not, what's important from what's trivial, and what should be considered from what can be ignored. It can find opportunity where others see only problems. It can see causal relationships where others see random events. Business writer Brian O'Reilly quotes psychologist Ted Bililies, who says that good mutual fund managers are exceptional in their ability to spot patterns: "Good fund managers have to be able to immerse themselves in minutiae one moment, zoom out and look at the big picture from thirty thousand feet, then dive back into the details again."[2]

A second critical aspect of intelligence is deductive reasoning (i.e., the application of general principles to concrete situations). A great mind sees how and where to apply general principles.

Great thinkers use both types of reasoning in concert. Consider this example: Businessman X observes the U.S. steel industry and sees that it is not prospering. He notes that its costs are higher and its technology is more backward than that of its international competitors. He observes a correlation between these two factors and low profits. He also sees that union work rules and wages contribute to the high costs. So far, his thinking is inductive. Next, he observes that there is a new technology that can make steel from melted scrap and calculates that using such scrap could save money. He also observes that union strength and wages are lower in the South than in the North. He deduces that by opening a new plant using scrap metal for raw material and hiring nonunion labor from the rural South, he can make steel for a lot less than the big steelmakers. He tries it and it works (induction). This implies that it might work on a bigger scale, so he decides to open another plant (deduction). It works again. Then he wonders if he might make more than one type of steel using the same formula (deduction), so he tries it and it works once again. He concludes that he is onto something big (induction)—and so on.

No, building Nucor was not quite this simple, but these were some of the key inductions and deductions that made it possible. It seems simple in retrospect because Ken Iverson and the founders of Nucor were able to simplify a complex problem by identifying and applying certain key principles that they applied consistently.

I noted in Chapter 1 that it is fashionable to downgrade the achievements of Prime Movers (in business or any other field) on the grounds that they were lucky to have been born with ability. The implication is that it is unfair or unjust for some people to be born with less ability than others are. There are three flaws in this argument. First, innate ability is not a matter of luck (chance) at all; it is caused by the laws of genetics. Second, the concept of justice does not apply to the metaphysically given (e.g., the laws of nature); it only pertains to matters of human choice and action. It is not unjust (even if unfortunate) that the volcano near Person A erupts, whereas the volcano near Person B does not. It *is* unjust if Businessman A chooses to give a raise to Employee B and not to Employee C, even though Employee C did a much better job. Third, regardless of one's natural endowments, it requires sustained effort and choice to actualize the ability one starts with. Ability is only a potential, not a skill. Michael Jordan would never have become a basketball star without thousands of hours of practice. Nor would Bill Gates have become a billionaire without years of excruciating effort.

All Prime Movers use their intelligence to acquire knowledge and specific competencies in the realm of their business. This does not mean that they are experts at every specialty in their organizations, but rather that they become experts at something, including seeing the big picture—a prerequisite of formulating a vision. Lack of knowledge in a particular area can be compensated for, as CEO Doug Becker of the rapidly growing Sylvan Learning Systems does by hiring people with the needed expertise, provided one knows what expertise is needed and has the ability to pick people with expertise (an issue I shall address in more detail in Chapter 7).

Confidence

Confidence is, to a considerable extent, a consequence of skill or mastery. Stanford University psychologist Albert Bandura calls task-specific confidence self-efficacy.[3] Self-efficacy is the conviction that one can perform at a certain level of skill on a certain task. Self-efficacy reflects how one assesses one's past attainments; usually it predicts future performance better than one's own past performance does. For example, consider two students who got A's in introductory algebra. One felt overwhelmed despite hundreds of hours of work, had to get extra tutoring, felt lucky that just the right problems were given on the final, and was given a few hints by the professor beforehand, whereas the other student, though he had to work hard, had no trouble understanding the material. The self-efficacy for algebra of the second student would be higher than that of the first student; this would affect their relative performance in the next course. In addition to directly enhancing performance, high self-efficacy leads to the setting of high goals, fosters persistence after failure, stimulates the use of better strategies, and builds morale. People with high natural ability, once they choose to use it, usually have high self-efficacy, and this encourages them to learn even more.

However, I believe there is another factor at work here, a more general type of self-confidence that can be called generalized efficacy. Generalized efficacy is an aspect of self-esteem; it refers to one's perceived capacity to deal with life's exigencies, to attain values, to achieve goals. Some children seem to develop this at an early age. The reasons are not fully known, but it may be due in part to early independence seeking. (Or is early efficacy the cause of early independence seeking?) Some children hide behind their mothers' skirts from day one, while others charge out into the neighborhood to find adventure. Those who seek independence become even more self-reliant, which gives them the confidence to become even more independent. Regardless of which comes first, independence and self-confidence are reciprocally related; each encourages and expands the other.

In some cases, early independence may be fostered by early deprivations (Steve Jobs was an orphan). But this is by no means a sufficient explanation of a child's later accomplishments. Some children, when confronted by early adversity, decide they cannot handle it, become frightened and self-pitying, and withdraw into themselves. Others, faced with the same threats, view them as a challenge to be overcome and proceed to take action. As noted in Chapter 1, a number of Prime Movers had very unhappy childhoods, but they did not let that stop their determination to pursue goals and succeed in attaining them. But for every Prime Mover with such a background, there are hundreds or thousands of people with the same background who lack the strength to overcome adversity.

In some cases, the parents' own confidence in the child may contribute to his or her confidence. When Thomas Edison's schoolmaster declared that he was "addled," his mother indignantly rejected the evaluation and decided to educate him at home, convinced that he was a lot more able than the teacher thought—which, of course, he was. It helped that Edison was impossibly curious and that he educated himself by opening his own chemistry lab in the basement. On the other side of the help coin, parents who give a child too much help may undermine his efficacy. If a child concludes after a success, "Yes, I did it, but only because Mom or Dad helped me," the child may reason that "Left to my own devices, I am helpless."

Another causal factor in childhood efficacy may be early experiences of success, especially successes that require a certain amount of tenacity and struggle. The reason for this qualification is that successes that come too easily may lead the child to conclude that success is due solely to natural ability, a premise that could tempt the child to give up when confronted by a task that was not effortlessly and immediately mastered (e.g., "I'm just no good at this"). This would lower his confidence in being able to tackle challenging tasks that require new learning and even make the child afraid to put himself in situations where failure was possible. On the other hand, if early success is achieved only by means of such exhausting, debilitating effort that one feels one could never do it again, as with the algebra student mentioned above, self-efficacy may be lowered. The bottom line is that if, all things considered, the child concludes (consciously or subconsciously) from early successes achieved with effort that "I am the type of person who can deal with anything life has to offer," he has the beginnings of high generalized efficacy. Edison, who certainly had high efficacy when working on his own projects as a child, wrote later in life, "I never allow myself to become discouraged under any circumstances."[4] This attitude was the leitmotif of his career.

I am not claiming that all Prime Movers have high generalized efficacy as children or that childhood self-appraisals are decisive. Not all Prime Movers brimmed with confidence from an early age. Sometimes the confidence develops later. Consider, for example, Will Kellogg.[5] For the first forty-six years of his life, he was totally dominated by his dictatorial, compulsively vain, older brother, John, who ran a health spa that catered to the rich and famous. In the course of preparing food for the spa guests, however, Will, partly by accident, invented cornflakes. Eventually he gained enough confidence to leave the spa and start his own cereal business. He proved to be a brilliant marketer and developed enough confidence in himself to defeat his brother in two lawsuits and overcome a disastrous fire. In the end, Will outshone his brother, whose spa went bankrupt. The bottom line is that one cannot start, develop, or expand a major business without confidence in one's ability. The job is too hard, the stresses too great, and the obstacles too daunting; no one who is faint of heart and mind could do it.

Prime Abilities

All business enterprises require quantification to some degree. Costs, sales, and profits are measured by numbers. Thus, it is not surprising that Prime Movers are often very skilled in mathematics. This is most obvious in (but not confined to) cases where finance is critical to their business.

John Pierpont Morgan, who helped make the United States the world's greatest financial power, was so good in math that his professor at the University of Göttingen (Germany) suggested that he become a professor of mathematics. He suffered throughout his life from many physical ailments and usually could not focus for long periods of time. But he could concentrate intensely for short periods of time and had a remarkable ability to get to the essence of a problem during those intervals. His accomplishments included saving the U.S. government and New York City from bankruptcy and the New York Stock Exchange from collapse as well as restructuring many U.S. industries—not to mention financing Thomas Edison's lighting company, which later became GE.

Michael Milken, the twentieth-century version of Morgan, was also a brilliant mathematician who graduated summa cum laude from Berkeley, having already discovered the potential value of junk bonds through his own research. His business professors at Wharton recognized his brilliance when one of them sent him to work at what was to become Drexel Burnham. He was so astute a bond trader that he would often make a 100 percent return on investments, an unheard-of rate. His star shone so brightly that he could not be a member of any committee, and he ended up running his own bond department. He then proceeded to restructure part of the U.S. economy and make billions for Drexel and for himself in the process until the government decided to destroy him. (For a documentation of the vacuity of the government's case against Milken and the identification of the real reasons why the government went after him, see Chapter 2, note 14.)

Investor Warren Buffett is another mathematical talent and was the only Columbia MBA student ever to get an A + from the legendary Benjamin Graham. His special ability is discovering a company's basic worth and then buying those companies that are undervalued—something that every investor would like to do but which very few are able to do well. Buffett has enough confidence in his own analytical powers, including his own very painstaking research (which may include visits to the company), to be able to consistently reject convention and majority opinion. It is especially striking that Buffett puts large amounts of capital into a few stocks rather than hedging his bets through diversification, as most investors do. He also abandoned the market altogether in 1969 when he saw no good values to invest in and came back into the market in 1974 when everyone else was down on it. Ten thousand dollars invested with Buffett in 1956 would have been worth $80 million in 1994—not a bad rate of return.

John Bogle of Vanguard was no slouch at mathematics either. He graduated magna cum laude from Princeton (before the days of grade inflation), thanks mainly to a brilliant thesis on the topic of the investment company. He was known to work out problems with a slide rule before other people could do it with a calculator. Even Buffett praised Bogle's book on mutual funds.

Walt Disney's early talent was creative ability in animation. He started developing his artistic talent by enrolling in art classes when he was a boy and spent years refining his skills before opening his own company. Later, the scope of his imagination expanded. After hiring people more skilled in animation than he was, he spent his energies ensuring high-quality productions and developing totally new concepts (animated feature films, theme parks).

No one doubts that Bill Gates has a brilliant mind. Ann Winblad describes him as a "massively parallel thinker with extraordinary bandwidth."[6] Translated into English, this means that he can think along many tracks at the same time and integrate hundreds of facts in order to find the pattern behind them. Hidden behind all the whining of his competitors and their constant demands that the government protect them from Microsoft is the unacknowledged admission that Gates is simply smarter than they are. Like Morgan and Milken, he is exceptionally able in mathematics, but he first applied his expertise to the field of software programming. He began to develop this expertise in college (to the neglect of his courses). As his knowledge grew, his vision became progressively broader so that now he understands the whole industry and even sees its future. Unlike the CEOs of many companies, he thoroughly understands his own products and technology, which gives him a clear competitive advantage over those who do not.

Like Gates, Intel's Andrew Grove is consistently described as brilliant. Harold Geneen's intellect may have matched that of Gates. Anyone who can manage more than 200 profit centers at the same time and make them profitable over a long period of time has to have astounding integrative powers.

John D. Rockefeller was not a brilliant student in the manner of Morgan and Milken, but his favorite subjects were science and mathematics; the latter was the subject he most excelled in. This ability was especially useful in helping him master the art of cost control. At a glance, he could spot an error on a balance sheet and check the number of drops of solder required to make a barrel, even as he planned consolidation of the refining industry and vertical integration.

Another oil magnate, John Paul Getty, although not a very nice fellow in most respects, made a fortune by acquiring a detailed knowledge of the oil business, which included knowledge of geology at a time when most oil drillers were skeptical of the value of science to the oil business. This expertise enabled him to know the true value of oil properties better than anyone else and then to buy valuable properties at low prices, especially during the Great Depression. Getty also saw the potential value of Saudi Arabian drilling rights in the 1940s and paid what was considered an outlandish price for them. After spending $30 million on exploration in Arabia, he struck it rich.

Henry Ford's special genius was mechanical. From an early age, he loved to take things apart and rebuild them. At age 7, he was repairing watches. He would take apart mechanical toys to see how they worked. Later he learned how to repair farm engines. He acquired engineering skill working for Detroit Edison. By the time he started building cars, he had a thorough knowledge of every part that went into them. For more than two decades, he tinkered endlessly with these parts (ignition, clutch, brakes, carburetor, chassis, motor, etc.) and continually improved every one of them. He also learned the intricacies of production and revolutionized how cars were put together. Ford's genius was described by William Knudsen: "Say we are going to buy a certain part for an automobile. . . . The samples come in . . . the technicians spend days going over them, taking them apart, testing one against another, making notes and tying labels to them. Then they are all spread out on a table, maybe thirty of them, ready for Ford. He comes in, looks at them for two or three minutes with his squinted eyes, says, 'That one,' and walks out. It's that one, sure enough."[7]

Steve Jobs was no software expert or electronic engineering wizard, but he knew how to identify those who were. He also knew how to fully utilize the talents of experts and how to judge the value of what they produced. For example, he knew the value of what had been discovered at Xerox Parc (e.g., user-friendly graphics, the mouse) better than Xerox did. Although Jobs was not a master of the small pieces of the big picture, he was able to see how they could fit together to create a masterpiece. His lack of managerial skill and knowledge of business strategy, however, eventually came back to haunt him.

Ross Perot's special ability, in addition to being an expert salesman and seeing the value of data processing services, was mobilizing talent. He knew how to raid other companies and grab their best people and how to motivate them, through offering stock options and enormous responsibility, to stay with him and work preposterous hours in order to meet outrageous deadlines. Perot was tremendously confident from a young age and nothing—not even rescuing an employee from a Middle East dictatorship or running for President—daunted him.

Perot rarely failed (except in politics), but this is not the case for all Prime Movers. Bill Bartmann went broke manufacturing pipes for oil rigs. But a kid who left home at age 14 was not about to be crushed by a little failure. After he closed his business, debt collectors harassed him in a way that he thought was unproductive. Maybe he could do better. So he bought some bad debts at two cents on the dollar and attempted to collect some of what was owed. It worked. So he increased the scope of his operation, constantly learning as he went. He learned how to judge risk and how to collect. Then he thought of packaging debts and making them into securities. That worked too. In eleven years, his company, CFS, became the leading company in the field of consumer debt.

Many people have commented on Fred Smith's keen intelligence, although in his case mathematics does not seem to be its central focus. He was an excellent student in high school and has always read voraciously. His mind is crammed with facts, but unlike many people who know a lot, he is able to focus his knowledge around a specific purpose, discarding what is irrelevant and integrating what is relevant. He was even confident enough to think he could change FAA (Federal Aviation Administration) regulations and long-held prejudices of Congress, which blocked the expansion of FedEx. What others said would take ten years to change, he got changed in two.

Throughout history, few women have created fortunes. The reasons need not concern us here, but there have been exceptions such as Mary Kay Ash. Darla Moore is another one. Since taking charge of her husband's stock portfolio, she has increased its worth to $1.5 billion. Before that, she was the highest-paid woman in banking. One of her special talents is getting to the heart of business issues despite apparent chaos, and she has total confidence in her own judgment. An early sign of independence was rejecting her mother's career suggestions. Leveraging the power of her stock holdings, she has not hesitated to get badly performing CEOs dumped. There is no breech between her mind and reality. When one troubled Fortune 500 CEO demanded a lower interest rate on a loan, she snapped, "You are bankrupt."[8]

It is important to note that it is possible to make a lot of money doing something very mundane. What is critical is that one have at least one very good core idea, even if the idea is a narrow one, and then apply it skillfully on a wide scale for a long time. Consider, for example, pigs. Wendell Murphy, a farmer, was frustrated in his early attempts to make money in pig farming so he came up with a clever idea: Put together a database, which integrates everything that is known about how to raise pigs (breeding, disease control, feeding), and then pay other people to raise them using this knowledge and the latest technology. Today Murphy is the largest pig farmer in the United States and is worth a billion dollars. In fact, he is so good that, just as in the software industry, competitors are trying to use the government to protect themselves from their most competent rival.[9]

Risk

Prime Movers are usually seen as big risk takers, but this is really not the case. First, risk is partly a function of how skilled you are. If one knows one can control the outcome, the risk is much less than in the case of someone who lacks skill. A common misunderstanding about risk is that risk is only a matter of what is out there, that is, the market and the customers. But this is incomplete. Consider a football analogy. Let us say that a typical running play behind the left tackle gains, on the average for all National Football League teams, 1.7 yards. This makes it a seemingly high-risk play if you need 3 or 4 yards for a first down. But for a coach with a very good offensive line, an outstanding running back, and an identified weakness on the part of the defensive team, the risk is a lot less. The risk, then, is not just a matter of what action is taken but who is taking it—more specifically, the skill and ability of the actor. Prime Movers can make actions succeed that would fail if taken by others. Prime Movers are confident of their ability so that what would be risky for others may not be to them.

Second, Prime Movers typically take as many steps as they can to avoid risk (e.g., using other people's money, leasing instead of buying, getting guarantees that purchased materials will work as claimed). Third, they do not typically frame actions in terms of what can be lost (though they are aware of it) but rather in terms of what can be achieved. They are first and foremost value seekers, not loss avoiders.

Reaching Beyond One's Grasp

People with ability do fail, sometimes after considerable prior success. I mentioned one reason for this in Chapter 3: They stop using the thinking methods they used to earn their success. A second reason is that the scope of thinking that was sufficient to achieve a certain scale of success is no longer sufficient because the market or technology has became more complex. In short, their jobs grow, but they do not. They keep using the knowledge and skills that worked before but fail to see that they need new, higher-level skills in order to keep growing. They gloss over or evade things they do not understand and deal only with aspects of the business that they do understand. They look at only one part of the picture—often it is the one part they feel they can master.

Such people may even attempt to move in the direction of growth, but they do not really understand what they are getting into. They assume that if they can do X, they can do Y. Sometimes they are smart or knowledgeable enough to do Y, but often they are not. They may hold it as a matter of pride that they can handle anything. The critical flaw here is that they are not objective about their own capabilities or knowledge. They do not realize when they are getting in over their heads. Consider the hapless Robert Citron, past treasurer of Orange County, California. He did fairly well investing the county's funds for many years in traditional, conservative instruments but gradually began to undertake more and more risks without fully understanding the implications of what he was doing. Furthermore, he reacted with fury toward anyone who questioned his competence. The bluff worked—until he bankrupted the county and lost his job.

Contrast Citron with Dave Thomas, founder of Wendy's. All he ever wanted was to be in the restaurant business. He learned about the business through working in restaurants, through running them, and then through owning them. When he started Wendy's, he knew the business that he was in as well as anybody, and better than most. He did not try to enter the automobile business or the steel business but stayed with what he was expert at, continually upgraded his knowledge, and became a multimillionaire in the process.

It is not always the case that the new skills that are needed cannot be learned; this depends on the individual's capability. But nothing can be learned unless the individual fully grasps what is not known and figures out what needs to be known. Disaster occurs when subjective confidence is divorced from objective competence. (Psychologists have shown that a slightly optimistic view of one's capabilities is healthy, but this is different from confidence that deviates substantially from the facts.)

I was shocked when an industrial psychologist, who frequently assesses middle- and upper-middle-level managers, told me that a remarkable number of the managers he has assessed do not intellectually grasp their own jobs, that is, they do not really understand what they are doing. One would think that they would see this and do everything in their power to gain the understanding they needed, or at least try to do so, but such was not the case. Rather, they denied or tried to cover up their ignorance. One can be sure that such managers will never become Prime Movers.

Overconfidence

Businessmen (and others) can become overconfident, not just as a result of past success but because they are very bright. They are able to grasp ideas and relationships rapidly. This is very beneficial except when it turns into arrogance. The arrogance pattern goes something like this: "I am brilliant; therefore, I do not have to get my hands dirty digging into the nitty-gritty of things. My reasoning power is so great that I can dispense with getting bogged down in details and facts. Nor do I have to bother to listen to the opinions of the inferior intellects around me. And if my decisions do not seem to work out, the setback is only temporary because I cannot be wrong."

Intelligence and knowledge need to be combined with a certain type of (nonreligious) humility: humility before the facts (i.e., reality). This includes the recognition both that no matter how much one knows, one does not or cannot know everything and that no matter how smart one is, one cannot know the future insofar as it is a result of human choice—with certainty. Intelligence must be applied to experience, not used as a substitute for experience, that is, for information gained from studying the real world.

Some intelligent people base their self-esteem on their intelligence rather than on their adherence to reality. So when there is a conflict between their self-image and the facts, it is the facts that have to be dispensed with. This is, of course, a recipe for disaster. No one can be omniscient. Being wrong should not be viewed as a threat but as a stimulus to gain new knowledge. Genuinely bright people with an ego problem (i.e., easily threatened self-esteem) are not reaching beyond their ability; rather, they are not fully using the ability they have.

Fear of Failure

It is often claimed that great businessmen are moved not by confidence but by fear—specifically, fear of failure. From a certain viewpoint this is true, but the formulation is misleading. No one could successfully engage in any difficult undertaking motivated solely or predominantly by doubt. Thomas Watson, Jr., was somewhat frightened when his father retired (and soon died), leaving him solely in charge of IBM, but at a deeper level he knew that he had excellent skills, including the ability to recognize talent. Ken Iverson of Nucor stresses that executives must not fear making mistakes, or else they will be unable to experiment and try out new ideas.[10] This will prevent them from taking calculated risks that could have a big future payoff.

I am reminded here of an example from history. Toward the end of the Peloponnesian War, the Athenian, Nicias, argued against the decision of Athens to invade Syracuse. Nevertheless, the Athenians decided to go ahead with the invasion and even made him the leader (*strategos*) of the expedition (along with Alcibiades, who later deserted). But plagued by doubt and hesitation, Nicias was unable to mount an effective campaign despite having an overwhelming force at his disposal. Ultimately, the Athenian army and navy—and Nicias—were destroyed.[11]

Fundamental doubt is different from healthy fear, fear based on the knowledge that one is neither omniscient nor omnipotent and that unforeseeable circumstances, including creative or aggressive action by competitors, could endanger one's plans or one's enterprise. Consider Gates's statement: "I have a fear of failure. Absolutely. Everyday that I come in this office, I ask myself: Are we still working hard? Is someone getting ahead of us?"[12] Such a premise is *not* a reflection of fundamental doubt (i.e., deep-seated feelings of inadequacy). Rather it is a way of showing awareness of the nature of capitalism: Everyone is trying to beat you and is free to do it if they are good enough. This attitude is supremely healthy and far better than its opposite: "We are the greatest thing since starched shirts, so why worry about anything."

Andy Grove of Intel also uses healthy fear as an antidote to complacency. To put it in his own words (which he also used as a book title), "Only the paranoid survive." This involves constantly checking one's mental map of the industry to make sure that one has not missed developing trends and new technologies. Grove constantly worries about everything: product quality, production, employee morale, hiring of the right people, and competitors.

So how can we put these two ideas—confidence and fear—together in a noncontradictory way? Lucent's (now Hewlett-Packard's) Carly Fiorina, rated by *Fortune* magazine as the most powerful businesswoman in the United States, combines these views as well as anyone. She describes herself as possessing basic self-confidence combined with humility before reality accompanied by the fear that she could fail if she did not make the right choices. I believe this view to be quite characteristic of Prime Movers.

Conclusion

If one looks closely at the role of ability in wealth creation, the pattern typically goes like this. Prime Movers have some natural ability, confidence, and the willingness to exert effort in order to develop and utilize their ability. Over time, they acquire a very high level of skill and knowledge in one or more aspects of a particular business. As their skills and knowledge increase, the scope of their thinking widens. Their vision expands, and they begin to see possibilities on a larger and larger scale. As their skills, knowledge, and vision expand, they expand the scope of their actions. This builds their confidence and encourages further thinking and expansion, and so on. Those with ability and active minds are best able to formulate and execute visions that will work. *Observe that this process is incremental and not grandiose.* The Prime Mover does not declare, "I am going to be a big shot and dominate the steel business," and then proceed immediately to take pretentious, rash actions that exceed the scope of his knowledge. The Prime Mover thinks big but also thinks objectively.

The difference between Prime Movers and the non–Prime Movers is that the latter (1) cannot acquire a high level of skill and knowledge, (2) acquire a high level of skill and knowledge but fail to recognize what they do not know, or (3) possess knowledge and skill but fail to act on them. This last issue pertains to motivation. A vision, as such, is really only a dream. To create wealth, the vision has to be actualized in reality. Knowledge and foresight must be combined with motive power. In the next two chapters, we discuss what Prime Movers' motive power consists of.

Notes

1. A. Rand, *Atlas Shrugged* (New York: Signet, 1992), p. 54.
2. Quoted in B. O'Reilly, "Does Your Fund Manager Play the Piano?" *Fortune*, December 29, 1997, p. 130.

3. A. Bandura, *Self-Efficacy: The Exercise of Control* (New York: W. H. Freeman, 1997).
4. D. Runes, ed., *The Diary and Sundry Observations of Thomas Alva Edison* (New York: Philosophical Library, 1948), p. 43.
5. See B. Folsom, *Empire Builders: How Michigan Entrepreneurs Helped Make America Great* (Traverse City, Mich.: Rhodes and Easton, 1998), Chapter 5.
6. Quoted in J. Wallace and J. Erickson, *Hard Drive: Bill Gates and the Making of the Microsoft Empire* (New York: Wiley, 1992), p. 338.
7. B. Folsom, op cit., pp. 167–168.
8. P. Sellers, "Don't Mess with Darla," *Fortune,* September 8, 1997, p. 70.
9. D. Roth, "The Ray Kroc of Pigsties," *Forbes 400,* October 13, 1997.
10. K. Iverson, *Plain Talk* (New York: Wiley, 1998).
11. I am indebted to Professor Blaise Nagy of Holy Cross College for the information about Nicias.
12. Quoted in G. Landrum, *Profiles of Genius* (Buffalo, N.Y.: Prometheus Books, 1993), p. 130.

5

The Drive to Action

And because, were she lying crushed under the ruins of a building, were she torn by the bomb of an air raid, so long as she was still in existence she would know that action is man's foremost obligation, regardless of anything he feels.[1]

—Dagny Taggart in *Atlas Shrugged*

Action

A business vision is only a dream, a future potential, an idea of what could be or ought to be. Prime Movers have an extraordinary capacity to see the business potential of a market or product or technology, but they do not stop there. They are Aristotelians rather than Platonists. By divorcing reason from the sensory world, Plato made contemplation an end in itself and thereby divorced thought from action. In contrast, Aristotle made reason this-worldly, leading to an integration of thought and action. Prime Movers start with a vision, and through the power of their own motion (i.e., action), they make it real. There is no breach between mind and body, between the idea and its physical expression. As Henry J. Kaiser put it, "It is always good to get on high ground and see the vision. But I can never escape the urge to do something about it."[2]

In considering the relationship of thought to action, it is a common error to think that there are only two alternatives: mindless action motivated by a gut feeling (meaning unidentified emotions) or inaction resulting from paralysis by analysis.

79

Neither the prototype of the just-do-it hippie nor of the timid, ivory-tower intellectual reflects how the Prime Mover operates.

It is not a choice between taking action with no knowledge at all or taking action after achieving omniscience. The first is irrational; the second is impossible. The Prime Mover may be inspired through intuition, but intuition, as I noted earlier, is based on previously acquired knowledge that has been automatized by the subconscious.

Prime Movers act on the basis of some knowledge, but not necessarily total certainty in every respect. For example, Lee Iacocca knew that the minivan was a good product and that initial customer response was favorable, but he could not be certain that customers would buy it in large numbers because customers have free will and thus the power to make their own decisions. It was a totally new product with no market history. But he took the risk and saved Chrysler in the process.

Prime Movers in Action

Two recent articles in *Fortune* argue that a critical factor in CEO success—and failure—is the issue of speed, especially the failure to implement strategies in a firm and timely manner.[3] Decision, gridlock, the failure to act swiftly, and the failure to insist on results and to replace those who do not get them are fatal, especially in today's fast-moving economy.

Sam Walton was not the first person or the only person to enter the discount retailing business. Fed-Mart was earlier; K-mart was bigger. But Walton did it better than anyone, partly by borrowing principles used by others but applying them more effectively and more consistently. Added to this was an unceasing torrent of actions focused on such issues as information management (before the age of computers), distribution, cost control, choice of locations, and customer service. Walton's long-time secretary Loretta Parker said of him:

> His mind works ten times faster than everybody else's does. I mean he just gets going and stays two or three jumps ahead, and he's quick to go with what's on his

mind. If he gets something in his mind that needs to be done—regardless of what else might have been planned—the new idea takes priority, and it has to be done now. Everybody has their day scheduled and then *bang!* He just calls a meeting on something.[4]

One of the critical links between thought and action in Prime Movers is impatience. The Prime Mover can't stand to have an idea for a long time and not take some action on it. Sometimes for Walton, the action consisted of relentlessly pushing his ideas (e.g., the need for greeters in every store) in order to wear down the resistance of others. At other times, it was ignoring his appointments because some idea had caught his attention, and he was off in his plane without telling anyone.

When Michael Eisner took over a sleepy, unfocused Disney in 1984, he had to energize and refocus the whole company. In a whirlwind of activity, Eisner expanded into international markets; produced dozens of new movies appealing to a wider market; expanded into video, satellite, and cable distribution channels; enforced stricter cost controls; at the same time, he increased admissions prices at Disney's theme parks, improved marketing, and built new hotels. The whirlwind reaped a stunning increase in growth and profits.

Eisner was famous for making rapid decisions in response to his subordinates' suggestions for new projects. An idea suggested on Saturday would have a decision by Monday morning. His predecessor might have waited weeks or months to make a decision and have come back with a maybe.

The impatience that drives Prime Movers to act reflects their desire not to waste time. They think along several tracks at the same time, they think quickly, they talk quickly, they change subjects quickly, and they often drive quickly. Michael Milken used to try to read financial reports while driving to work, with sometimes unfortunate consequences. Steve Jobs was notoriously impatient. No amount of work on the part of his staff seemed to be enough, no deadline too short, no product improvement sufficient. He drove his people to continuous, unrelenting action until the product met his standards.

Michael Bloomberg specialized in doing things faster than

his competitors. It helped that he did not have to go through any bureaucracy to get things done. "Instead of doing what our bigger competitors do, which is to take two or three years to perfect a technology that is then a fossil when they put it into the market, we just throw it out there and work with our customers to perfect it."[5] The "don't think, do" credo that gurus love to quote is a bit exaggerated; the actions of Prime Movers are not thoughtless. One reason they seem so to an outside observer is that Prime Movers (like Bloomberg) think so much faster than most other people that their actions seem impulsive even though there is sound reasoning behind them. The real meaning of "don't think, do" is: Do not get lost in endless analyses or in planning that is so long-range as to be meaningless. "Everyone talks about multi-media," says Bloomberg, "but we're doing it."[6]

Prime Movers usually do more analysis and planning before acting when the price of failure is steep, but they are still driven to act fast. When Ken Iverson debated buying a German strip-casting machine, which had never been proven to work before, he took the trouble to send his best people to visit the plant that made it and study the machine carefully. They placed their order so fast that the seller was shocked, but Nucor also got a money-back guarantee in case it did not work. Nevertheless, it was an enormous, bet-the-company investment, given that the buildings that would house the machine cost more than the machine itself. Nucor also built the buildings at the same time as it installed the machine in order to save time. Iverson, however, did not fear failure and even expected to encounter some failure. "As a manager," he said, "you have to make decisions. If you don't make decisions, you are going nowhere and doing nothing."[7] As Nucor was installing its new machine, "big steel" was spending thousands of dollars on reports that "proved" the new machine would not work and that even if it did work, it would not be cost-effective. Of course, the machine made millions for Nucor, and it proceeded to build other, similar plants.

Unlike men of lesser ability, who may take a flurry of actions that add up to nothing—often just to show who's in charge—Prime Movers know which actions are important. When Cornelius Vanderbilt went into the railroad business, he focused both on lowering fares by lowering his own costs through consolidation and on upgrading service through improving the rails, the locomotives, the terminals, and the routes. Customers flocked to his railroads and made him rich.

When Eckhard Pfeiffer took over the helm of Compaq Computer Corp. in 1991, he immediately slashed prices of Compaq's PCs, a move that increased sales dramatically. He also reorganized the company, bought other companies with needed technological expertise, and placed special emphasis on developing Compaq's server business, which expanded dramatically. Under Pfeiffer's driving leadership, Compaq's stock price increased dramatically. (In 1999, when Pfeiffer seemed to slow down, the company took a turn for the worse, and he was fired.)

Taking action means showing initiative rather than waiting until circumstances force one to react. As soon as Roberto Goizueta grasped that return on capital was a critical determinant of wealth creation, he sold off peripheral businesses (plastics, wine, coffee, water purification) that were not showing a sufficiently high return. When he decided that Coke should not be in the movie business, he sold Columbia Pictures and used the money to expand overseas. When he discovered that the fountain business was doing poorly, he cut delivery costs so that the profit margin exceeded the cost of capital. And when New Coke proved a failure as a replacement for old Coke, he reintroduced and renamed old Coke. After he grasped that bottlers had too much power and were not acting in a concerted fashion, he bought control over them and joined them together into a juggernaut. No wonder Goizueta liked the story of the two vultures waiting in the middle of the desert for something to eat: One turns to the other and says, "Patience, hell. Let's go kill something."

To Cyrus McCormick, defeat simply meant a delay and was quickly remedied by the next action. When no one would buy his reaper, he developed a slew of innovative policies, including public demonstrations, to call attention to his product. When the Great Chicago Fire demolished his huge factory, which manufactured 10,000 harvesters a year, he ordered a new and larger one built even before the cinders were cool. A temporary factory office was opened the next morning, and temporary factory buildings soon followed. Generally, he chose to do the hardest thing first on the grounds that the remaining actions would follow easily.

Actions off Course

The potential danger in being action-oriented is that you may take the wrong action or, worse, take a series of wrong actions, each wrong choice leading to another wrong choice, until the garden path becomes a bottomless pit. There are two primary causes of such fiascoes.

The first is overconfidence. Prime Movers are of necessity confident; if they were not, they would not be able to move anything. But they are not omniscient, so some errors are inevitable. Confidence served Thomas Edison well—but not always. Continued action proved successful with respect to the phonograph, the lightbulb and electric systems, and the movie camera and projector. But persistent action in the iron ore–crushing business led to the loss of almost all of his wealth, which fortunately he was able to rebuild thanks to income from his successful businesses. In this case, Edison was overconfident.

The second cause is, surprisingly, the opposite of self-confidence: self-doubt. It is very threatening to many people to be wrong. Thus, if a course of action does not work out, it is tempting to try to prove that the failure is only temporary. Typically, the individual puts self-esteem on the line and is loath to admit to anything less than perfection or 100 percent success in every undertaking. In either case, the response is often to redouble effort with the same strategy and, often, additional financial commitment. The result can be eventual success, but often it is financial disaster. Professor Barry Staw of the University of California at Berkeley has written at length about disasters caused by overcommitment to losing courses of action.[8]

Regardless of motive, the antidote to remaining overcommitted to a losing course of action too long is to focus not inward on how one feels but outward on reality. A favorite and useful tactic used by business leaders to avoid pouring bad money after bad money is to ask themselves this question: If I were starting from scratch, would I go into this business right now? Intel's Andy Grove and Gordon Moore saved their company this way. They decided that, due to Japanese competition, there was no future in memory chips even though the company had defined itself as a memory chip producer. Their road to salvation was to get into the microprocessor business, which subsequently made a fortune for them and their stockholders.

Drive

He did not have the strength to feel—not even to suffer. He had burned everything there was to burn within him; he had scattered so many sparks to start so many things—and he wondered whether someone could now give him the spark he needed, now when he felt unable ever to rise again. He asked himself who had started him and kept him going. Then he raised his head. Slowly, with the greatest effort of his life, he made his body rise until he was able to sit upright with only one hand pressed to the desk and a trembling arm to support him. He never asked that question again.[9]

—Hank Rearden in *Atlas Shrugged*

For man, action is not an uncaused primary; it is caused from within. That inner fire that moves men to action, which (for want of a better term) I called drive, is a conglomeration of several interrelated sparks: ambition; high goals and standards; stamina; effort and energy; and tenacity.

Ambition

Ambition means the desire to better the conditions of one's life, to improve one's lot, to achieve one's important values. Conventionally, however, ambition is regarded with suspicion at best and with distaste or repugnance at worst. There are, I believe, four main reasons for this:

1. *Pretension.* Some people's ambitions are totally divorced from their actual knowledge, ability, and efforts. Pretentious ambitions are held not as a guide to action but as a substitute for action for the purpose of faking one's self-esteem. The sign of a genuine ambition is that one is actually doing something to attain it.

2. *Envy.* Many people resent other people trying to move ahead, especially when they themselves are not. Such envy is not confined to ethnic backwaters but can occur anywhere. It is often expressed by the catchphrase, "So you think you're too good for the rest of your old chums, do you?" Of course, the budding Prime Mover *is* too good for the type of person who would resent his determination to achieve something great.

3. *Morality.* President Nixon's staffer John Dean was guilty of blind ambition, which means ambition divorced from moral principles. Many people assume that ambition is always blind, but, in reality, this depends on the person. Ambition, as such, is a morally neutral concept. Its meaning does not specify either the content of the ambition or the means to be used in achieving it. Moral people will choose moral goals and use moral means to attain them; immoral people will do the opposite. There are plenty of businesspeople around who want to *get* but not to *earn* money. Some are just plain crooks; others want government favors and handouts so they can escape the responsibility of winning their wealth through free competition in the marketplace. As I have noted previously, Burton Folsom calls them "political entrepreneurs." Even people of genuine productive ability are not always consistent in their advocacy of economic freedom. The mixed economy is partly to blame in that it rewards those who have enough pull to gain special favors from the government and penalizes (and even ruins) those who do not.

4. *Values.* Ambition is often associated in people's minds with values that are not independent but rather secondhand, that is, focused on what can be gained from or through other people. The two most common examples are fame[10] and power. (Conventionally, people who renounce such values in favor of love for their work are described as selfless, but this is the exact

opposite of the truth—see Chapter 6 for details.) By implication, such examples rule out authentic, firsthand values, that is, values one chooses and wants for oneself, such as the desire to do exceptional work or make an outstanding product or grow a business. As noted, the concept of ambition is content-neutral: It is no better and no worse than the nature of the values people choose to pursue. Thomas Edison was ambitious; so was Hitler.

Prime Movers are enormously ambitious. They differ from other people in the scope and intensity of their ambitions, in the fact that they love the work, and in their actions taken to succeed. These ambitions may be expressed in terms of money or in terms of work accomplishments that will earn money, or both. John D. Rockefeller, for example, at age 13 told a schoolmate that he wanted to be worth $100,000 someday. Although that does not seem like much, it was a fortune in 1852. (Little did Rockefeller know that he would someday be worth 10,000 times that much.) He also had the desire to do something "big [important]," which of course he did.

James J. Hill, builder of the Great Northern Railroad, had the same financial goal as Rockefeller, although he was in his twenties when he set it. Later he set his lifetime work goal: to build a transcontinental railroad. Success in reaching this goal allowed him to easily surpass his financial goal.

Cyrus McCormick's ambition was to become a millionaire. He achieved it at age 57, thanks to shrewd real estate deals and the reaper. Jack Welch of GE had the same million-dollar ambition when he was in high school and exceeded it with a vengeance.

Typically, the content of the Prime Movers' early ambition is in the general form of "I want to do something great," and the specific content (e.g., career, profession, business) comes later. Thomas Edison was greatly inspired by a book on electricity by Michael Faraday, which he read when he was in his early twenties. He asked himself, "Can I get as much as he did? I have got so much to do and life is so short, I am going to hustle."[11] Later in life he complained that he had too much ambition, which led him to try too many things.

It is an interesting hypothesis that Prime Movers were

themselves inspired in childhood by real or fictional heroes. Edison was inspired not just by Faraday but by the character of Gilliatt in Victor Hugo's novel *Toilers of the Sea*. The book focuses on Gilliatt's desperate struggle to salvage a steamship engine from a treacherous reef. James J. Hill's favorite reading as a young boy included *Ivanhoe* and a biography of Napoleon. (Hill's middle name, Jerome, was the name of Napoleon's brother.) Fred Smith's boyhood heroes were great military generals. Tom Monaghan of Domino's Pizza was enamored of P. T. Barnum, Frank Lloyd Wright, and Abraham Lincoln. Reading about great achievers can implant in a child's mind the idea of greatness in concrete, directly perceivable form. Such role models can help convince the child that greatness is both possible and desirable.[12]

Some Prime Movers may not have needed any such models. Sam Walton wrote, "I have been overblessed with drive and ambition from the time I hit the ground."[13] His early ambition in retailing was to make his "little Newport store to be the best, most profitable variety store in Arkansas within five years."[14] It did not take him long to surpass that goal. Helen Walton said to her husband, "Sam, we're making a good living. Why go out, why expand so much more? . . . After the seventeenth store, though, I realized that there wasn't going to be any stopping it."[15] Most men are quite willing to rest on their laurels after they achieve some success. But like most Prime Movers, success only made Walton set his sights higher.

Wayne Huizenga's friends told him to retire after his stunning success at Blockbuster, but he would have none of it. "[T]hat's what gets the adrenaline going—that's why people climb mountains. . . . Life would be a lot simpler if . . . we didn't have to set the world on fire and re-invent the used-car business. But it's a huge challenge, and if we can make this thing work—and I think we can—it's another Wal-Mart."[16]

International Management Group CEO Mark McCormack makes it a matter of pride never to become complacent after a success but always to strive for more. He practices the same philosophy as the sports champions he represents: Strive to be number one; if you are number one, win by even more the next time.

Prime Movers who inherited money were not concerned about spending it in a life of leisure or trying to protect it, but rather they used it to make an even bigger fortune. J. P. Morgan was born to wealth, but he died much wealthier, having helped make the United States the number one financial power in the world. Fred Smith inherited $8 million but put it all (as well as other family members' money) into his FedEx venture and nearly lost it all on more than one occasion. But he is now worth more than fifty times what he put in.

High Goals and Standards

Ambition, the desire to improve or do something great, is manifested in the specific goals one sets for oneself and one's business, including one's own employees. Hundreds of studies of goal setting show clearly that setting high goals leads to better performance than setting easy goals. Assuming adequate knowledge and ability, the higher or more difficult the level of the goal, the better is the performance.[17]

Prime Movers march to their own clear and challenging drum beats and make their followers march to them, too. Lucent's Carly Fiorina, who managed its biggest division with sales exceeding $20 billion, argues that one of the key jobs of a leader is to define the meaning of success and failure. This is done by identifying the specific goals that executives and managers must achieve. She obviously did a good job of this because she was appointed CEO of Hewlett-Packard. She is the first woman ever to run a top Fortune 20 corporation.

When Michael Bonsignore took over a moribund Honeywell in 1994, stock analysts had given up on the company. One of the changes he made was to end the process of managers setting their own goals, which they had set at very easy levels, and insist on a 15 percent per year growth rate. This sent shock waves through the management ranks, but these goals, in conjunction with many other changes (including the building of employee confidence), jump-started the company's earning growth.

American Express President Ken Chenault set out to boost earnings per share by 25 percent or more, maintain a return on equity of 20 percent, and increase revenues by at least 8 percent a year. When the latter figure reached only 7.5 percent in the first three quarters of 1998, Chenault wasn't satisfied. "We need to improve dramatically," he urged.[18]

Prime Movers are not participative about where the company is going, though they typically allow considerable discretion about how their managers will get there. Company goals are often used to galvanize and integrate the efforts of all employees. When Gordon Bethune took over a demoralized Continental Airlines, he rallied the troops by making on-time flights the central goal of every department. Within two months, Continental had gone from last to first in the on-time rankings. This increased efficiency and helped make the company profitable.

The goals set by Prime Movers come in two levels: very difficult and impossible. Thomas Edison wanted his research laboratory to make a major invention every six months and a minor invention every ten days. Although Edison had a habit of promising products faster than he could deliver them, this only expressed his enormous self-confidence and irrepressible urge to create.

Hank Greenberg has been CEO of insurer American International Group (AIG) for thirty-one years, during which time its market value has increased from $300 million to $88 billion. He is described as "tough, demanding, impatient, focused, tireless, [and] tenacious."[19] His goal: 15 percent growth per year in a highly competitive industry. Of course, he is very smart and has a very good eye for detail so that he is driven to do things that work.

Annuity billionaire Eli Broad is unrelenting in his desire to grow his company, SunAmerica. Says one senior vice president, "Eli's style is tough. Demanding doesn't even begin to describe it."[20] Broad is not so different from GE CEO Jack Welch. At GE, every business has to be number one and number two in its industry. Dr. Steve Kerr of GE describes the GE stretch targets as follows: "A stretch target, which basically is an extremely ambitious goal, gets your people to perform in ways they never imagined possible. It's a goal that, by definition, you don't know how to reach."[21] If you are Welch's type of manager, however, you find out how in a hurry.

Given that GE attained a record 14.5 percent operating margin and 25 percent return on equity in 1997, one would think that Welch would now be satisfied. One would be wrong. He next planned a major restructuring because he did not think GE was competitive enough in several of its business units.

Both Welch and Goizueta agree that there have to be benchmarks to galvanize company efforts.[22] Often the benchmark is the performance of competitors, and the goal is to beat them. This can be a dangerous game when one becomes so focused on what others are doing that one does not take the initiative to lead rather than follow the pack. But competitors do have to be taken into account when setting goals.

British Petroleum CEO John Browne likes to convince people that they can achieve more than they think they can.[23] The Japanese concept of *kaizen*, which means continuous improvement, used to be the watchword for goal setting. Not any longer. Great business leaders now demand discontinuous improvement, which means improvement in fast, large, and outlandish increments. Browne was told once that developing a new oil and gas field would cost $675 million, which was not nearly good enough for Browne. Nor would an incremental improvement of $10 million do the trick. The goal was set at $405 million, 40 percent under the original estimate, and the job came in at $444 million. Nor is Jack Welch a fan of incremental change; to him, it is not big or revolutionary enough to keep your company competitive.

Many Prime Movers have lists of their own daily goals and make sure that they do not stop working until they achieve them. Mark McCormack's wife claims that his favorite thing in life is to cross things off his daily list. Mary Kay Ash wrote a list of goals to be attained each day, and these were tied to longer-term goals. Typically her daily list would include six goals ranked in order of importance or in order of difficulty, with the most difficult one put first.

Andy Grove of Intel is unrelentingly goal-oriented. Everyone in the company has medium-term objectives to meet, and these are documented by means of key results that reveal success or failure in relation to the objectives. Feedback is ensured by means of frequent meetings both between employees and supervisors and between Grove and his managers.

Nucor general managers are required to generate a return of 25 percent on their assets. They have to submit two brief but detailed quantitative reports weekly and a more detailed report each month in order to track progress in relation to goals.[24] Disney's Michael Eisner encourages his people to come up with creative ideas and then imposes strict deadlines for completing the projects.

Perhaps no company in the United States is more goal-oriented than Cypress Semiconductor. President T. J. Rodgers has set up a goal system that is so detailed it would make a type A accountant wince.[25] Everyone at Cypress must set goals that are integrated with the company's goals and the goals of their unit. These are tracked by a computer program that anyone, including the president, can access (and other people can also access his goals).

On a typical day, the system may list more than 10,000 separate goals. A single new chip requires 48 separate milestones and may involve thousands of individual goals, including goals for quality. Each goal has a time deadline, a relative priority in relation to other goals, and a specific person who is responsible for achieving it. Progress is usually checked weekly; people with delinquent goals are questioned about why they are behind schedule and what they plan to do about it or what help they need to succeed. The goals are coordinated both by functional area and by project. Computer tracking allows problems to be spotted before they become critical.

Effort, Stamina, and Energy

Achieving any large-scale goal requires relentless effort. Earning money at any level of ability is hard work, and earning a lot of money is very hard work. Those who argue for the benefits of leading a balanced life will not find any adherents among Prime Movers. They are bursting with restless energy of a type rarely seen outside of a blast furnace. That is why they love the slogan, "Lead, follow, or get out of the way." They want a clear road in front of them. Both Welch and Goizueta view energy as one of the most important traits of a business leader; Goizueta ranks it number one.[26] More energy is needed today than ever before because the pace of modern business is very fast and a person without enormous energy simply cannot keep up, much less lead.

Obsession is not an inappropriate term for Prime Movers' attitudes toward their work, but their motivation is not necessarily neurotic. Neurotic motivation is based on fear (self-doubt), whereas healthy motivation is based on love (desire). Some Prime Movers are no doubt motivated by both. J. Paul Getty would be one example. On the other hand, Walt Disney, though he had an unhappy childhood that he did not entirely overcome, genuinely loved animation and even paid for his own art training with money earned on a secret job so that his cruel, exploitative father could not interfere.

One measure of effort is hours worked. Stamina is the ability to sustain effort over a long time period. It is common for Prime Movers to work hard even as children, though not necessarily on schoolwork. Many had newspaper routes and had other children working for them. Warren Buffett resold lost golf balls, installed pinball machines, and supervised fifty kids when he was in high school. Gates spent his spare time playing with the school computer. Mary Kay Ash took care of a sick father as well as going to school and selling Girl Scout cookies. Her mother, who worked fourteen hours a day, was an inspiring role model.

As adults, the hours became even longer. Bill Gates's workweek was originally ninety hours, although lately he has trimmed it back to sixty to seventy hours. Larry Bossidy, CEO of Allied Signal, works twelve hours a day and is renowned for his stamina. Roberto Goizueta worked ten-hour days; Mary Kay Ash sometimes worked sixteen to eighteen hours a day. Tom Monaghan of Domino's worked eighteen hours a day for ten years. Cornelius Vanderbilt started a new, full-time career in the railroad business after he was seventy years old. Thomas Edison worked eighteen-hour days for some forty-five years and often worked for days at a stretch with nothing but short naps. It helped that Edison only needed four hours' sleep a night; New York real estate magnate Samuel LeFrak gets by on the same number. Michael Eisner set the tone for Disney when he became CEO by coming to work every day at 7:00 a.m. and staying into the evening. The Disney motto became, "If you don't want to come in on Saturday, then don't bother coming in on Sunday."[27] An article in *Fortune* provided information on the work habits of eight CEOs, including Gates. The average workweek was close to seventy hours, and the average amount of sleep per night was a little over six hours.[28]

Prime Movers today do not take many vacations or take working vacations like Gates. Those who actually go somewhere may spend most of their time on the phone talking to subordinates and clients and sending and answering faxes. Sam Walton used to sneak away during family vacations and check out the nearest Kmart.

In today's global economy, extensive travel is a must for senior executives. The *Fortune* survey noted above revealed that most CEOs traveled twelve or more days a month. Stamina may be partly inherited, but it also stems from one's internal commitment to one's work and, of course, to being in good shape.

For pure energy, few business leaders can beat David House. His grueling work, travel, and workout schedule has earned him the nickname Captain Adrenaline. By the force of his energy and judgment, he has taken a near-defunct company, Bay Network, from a $167 million loss to a projected $243 million profit after only fifteen months on the job.

The theory is that people who work very hard will soon burn out; some people do, but Prime Movers just turn up the flame. When Jobs and Wozniak were working unholy hours on the Apple, Wozniak burned out, but Jobs did not.

It is fashionable to imagine that, on their deathbeds, people who have worked monomaniacally at their careers say, "I am sorry I did not spend more time with my family." Maybe some do, but not Cyrus McCormick. Upon awakening momentarily from a death stupor, he blurted out, "Work. Work!"[29] and then expired. This shows how far his love of work had penetrated into his subconscious. There is a reason why Prime Movers do not burn out, which I will explain in the next chapter.

Tenacity

Tenacity or persistence is a form of effort but refers specifically to the willingness to put forth effort even in the face of setbacks and failures. Prime Movers love to quote Calvin Coolidge:

Nothing in the world can take the place of persistence.
Talent will not; nothing is more common than unsuccessful men with great talent.
Genius will not; unrewarded genius is almost a proverb.
Education will not; the world if full of educated derelicts.
Persistence, determination alone are omnipotent.

Although Coolidge overstates the point—persistence alone is not enough and no one is omnipotent—the emphasis he gives to persistence is fully justified. Tenacity is critical in any difficult undertaking precisely *because* no one is omniscient or omnipotent, and thus some failures in the course of pursuing one's values are inevitable. Those lacking in tenacity give up and fail to achieve what they want; those who keep going still have a chance.

Thomas Edison is the perfect embodiment of this trait. To develop the filament for the first commercially feasible lightbulb, his lab tested 1,600 different materials and, later, 6,000 types of vegetable fiber before discovering that a cotton thread coated with carbon would work and that bamboo did an even better job. After the first 1,000 failures, a laboratory worker became discouraged, but Edison reassured him that they had learned a great deal; he had discovered 1,000 types of fiber that did not work. Edison and his staff labored for almost ten years to develop the storage battery. They had to consider the simultaneous effects of many different variables without the benefit of modern mathematics or computers and without any knowledge of theoretical chemistry; 10,000 different experiments were run before they got it to work right. No wonder Edison admired Gilliatt in Hugo's *Toilers of the Sea*.

Fred Smith started FedEx in 1973 and did not make a profit until 1976. During that period, the company was constantly on the verge of bankruptcy. Once Smith helped meet the payroll through gambling winnings. Add to this a hit-and-run accident, an FBI investigation, a divorce, lawsuits, and his temporary demotion from CEO to president and you have all the ingredients for a mental breakdown, not to mention business failure. But toughened by death-defying combat experiences in Vietnam and his own resilience, he struggled through and made FedEx immensely profitable.

Tom Monaghan endured three near-bankruptcies, lawsuits, angry creditors, a fire that burned all his records, three partners who tried to oust him, and several almost-fatal plane crashes. Despite a poor education, an unhappy childhood, and little in the way of resources, he made Domino's successful after a twenty-year struggle.

Ross Perot loved Winston Churchill's phrase, "Never give in, never give in, never, never, never, never," and lived it. Furthermore, he made his employees live it. Sixty-, eighty-, hundred-hour weeks were routine if that's what was necessary to complete a difficult job on time.

Walt Disney was the victim of many failures and betrayals. Most of the income from his first animated film was taken by another studio. He came back with *Mickey Mouse* in synchronized sound. An investor took much of the earnings from this, sending Disney into a deep depression. He bounced back with Technicolor and *Snow White*, followed by financial failures with *Fantasia*, *Bambi*, and *Pinocchio* that put the whole studio at risk. He came back by selling stock in the company, only to be shut down by World War II. But he kept making films, hooked up with a TV network, and built the hugely successful Disneyland. Only poor health was able to stop him permanently.

UPS's James Casey believed that "Determined men make conditions—they do not allow themselves to be victims of them."[30] He overcame an early failure in the gold prospecting business, the murder of one of his business partners by a hoodlum, the Great Depression, and thirty years of legal battles against government regulations that limited interstate commerce. But in the end he won; UPS became the dominant company in package delivery.

Cyrus McCormick was described by others as possessing bulldog tenacity. He was ruined his first big venture, making iron ore into pig iron. He also suffered through endless litigation over patents for the reaper. It took nine years of effort before he sold his first reaper. His early advertisements were a failure;

when demand finally picked up, he was unable at first to find a manufacturer to build his reaper. But in the end he prevailed.

Mary Kay Ash's second husband was to have been her right-hand man, but he died just before the opening of her company. She went on without him. Her first beauty show was a flop, but she treated failure as a learning experience, not as proof of inadequacy. She improved her techniques, and her subsequent shows were increasingly successful. Her third husband died, but she pushed on. In the mid-1980s, sales fell dramatically and the company's stock price along with them. The company came back with a massive sales increase spurred by an expansion into international markets. "I've told my consultants and sales directors countless times," she says, "if we ever decide to compare knees, you're going to find out that I have fallen down and gotten up so many times in my life."[31]

Stewart Alsop describes Bill Gates as follows: "Gates is tenacious. That is what's scary. . . . Bill always comes back, like Chinese water torture. . . . People are scared of Microsoft because they are so persistent."[32] The first Windows program took seven years to develop and suffered from cost overruns, delays, lawsuits, and widespread skepticism, even from within the company. At the end of this road has been market dominance and billions in profits.

When Nucor bought its new, unproved, continuous steel-making machine from Germany, it failed repeatedly. Every part of the machine broke at least once. In some catastrophic failures, almost the whole plant was lost. One man died in an explosion that could have killed many more. Nucor was losing $1 million a week; weeks and months went by without success. But for CEO Ken Iverson and Plant Manager Keith Busse, there was no question of quitting. Finally they got the machine to work and then built a second plant like the first, and then a third.

Sam Walton went through many bad times in the retail business. Consider David Glass's description of the opening of one of the earliest Wal-Mart stores:

> It was the worst retail store I had even seen. Sam had brought a couple of trucks of watermelons in and stacked them on the sidewalk. He had a donkey ride

out in the parking lot. It was about 115 degrees, and
the watermelons began to pop, and the donkeys began
to do what donkeys do, and it all mixed together and
ran all over the parking lot. And when you went inside
the store, the mess just continued, having been tracked
in all over the floor. He was a nice fellow, but I wrote
him off. It was just terrible.[33]

The write-off was a bit premature. This fiasco did not faze
Walton at all, as history shows, and David Glass soon changed
his opinion and come to work for Walton—he is now CEO. Incidentally, Walton had several other failures, including a discount
drug chain, a home improvement center, and two Hypermarts.

When Is Enough, Enough?

History is full of examples of businesspeople who persisted in
doing the wrong thing. When does tenacity turn into stubborn
foolishness? When does losing money in the short run lead not
to later profit but to financial disaster in the long run? Typically,
it is when a business persists in selling an old product or pursuing an old strategy in defiance of changes in the market, technology, customer expectations. Many large corporations (e.g., GM,
Kodak, Xerox, AT&T, IBM) have been severely hurt by looking
backward instead of forward. New leadership is usually required to shake up stodgy companies and move them in a new
direction. For example, in his few weeks on the job, C. Michael
Armstrong, the first outsider in eighty years, shook up AT&T by
promising draconian cost cuts, making key acquisitions, speed-
ing up decision making, streamlining management, stretching
the executive workday, revamping the executive bonus system,
and rethinking the company strategy. He has made a slew of
acquisitions and entered into numerous joint ventures.
    Jack Welch is now looking for a successor at GE. What traits
is he looking for? "Vision. Courage. The four E's: energy, ability
to energize others, the edge to make tough decisions, and execu-
tion, which is key because you can't just decide but have to follow up in 19 ways."[34] Clearly he is looking for driven men.

Conclusion

Prime Movers are ferociously committed to action, which means they are committed to reality and to the necessity of bringing their ideas into concrete, material form. They are determined to overcome any challenge in order to achieve goals that leave lesser men gasping. But what is the deepest root of this drive? This is the subject of the next chapter.

Notes

1. A. Rand, *Atlas Shrugged* (New York: Signet, 1992), p. 312.
2. A. Heiner, *Henry J. Kaiser: Western Colossus* (San Francisco: Halo Books, 1991), p. 21.
3. G. Colvin, "How to Be a Great CEO," *Fortune,* May 24, 1999, pp. 104ff. R. Charan and G. Colvin, "Why CEOs Fail," *Fortune,* June 21, 1999, pp. 69ff.
4. S. Walton and J. Huey, *Made in America* (New York: Doubleday, 1992), p. 116.
5. R. Stern and J. Zweig, "A New Guy Can Do It Better," *Forbes,* November 25, 1991, p. 125.
6. J. Mandese, "Bloomberg Plays Rhythms of Finance, News Service Looks for More Media to Grow," *Advertising Age,* June 12, 1995, p. 4.
7. R. Preston, *American Steel* (New York: Prentice Hall, 1991), p. 88.
8. For example, see B. Staw, "The Escalation of Commitment to a Course of Action," *Academy of Management Review,* 1981, vol. 6, pp. 577–587.
9. A. Rand, op. cit., p. 36.
10. It is not always a symptom of secondhandedness to want fame. It can be proper to want to do something one considers great by one's own standards and hope that it will be appreciated (e.g., writing a great novel).
11. M. Josephson, *Edison* (New York: McGraw-Hill, 1959), p. 62.
12. For an analysis of the role of art in human life, see A. Rand, *The Romantic Manifesto* (New York: Signet, 1971).
13. S. Walton and J. Huey, op. cit., p. 11.
14. Ibid., p. 22.
15. Ibid., p. 78.

16. K. Kerwin et al., "Hurricane Huizenga," *Business Week*, February 24, 1997, p. 93.
17. E. Locke and G. Latham, *A Theory of Goal Setting and Task Performance* (Englewood Cliffs, N.J.: Prentice Hall, 1990).
18. A. Bianco, "The Rise of a Star," *Business Week*, December 21, 1998, p. 62.
19. C. J. Loomis, "AIG: Aggressive. Inscrutable. Greenberg.," *Fortune*, April 27, 1998, p. 108
20. J. Martin, "Eli Broad Runs Things His Way," *Fortune*, October 13, 1997, p. 178.
21. S. Sherman, "Stretch Goals: The Dark Side of Asking for Miracles," *Fortune*, November 13, 1995, p. 231.
22. B. Morris, "Roberto Goizueta and Jack Welch: The Wealth Builders," *Fortune*, December 11, 1995, pp. 80ff. (including interview that follows).
23. S. Prokesch, "Unleashing the Power of Learning: An Interview with British Petroleum's John Browne," *Harvard Business Review*, September/October 1997, pp. 147ff.
24. K. Iverson, *Plain Talk* (New York: Wiley, 1998).
25. T. Rodgers, W. Taylor, and R. Foreman, *No Excuses Management* (New York: Doubleday, 1992).
26. B. Morris, op. cit., p. 102.
27. R. Grover, *The Disney Touch* (New York: Irving Professional, 1991), p. 56.
28. L. Smith, "Stamina: Who Has It. Why You Need It. How You Get It," *Fortune*, November 28, 1994, pp. 127ff.
29. H. Casson, *Cyrus Hall McCormick: His Life and Work* (Chicago: A. C. McClurg, 1909), p. 187.
30. J. Casey, "Our Partnership Legacy," *United Parcel Service of America*, 1985, p. 7.
31. M. K. Ash, *Mary Kay* (New York: Harper & Row, 1981), p. 11.
32. J. Wallace and J. Erickson, *Hard Drive: Bill Gates and the Making of the Microsoft Empire* (New York: Wiley, 1992), p. 400.
33. S. Walton and J. Huey, op. cit., p. 45–46.
34. T. A. Stewart, "Who Will Run GE?" *Fortune*, January 11, 1999, p. 27.

6

Egoistic Passion

The creators were not selfless. It is the whole secret of their power—that it was self-sufficient, self-motivated, self-generated. A first cause, a fount of energy, a life force, a Prime Mover. The creator served nothing and no one. He . . . lived for himself.[1]

—Howard Roark in *The Fountainhead*

The only man never to be redeemed is the man without passion.[2]

—Francisco d'Anconia in *Atlas Shrugged*

In the previous chapter, I showed that great wealth creators are driven. Here I will answer the question, Driven by what? The answer is: ego. Ego is the motive power of Prime Movers; above all, they work for themselves. But what does this actually mean?

Counterfeit Egoism

For most people, egoism is a dirty word. To them, it connotes unthinking louts who act on their feelings of the moment without regard to reason, reality, or the rights of others. Such alleged egoists do whatever they want and reject all moral principles. Of course, there are people like this, but as I will demonstrate, they are counterfeit or inflated rather than true egoists. Let us consider a hypothetical but representative business example—the type of person that business magazines write about all the time, the businessman with the so-called big ego. Let us call him Mr. Big.

Mr. Big is CEO of Titanic Corp., a multibillion-dollar global company. Mr. Big has five corporate jets, apartments in four cities, and membership in three posh country clubs—all paid for by the company. He has a trophy wife bedecked with diamonds and emeralds. He owns a plush mansion where he gives frequent parties for the power elite; he has a private staff of yes-men who do his every bidding and never say no. He rarely leaves his office except for public functions. He eats in the executive dining room and has his own personal chef.

He vacillates between starting new projects based on his own whims and blindly copying what other companies are doing. His copycat actions are always in form rather than substance. If he hears that total quality management (TQM) is good, he starts a TQM program with much fanfare and then forgets about it a month later. He never gives reasons for starting or stopping a new initiative but demands unquestioning obedience from his employees. He makes it very clear to people who try to question him that he is the boss and knows it all.

He has spies everywhere in the company so he can be informed of what is going on, but he never shares his own knowledge with others. He lies or cheats whenever it is convenient, if he can get away with it. He gives inspiring speeches about delegation and empowerment but micromanages everything when he is around—which is only sporadically. He bullies subordinates and fires anyone who openly disagrees with him. He enjoys the feeling that people fear him. He plays top executives against one another, especially if they seem to be exceptionally able. He takes credit for the achievements of others but blames them for any failures. Mr. Big is stingy with rewards for employees, but he is generous with rewards for himself and makes sure his handpicked cronies on the board of directors always approve them. His compensation consists of a high fixed salary and perks, plus bonuses whose basis is unclear (except that they are not based on the creation of stockholder value). If he happens to get stock options and the price drops, he makes sure that the board reprices them at a lower level.

Mr. Big does not pay consistent attention to running the

business, preferring to spend his time, when not hobnobbing with important people, looking at the big picture, although nobody seems to know just what this picture consists of. He likes to call news conferences during which he boasts of his genius. His PR man makes sure that his name is constantly in the press.

Eventually, the company starts going downhill. The best people, especially top executives, start leaving. They reveal, privately, that they do not trust Mr. Big. Morale is low throughout the company. Key initiatives are stymied; new technological innovations die on the vine. Threats from competitors are ignored. A series of bad decisions are made; market share is lost and profits turn to losses. Stockholders sue the company as the stock plummets. Finally, Mr. Big is fired, his career in ruins. The business press solemnly declares that the downfall of Mr. Big was caused by his big ego.

But was it? Let us look at Mr. Big more closely. The actual meaning of egoism is concern with one's own interests. If we can assume that Mr. Big wanted to succeed, then he was certainly not acting to further his own interests as a CEO. Consider how he spent his time: Instead of attending to the business, he attended prestigious social functions, remained holed up in his office, or gave boastful speeches. When he did show up for work, observe the way he treated employees: He bullied, deceived, manipulated, and terminated them but never developed them or let them use their initiative. Note his lack of moral principles: He lacked the virtues of rationality, honesty, integrity, independence, and justice. He made decisions on whim, not on facts or reasoning. He lied, and he preached one thing and did another. Mr. Big focused on making an impression on others, but not on getting the job done; he copied what others appeared to be doing but failed to use his own judgment. He gave himself rewards he did not earn and denied others rewards they had earned. His policies were pragmatic; he did what seemed to work in the short run, but he failed completely in the long run. In sum, everything Mr. Big did undermined rather than enhanced his ability to succeed. His policies were not pro-self but anti-self. He was not furthering his own career; he was committing professional suicide.

Mr. Big clearly has much in common with the egotist (as

opposed to egoist) that Harold Geneen complained about at ITT. He describes the egotist as a person who lives in a world of his own imagination, oblivious to what is really going on around him, and who assumes that he knows everything and that everyone else knows nothing. Obviously, any such executive is doomed to failure because he looks inward at his own feelings and image rather than outward at reality to make decisions.

It is obvious that Mr. Big is, in fact, very small. Notice that he seems to have no values of his own, even in the realm of work. He lives for the appearance of success, for the prestige and power of his position, for the positive vibes supplied by others. He needs others to fill the void where his own values should have been. He feeds on the admiration given him by others as a substitute for the admiration he does not feel for himself. Inside such men there is no ego at all but a hollow shell desperate to be filled by other people's values and esteem. Such men are not wealth creators, but wealth getters and wealth flaunters.

Mr. Big does have an ego problem, but the problem is not that his ego is too big; it is too small and, at the same time, inflated. An inflated ego is a counterfeit ego; it reveals a desperate attempt to hide profound self-doubt by substituting the symbols of power and success for real accomplishment. The two dead giveaways of the inflated egoist's deep insecurity are a fear of employees with ability and a compulsive need to call attention to himself or herself. Egomania is not egoism.

Former Chrysler Vice Chairman Bob Lutz agrees: "You sometimes see CEOs who have big [inflated] egos, which come from insecurity. They have to be the center of attention, they intimidate people and take the upper hand right away in discussion, and they lead by creating the kind of fear where the employees live in trepidation of their reaction."[3]

Is Mr. Big just fiction? Consider Harding Lawrence, "The Man Who Killed Braniff."[4] He was described as a flamboyant showman and was convinced that he was brilliant. To show his persuasive ability, he liked to talk people into believing things that they knew were not true! He threw childish tantrums when he flew if the service personnel did not do what he wanted, even though he did not tell them what it was he wanted. He humiliated attendants and bullied and threatened managers. The managers were chosen for their ability not to displease him. After deregulation, he bought new routes without bothering to check whether or not they were profitable. (They weren't.) As the company sank into debt, he increased spending. He built a luxurious new headquarters building, where he holed up in a suite with his personal valet and housekeeper. He would call subordinates at 3:00 a.m. and harangue them about their incompetence. Not surprisingly, Lawrence was eventually fired in disgrace, and Braniff went bankrupt. If Lawrence was being selfish, then it is hard to imagine what he would have done differently had he been trying to be self-sacrificial.

John DeLorean, the former GM executive who tried to start his own automobile company, is another tragic example. His major focus was on polishing his own image, exaggerating his past achievements, getting press coverage, and making a good impression on investors through inflated sales estimates. At the same time, he neglected the details of the actual business, other than issuing occasional arbitrary orders based on his whims of the moment. The result was ignominious failure.[5]

True (Rational) Egoism

True egoists are not narcissists; they are not preoccupied with grandiose fantasies or obsessed with being the center of attention and getting constant approval. They are not concerned with self-inflation because they are secure within themselves and confident of their own value. They do not feel they have to disprove an inner sense of worthlessness. Their primary focus is not inward on their inner feelings, but outward on reality.

True egoists take the actions needed to succeed on the job. They look at the facts and use reason, not whim, to make decisions. They think and plan long-range. They learn what is going on and persuade others through two-way communication. Egoists spend their time learning about the business and about competitors; they learn from others but always use their independent judgment. They crave people of ability and strive to give them as much responsibility as they can handle. They reward people fairly and do not take more—or less—than they deserve. Egoists practice the virtues of honesty and integrity because they know that trust is critical for business success (see Chapter 8 for details). True egoists possess what Geneen calls normal or healthy self-esteem and self-confidence that are based on making decisions in accordance with the facts and the knowledge that they are continually learning and improving their knowledge and skills.

Mark Fraga of the Wharton School puts the issue as follows: "The person with the [genuinely] big ego is committed to the venture and will do whatever it takes to succeed. His attitude is, 'I'm here world. I'm going to turn air into gold [metaphor], I am going to make the impossible mundane.' "[6] Ego is essential to commitment. Venture capitalist Audrey MacLean explains: "Starting a company is like going to war. You can't do anything else but be fully engaged. You have to be insanely, passionately, nothing-can-stop-me committed.[7]

People are most often confused by executives who seem to share attributes of both the inflated and the genuine egoist. These are usually people of genuine ability who are independent in their work but who are dependent outside it, as shown by their cravings for attention and publicity. For example, in reviewing a book about Oracle Corp. CEO Larry Ellison, reporter Steve Hamm writes, "Ellison is a larger-than-life personality who wants desperately to be admired—and believes in nothing but himself."[8] Observe the contradiction here: If Ellison really believed fully in himself, he would not be desperate for the attention of others. There are a number of great wealth producers who are independent in their work and dependent outside of work, but allowing themselves to hold such contradictory premises is a dangerous indulgence. It is easy (and not uncommon) for such people to begin to neglect their work in favor of the limelight and also to let the secondhander attitude begin to affect the way they make work decisions. Many such people lose their effectiveness over time.

The alleged alternative or antidote to an inflated ego is no ego. Management gurus urge leaders to take the ego out of leadership. The new catchword in leadership today is servant leadership. Servant leaders, it is claimed, want nothing for themselves and only work altruistically for their employees, their customers, and the public.

This, of course, is utter nonsense. I am not being cynical here; I am not saying that wealth creators are not morally good enough to practice such an (allegedly) noble moral code. I am saying that they are too good to practice such an ignoble moral code (i.e., self-immolation). No self-respecting person would want to be a leader if all it meant was being a slave to the wants of others. No one could endure the stress, the long hours, the worry, the exhaustion, the risk and uncertainty, the endless problem solving, the frustrations and failures, the relentless pressures and demands that are the price of success in business—motivated by a selfless concern for the welfare of everyone but oneself. I do not know of a single wealth creator in history who was so motivated.

A selfless person like Mother Teresa might have been able to minister to the sick and the dying, using money donated by people who have earned it, but she would have been unable to create the wealth that made her work possible or to move an industrial civilization forward.

True egoists have strong passions based on their personal values but operate on the premise of reality and reason first. They do not sacrifice their own long-term interests to spur-of-the-moment whims. Nor do they sacrifice others by deceiving or defrauding them. True egoists treat other people with respect and trade with them honestly. They decide what they want to achieve, decide objectively on the proper means to achieve it, and act accordingly. *The proper antidote to counterfeit egoism is not altruism but genuine—rational—egoism.*

Management guru Lanny Goodman has this to say about the proper motivation of owner-entrepreneurs:

> Conventional wisdom would have us believe that a company has a life of its own and we're all there to serve it. . . . We're taught to be good soldiers, to serve others and sacrifice ourselves. I say, poppycock. . . . The founder's first obligation is to himself. If that obligation isn't satisfied, none of the others [to employees, customers, etc.] can be satisfied, either.[9]

Goodman advocates creative selfishness, by which he means the owner should pursue his or her legitimate interests and figure out how to make these interests converge with those of his or her employees and customers. Business, he says, is a bilateral process (i.e., a process of trade).

Focusing now on the motivational aspect of egoism, I believe the real key to the wealth creator's motivation is, surprisingly, love—not selfless love for others, but a profoundly personal, selfish love of the work, the product, the process of creation, growth, success, and the rewards earned through success. The old songwriters were right—in the wrong way: Love does make the world go 'round, but it is not romantic love (as wonderful and precious as that is) that produces the world's goods. It is love of achievement. Chrysler's Bob Lutz agrees with Tom Peters that the greatest breakthrough products are made by people who do it for "the sheer joy of creating for themselves."[10]

It is worth asking whether Prime Movers value the work more than the money or the money more than the work. My research indicates that they love both, but the work is more fundamental. A true egoist will not want to spend time and effort doing something he or she does not enjoy just for an extrinsic reward. Prime Movers love the process of making money as well as the money. Some consider it chic to say, "I really did not do it for the money," but somehow one never observes these people working for free. What they really mean by such a statement is that the work was their primary focus. Prime Movers, however, understand the causal relationship between work and money. If businessmen are good at their work, the money follows. Under capitalism, the two are inseparable. Unless the producer does good work and makes money, he or she will not be able to continue working; the money he or she makes is not only a way to keep score and a source of pleasure but also fuel to expand the business.

In view of this, it may seem puzzling that biographer Matthew Josephson seemed to worship Thomas Edison, a very successful businessman as well as inventor, at the same time that he disparaged other nineteenth-century capitalists, whom he called "robber barons."[11] I believe the reason for this is that Edison claimed that he made money in order to invent (create), while the so-called robber barons created so that they could make money. To Josephson, Edison's motivation must have seemed more intellectual and pure and the robber barons' motivation more earthly and materialistic. But this Platonic splitting off of man's faculties into higher and lower types is fallacious. Creation and moneymaking are reciprocally related: Each makes the other possible. The creation of wealth is a result of the creative use of one's mind; wealth, in turn, makes further creative efforts possible.

Now let us look at the motivation of some actual wealth creators.

Prime Movers at Work

John Allison, CEO and architect of BB&T Corp.'s expansion into a $30 billion banking powerhouse, says, "I love my work. I love the process of building a financial institution. And I love the fact that [due to stock appreciation] we have made many employees wealthy."[12]

Mary Kay Ash advises that the first priority in selecting an entrepreneurial career is to choose something you will enjoy. She writes, "Find something you like to do so much you would do it for free—and somebody will pay you well."[13] She mentions explicitly the need to love the work enough to be able to endure the long hours it will require. Mary Kay does enjoy the fact that she provides thousands of women with excellent jobs and that people get pleasure from using her cosmetics; but for her, the career starts with personal goals and priorities that are the means to personal happiness.

Michael Bloomberg believes that "all successful people love what they do, because a great percentage of success is just [to] keep doing it more often. . . . Sunday night," he says, "is the happiest night of the week because I know that when I fall asleep, I'm going to have a week of work. I can't wait to get back to work."[14]

Warren Buffett says, "I get to do what I like to do every single day. . . . It's tremendous fun."[15] For Buffett, this includes

being able to work with people he likes and to avoid people he
does not like.

James Casey of UPS inspired employees with his passion
for more than fifty years. He wrote that "we are in a company
where inspiration can flourish without frustration and where
individual initiative and self-expression are encouraged, not stifled. This condition is engendered among us largely because we
are an employee-owned company. We are not working for out-
siders. We are in business for ourselves."[16] It is not the case that
publicly owned companies necessarily destroy the ego, but they
do have more outside pressures than do privately owned ones.

Walt Disney was among the most passionate of Prime Movers. His first love, which began in childhood, was animation. He
did not hesitate to work twenty-hour days, to drive his people
incessantly for better quality, and to scrap entire projects if they
did not meet his standards. He constantly exceeded budgets in
an effort to make his films perfect. He became obsessed with his
desire to build Disneyland and would not rest until he got what
he wanted.

Michael Eisner, who is the current CEO of Walt Disney Co.,
and who returned stunning gains to shareholders over his first
fourteen years, discovered earlier in his career that "I loved the
concept of creating intellectual property." More, generally, he
claims, "I have a very strong sense of work; I enjoy working."[17]

Henry Ford's passion for mechanical devices manifested itself as early as age 7, when he began taking apart and repairing
watches and, later, machines such as steam engines. His passion
for the concept of a self-propelled vehicle began at age 12, when
he and his father came upon a wagon powered by a steam engine with a chain connected to the rear wagon wheels. This was
his original inspiration for the idea of the automobile. The Model
T became his later passion, and he spent almost twenty years
improving and perfecting the car and the method of assembly.

Ford's hero, Thomas Edison, had a lifelong passionate curiosity. He set up his own basement laboratory as a child. He took
night jobs so he could have the days to run experiments. He
spent his money on books and equipment rather than on food
or winter clothing. He lived in rat- and roach-infested rooming-

houses. He lost his whole fortune at one point in a failed venture, but nothing could stop him from inventing (and recouping his fortune). Unlike many people, he loved to think.

Bill Gates's passion for computers started when he was in the seventh grade; the private school he attended bought a teletype machine, which was connected to a primitive minicomputer in downtown Seattle. Gates became obsessed with the machine and with computers in general and spent all his spare time in the computer lab. When Gates and his friends (including Paul Allen) were given free computer time, they spent days and nights working at the computer to the neglect of everything else, including washing, sleeping, eating, and schoolwork. Gates was a true computer nerd—and a genius. Soon he and his colleagues were making money in return for their computer expertise. Gates's passion has not diminished to this day, although his range of activities is now much wider than it was as a teenager. He agrees with Buffett that "you've got to enjoy what you do every day."[18]

One often thinks of the Japanese as working selflessly for the company regardless of their own interests, but Honda Motor Co. founder Siochiro Honda rejected this philosophy completely. "First, each individual should work for himself—that's important. People will not sacrifice themselves for the company. They come to work at the company to enjoy themselves. That feeling would lead to innovation." He applies the same credo to himself: "The most important thing for me, is me."[19]

Steve Jobs is routinely described as having a passionate nature. Like Gates, he would think nothing of working day and night for weeks or months on end to get a job done (e.g., inventing the Macintosh). Jobs was especially effective in inspiring others with his passion, whether they were purchasing managers, investors, or employees. Jobs's passion was not always accompanied by good business judgment, but it was combined with enough vision to bring him stunning success.

Ken Iverson of Nucor loves making steel. "Hot metal has a fascination all of its own," he explains. "There is a fascination about melting a metal and pouring it into a shape. A hot metal man has to feel that fascination. That's why he works around metal."[20] Iverson made sure that Nucor employees felt the same way. He describes one new hire, who had never worked with steel before, straddling a red-hot billet of steel trying to hold together a broken hydraulic hose. "I was terrified he would burn himself. The hoses blew apart again and he got hydraulic fluid in his eyes. We took him down to wash his eyes out, and he turned to me and said, 'This is the best job I ever had.' He was a hot metal man, only he didn't know it."[21]

Roberto Goizueta's heir at Coca-Cola, M. Douglas Ivester, is described by a colleague as a man who "thoroughly enjoys what he is doing—his work is his hobby."[22] This is one reason he can visit forty-six different countries in 200 days and not feel stressed. Stress can come from perceived inability to get the job done, but it can also come from feeling compelled to expend enormous effort at a job (or career) one does not really love. Loving the work as such, however, is no guarantee of success as Ivester, who was recently fired, discovered.

International Management Group CEO Mark McCormack is unusual in terms of the longevity of his passion. Even though he is well past the normal retirement age of 65, he has no intention of retiring. He explains, "Why should I retire? Most people retire to something they have wanted to do all their lives. I am already doing it."[23] He believes that doing what he loves—"my passion is my work"[24]—gives him a competitive advantage over his competition with respect to having the motivation to persist in the face of hardships and difficulties.

When Dick Notebaert, the dynamic CEO of Ameritech, was asked how he had the energy to keep working so hard day after day, he replied, "Because it's fun. . . . I don't understand how people . . . can do something that's not fun."[25]

Wendy's founder Dave Thomas loved restaurants, even as a young boy. His adoptive grandmother worked in a restaurant, and he spent a good deal of time with her. Due to an unstable family situation, Dave and his adoptive father ate out frequently. He loved the bustling atmosphere, the sight of happy families, and the juicy burgers. At age 8, he decided he would someday own his own restaurant business. Starting at age 12, he took a series of restaurant jobs including a stint with Kentucky Fried Chicken, where he made his first million. His passion never flagged; eventually he started Wendy's and grew it into a global corporation.

Cornelius Vanderbilt loved to make money. He started with a $100 loan from his mother and ended with a $100 million fortune made in shipping and railroads, accumulated over a career that lasted more than sixty years. One critic complained: "He envisioned a chance, an opportunity, an invention, a trend in commerce, not as it would react to the advantage of the community, but in terms of his own profit. There was nothing in him of that will to public service which moved families . . . to sacrifice their energies and wealth to the attainment of an ideal."[26] The critic's ideal, presumably, was anything that benefited others but not himself. Vanderbilt's own philosophy was that "I have always served the public to the best of my ability. Why? Because, like every other man, it is in my best interest to do so."[27] In short, he made money for himself by trading value for value with the public.

It was Cornelius Vanderbilt's son William who uttered the immortal phrase, "The public be damned!" But few people know the full context. William had been asked by a reporter whether the public had been consulted about the proposed discontinuance of a mail train that was not profitable. The reporter asked, "Are you working for the public or your stockholders?" Vanderbilt replied, "The public be damned! I'm working for my stockholders." What he meant was that he was not in the business of sacrificing the interests of the owners to those members of the public who wanted him to run an unprofitable train.[28]

Sam Walton loved merchandising. He said, "It has been an absolute passion of mine. It is what I enjoy as much as anything in business. I really love to pick an item—maybe the most basic merchandise—and then call attention to it."[29] No wonder he was willing to spend so much time at it.

Legendary inventor Warren Buffett got it right when he said, "Find the leader who loves his business." Southwest Airlines' Herb Kelleher is Buffett's kind of CEO; says Kelleher, "I love it, I love it—I sure as heck do."[30]

Egoism and "The Public Interest"

In a revolt against egoism, modern public-spirited gurus have advocated what is called stakeholder capitalism, which means that every group that has an interest in what the company does (e.g., employees, customers, the community) should have a say in how the company is governed. No company could be successfully governed if such a theory were applied consistently; such a policy would produce chaos. The only legitimate stakeholders (assuming the company is not physically harming anyone) are the owners (stockholders) who have risked their own money in the venture. *Stakeholder capitalism is nothing more than an attempt by some people to plant their stakes on other people's property.*

A rational CEO will consider the interests of employees and customers not because either group necessarily has any ownership stake, but because they are the means by which he or she makes a profit. Disgruntled employees, high turnover, and customer dissatisfaction will undermine or destroy any business.

Great wealth creators do benefit the public—in the sense that many individuals benefit from their achievements—if the wealth creators are honest and left free to function (free, that is, from government coercion); but that benefit is a by-product of the capitalist system in which profit is made through trade. Under capitalism, the most creative, industrious, innovative, cost-conscious, customer-service–focused, visionary leaders make the greatest fortunes. But the prime motive for their work is not public service; it is their own selfish love of the work, the process of creating, and the financial rewards they earn as a result.

To quote Ayn Rand:

> The creator stands above any humanitarian.
>
> It is true that the real benefactors of mankind have been the creative, productive men. No humanitarian ever has or can equal the benefits men received from a Thomas Edison or a Henry Ford. But the creator is not concerned with these benefits; they are the secondary consequences. He considers his work, not love or service to others, as his primary goal in life. Thomas Edison was not concerned with the poor people in the slums who would get electric light. He was concerned with the light.[31]

Cypress Semiconductor President T. J. Rodgers is one of the few wealth creators who has stood up for the virtue of wealth creation. He defied the left-leaning nun, Sister Doris Gormley, who demanded that Rodgers choose corporate board members on the basis of racial and sexual quotas rather than competence. Rodgers is too selfish to jeopardize the company for the sake of social agendas. He also serves his self-interest by taking a modest salary and making his fortune by trying to ensure that the value of his stock is constantly appreciating.

Both the thinking and the action Prime Movers take to bring the thought into material form are motivated by ego, by their desire to achieve their values and to better themselves and their lives through productive work.

The Prime Mover's Attitude toward Himself

Given that true Prime Movers are egoists but not inflated egoists, what is their attitude toward themselves? For the best of them (that is, the most genuinely confident), it is this: They are aware and proud of their own ability and achievements, but not self-consciously so. They are not self-obsessed because they have no fundamental doubts to overcome. They have no need to convince themselves or others that they are great. They are not primarily focused on themselves, but on reality—on the facts and the work to be done. They project an inner self-sufficiency that requires no artificial reassurance. They may even appear modest by conventional standards because they do not have a need to boast or protect their self-image. They know their own value, they are confident of their own judgment, and other people's view of them is not important.

Passion and Reason

A caveat: Successful Prime Movers must be passionate, but they cannot succeed if they are dominated by passion (i.e., if they are emotionalists). Their love of the work gives them fuel, but it does not give them knowledge and judgment. Passion must be directed by reason, by focusing on reality, by taking facts seriously, by identifying what needs to be done to make the enterprise successful. When passion dominates, as it has from time to time for Steve Jobs, poor decisions can be made that alienate employees and may even threaten company viability. Jim Carlton's *Wall Street Journal* headline (April 14, 1998) says it all: "At Apple, a Fiery Jobs Often Makes Headway and Sometimes a Mess." If one's desire to make something work obscures one's knowledge of whether it is really working or not, then reality is denied. If it is denied consistently, then only disaster can ensue.

Conclusion

Ayn Rand summed up the motivation of what she called "the Money-Making Personality" as follows: "Behind his usually grim, expressionless face, the Money-Maker is committed to his work with the passion of a lover, the fire of a crusader, the dedication of a saint and the endurance of a martyr."[32] Prime Movers are motivated at root by ego—in the highest and most reverent meaning of that term. However, they do not operate as one-man firms. They have hundreds or thousands or hundreds of thousands of people working for them. How they choose, develop, train, and motivate such people is the subject of the next chapter.

Notes

1. A. Rand, *The Fountainhead* (New York: Signet, 1993), p. 678.
2. A. Rand, *Atlas Shrugged* (New York: Signet, 1992), p. 745.
3. Quoted in D. H. Freedman, "Got Guts?" *Inc.*, March 1999, p. 54.
4. B. Harris, "The Man Who Killed Braniff," *Texas Monthly*, July 1982.
5. J. Conger, "The Dark Side of Leadership," in R. Vecchio, ed., *Leadership* (Notre Dame, Ind.: University of Notre Dame Press, 1997).
6. Quoted in B. O'Reilly, "What It Takes to Start a Startup," *Fortune*, June 7, 1999, p. 138.
7. Quoted in M. B. Grover, "Starting a Company Is Like Going to War," *Forbes*, November 2, 1998, p. 186.
8. S. Hamm, "The Outrageous Enigma of Silicon Valley," *Business Week*, December 8, 1997, p. 19.
9. "The World According to Me" (interview with Lanny Goodman), *Inc.*, January 1998, p. 66.

10. Quoted in D. H. Freedman, op. cit., p. 52.
11. M. Josephson, *Edison* (New York: McGraw-Hill, 1959).
12. Presentation at the University of Maryland, College of Business and Management, March 2, 1998.
13. M. K. Ash, *Mary Kay: You Can Have It All* (Rocklin, Calif.: Prima Publishing, 1995), pp. 140–141.
14. W. Hearst, "The Terminal Man: A Conversation with Michael Bloomberg, Business News Magnate," *San Francisco Examiner*, July 10, 1994, p. B14.
15. "The Bill & Warren Show," *Fortune*, July 20, 1988, p. 52.
16. J. Casey, "Our Partnership Legacy," *United Parcel Service*, 1985, p. 103.
17. Michael Eisner interview, Las Vegas, Nevada, June 17, 1994. Interviewer unknown. Downloaded from Internet posting at <http://www.achievement.org/autodoc/page/eis0int-1>.
18. "The Bill & Warren Show," op. cit., p. 53.
19. R. L. Shook, *Honda: An American Success Story* (New York: Prentice Hall, 1988), p. 13.
20. R. Preston, *American Steel* (New York: Prentice Hall, 1991), p. 8.
21. Ibid., p. 78.
22. N. Deogun, "Can His Successor, Douglas Ivester, Refresh Coca-Cola?" *The Wall Street Journal*, November 20, 1997, p. B-1ff.
23. M. McCormack, *The 110% Solution* (New York: Villard Books, 1991), p. 221.
24. A. Robbins, "Power Talk: Anthony Robbins with Mark McCormack" (audiotape). Robbins Research International, 1993.
25. Quoted in N. Tichy and E. Cohen, *The Leadership Engine* (New York: HarperBusiness, 1997), p. 131.
26. A. D. Smith, *Commodore Vanderbilt: An Epic of American Achievement* (New York: R. M. McBride, 1927), p. 41.
27. W. J. Lane, *Commodore Vanderbilt* (New York: Knopf, 1942), p. 221.
28. B. Stevenson, *The Home Book of Quotations* (New York: Dodd, Mead, 1967), p. 1,480.
29. S. Walton and J. Huey, *Made in America* (New York: Doubleday, 1992), p. 57.
30. T. Stewart, "Why Leadership Matters," *Fortune*, March 2, 1998, p. 82.
31. M. Berliner, ed., *Letters of Ayn Rand* (New York: Dutton [Penguin], 1995), p. 82.
32. A. Rand, "The Money-Making Personality," *The Objectivist Forum*, vol. 4, no. 1, 1983, p. 4. (This article was originally published in *Cosmopolitan* magazine, April 1963.)

7

Love of Ability in Others

[M]y only love, the only value I care to live for, is that which has never been loved by the world, has never won recognition or friends or defenders: human ability. That is the love I am serving—and if I should lose my life, to what better purpose could I give it?[1]

—Ragnar Danneskjöld in *Atlas Shrugged*

To me—the foulest man on earth, more contemptible than a criminal, is the employer who rejects men for being too good.[2]

—Andrew Stockton in *Atlas Shrugged*

Prime Movers are neither omniscient nor omnipotent. They have to employ other people—lots of other people—in order to reach their goals. Just as they value ability in themselves, they value it in other people. Brainpower is always harder to find than muscle power. Managers can perform unskilled labor, but unskilled laborers cannot manage. Today, as more and more manual work is replaced by machinery (including computers), creative thought is the only permanent competitive advantage.

It follows that the more brainpower an organization has, the greater its potential for success. (I say potential because smart people alone are not enough. They have to be properly led and coordinated in order to be productive.) This need for brainpower is the proper meaning of the expression, "Our people [employees] are our most important asset." Excepting that the Prime Mover is the single most important asset, the expression is true.

Of course, many business leaders give lip service to it but do not mean it. At least five types of action are implied for those who, like Prime Movers, do mean it.

1. *Find.* Prime Movers look very hard for people with talent. Even when they are not actively looking, they keep their eye out for people they might want to hire in the future. Typically these are people they have met in the course of doing business or people they have heard about. Sometimes they are people who work for competitors. It is an interesting phenomenon that people tend to attract and be attracted to people who are like themselves; thus brilliant leaders (if they are not insecure) seek and attract very able subordinates, whereas mediocre leaders tend to attract mediocre talent. It is not clear whether mediocre performers prefer people like themselves for reasons of psychological comfort or whether less able people are simply less able to identify ability when they see it. I suspect it is both.

2. *Hire.* Prime Movers are typically very selective about whom they hire. They have an explicit hiring philosophy, and they put applicants through the wringer before deciding to make an offer. Only the very best make it. Thirty-five-year corporate veteran Joseph Goodell recommends a philosophy that many great business leaders practice: "Hire people who are smarter than you."[3] This does not mean that Prime Movers hire other Prime Movers who are even more capable than themselves (this is rare); rather, they hire people who know more than they do about *some aspect* of the business. CEO Doug Becker of Sylvan Learning Systems specifically recommends hiring executives who have strength in the CEO's major area(s) of weakness. Thus, a CEO who is a finance expert should hire someone with marketing expertise if marketing is critical to success, and vice versa.

3. *Develop.* Employees may be heavily trained, or they may simply be thrown into a difficult job and told to sink or swim. Either way, they are expected to learn a lot and learn it fast. Often they are given preposterous goals right from the start. This is actually an expression of confidence in the employee. Competent but inexperienced employees are ideal in one respect: They do not know that what they have been asked to do is impossible—which is why they so often succeed.

4. *Utilize.* Prime Movers, as with every effective leader, set the fundamental goals for the organization. There is no democracy here. But they delegate to able subordinates enormous responsibility for deciding how to reach the goals. Furthermore, they do not fear disagreement on the part of subordinates. Screaming fights are not unusual in dynamic organizations as a means of ensuring that conflicting viewpoints get a full hearing before any final decision is made. Intel is famous for such fights. Andy Grove calls his method "constructive confrontation"; it involves intensive debates about such issues as company strategies, technical issues, and markets; it even includes middle managers.[4] Prime Movers do not want obedience from their employees; they want ideas (i.e., thinking). Merck CEO Raymond Gilmartin says, "Where you want the contest is not among people but among ideas. It's very important for people to be able to challenge, to be very open."[5] Of course, organizational anarchy cannot be tolerated, so there have to be limits on disagreement. Typically, people who do not accept the CEO's basic vision are fired.

5. *Reward.* Able people are rewarded generously for their achievements. This topic will be addressed specifically in the next chapter.

A corollary of love of ability is the unwillingness to tolerate incompetence. An employee of a major U.S. corporation recently told me the following story. Her unit was very effective whereas a neighboring unit was not. She asked the director of the poorly performing unit what his philosophy toward poor performance was. The director replied, "You must love the nonperformers more." He evidently saw no connection between the poor performance of his unit and his management philosophy (the worship of incompetence). This is the exact opposite of the philosophy of Prime Movers. They love the nonperformers less. They are not above getting angry with them, humiliating them, or firing them. It is said that one of Bill Gates's favorite expressions is "That's the stupidest thing I ever heard of." Steve Jobs was prone to make equally belittling comments to employees whose work he did not like. Roberto Goizueta believed in an occasional "public flogging." Andy Grove frequently tongue-lashes people whose performance he considers below par.

Microsoft and Intel regularly weed out lower-performing employees. It is not that Prime Movers are deliberately insensitive (though some are); rather, they are simply too brilliant, too passionate about their visions, and too ambitious about their goals to tolerate people who are not doing a good job. Prime Movers can be very intimidating, but, at the same time (unless they are very insecure), they respect people who can argue back at them.

A recent *Fortune* article argues that the failure to implement strategy is the major cause of CEO failure, and the major reason for that is the failure to put the right person on the right job and the related failure to remove people who are not performing well.[6] This often occurs because the failed managers are personal friends or protégés.

Business and Friendship

It is not an original observation to say that mixing business and friendship is a very dangerous policy. Personal friendships involve a different type of currency than business relationships. The trade in friendship and romantic love is primarily spiritual: my character, ideas, and interests for your character, ideas, and interests. (Romantic love, of course, has an important physical aspect.) Sometimes, both types of trade involve the same people, but usually not. Keeping personal friends in positions of responsibility when they can no longer do the job not only reduces the effectiveness of the units under the incompetent manager, but also undermines the morale of the whole company when word gets around that "It's not what you can do but who you know that counts."

The proper relationship between employer and employee is functional, not personal. Prime Movers want people who can do the work, and that's usually all they want. They practice the code of competence. Their love of ability does not necessarily imply any type of personal friendship. I recently spoke to one seasoned executive who noted ruefully how one CEO had spent hours asking the executive about his views on various business matters and then had shown no further interest in him when the CEO had learned all he had wanted to learn. This is not atypical, nor is it improper. Business relationships involve a trade; from the viewpoint of the CEO, the trade is my money (and a chance to do something important and exciting) for your brains and work. Such relationships may, but do not normally, blossom into anything more. CEOs may show some interest in the personal lives of their employees, but usually this is very limited. (Yes, people do fall in love on the job, but this is an exception to the normal business relationship between people.)

It must be stressed that the same principle holds from the point of view of the employee. The employee very rarely takes a job because the boss is his or her closest friend or romantic partner. The employee wants a place to earn a living, to do interesting and challenging work, and to develop skills. The employee "uses" the boss in the same way that the boss "uses" him or her. Both agree to work together because each wants something from the other; an employment relationship involves a limited exchange, a mutual trade involving exchange of values. Such a functional or exchange relationship is fully appropriate given that the purpose of a business enterprise is to make a profit (i.e., to create wealth).

Once a company puts other goals on an equal footing with making an honest profit through voluntary trade, whether the other goals involve personal friendships or lifetime employment or something else, goal conflict inevitably results and profits eventually suffer. For example, it is in a Prime Mover's self-interest to have satisfied employees and, of course, satisfied customers. Customers who are satisfied stay loyal and come back for more. Employees who are treated well are more likely to be committed to organizational goals and to remain with the company than those who are unhappy. But employee satisfaction cannot become an end in itself, divorced from the need for profit. Paying everyone twice what they are worth and reducing the workweek to twenty hours might delight many people, but it will also lead to corporate suicide. *Putting people above profits means putting emotion above reason and reality.* The proper principle is: *profits through people*, using very capable people to earn profits.

An outstanding example of an unconflicted company is Coca-Cola under Roberto Goizueta, who said, "A publicly traded company exists for one purpose and one purpose only: to increase shareowner value."[7] And few people in history did it better than he did.

As for corporate donations (e.g., to charities, to educational institutions), these are pure acts of generosity and must be limited by the corporation's obligation to its stockholders. It is an interesting irony—but in fact totally logical—that Roberto Goizueta, by spending all his time building Coke's profits rather than doing civic projects, enormously benefited Atlanta. The increased value of the stock enabled individuals and foundations that owned Coke stock to undertake civic projects they could not have otherwise afforded.[8]

Let me make clear that I consider honest profit making to be fully moral as an end in itself—not because it serves society. The moral justification for profit is man's right to his own life, which means his right to trade freely with others and his right to reap the rewards of his efforts.[9] It is true that others benefit from the trade if the owner is able enough to create wealth, but that is not its moral justification. Man is not a slave of society, but a sovereign being.

Let us now observe how some Prime Movers demonstrate their love of ability in others.

Prime Movers as Ability Lovers

Most Prime Movers, at some point, hire one or more what I call right-hand men—people of extraordinary ability and skill—to help them with particular facets of the business. This is in addition to accumulating deep pools of talent at every level.

When Gordon Bethune became CEO of Continental Airlines, a perennial loser that no one thought could be saved, he fired fifty of the sixty-one executives. He also hired Greg Brenneman as second in command; together they hired an outstanding management team and brought the airline to profitability.

British entrepreneur Richard Branson has talent galore, including Gordon McCallum and Stephen Murphy. He needs it because his empire includes some 200 not always well-organized companies. One of the roles of Branson's top aides is to say no when his incurably active brain comes up with crazy ideas.

Michael Bloomberg's business empire was built on talent. For example, he hired Matt Winkler to be editor in chief of the *Bloomberg Business News,* and Winkler made it a sparkling success. Bloomberg pushes employees to develop their skills and is confident enough of his employees to promote from within rather than search for top executives from the outside. Bloomberg insists that all managers develop replacements. He says, "A good manager always has a replacement ready, and the best managers always have somebody who's better than they are."[10]

Prime Movers also take pains to develop the talent they have. Lawrence Bossidy, CEO of Allied Signal, has had brilliant success during his six years there and attributes it in part to his heavy emphasis on training, not only of executives but of all employees. He wants everyone to grow "six inches taller," which means growing markedly higher in terms of knowledge and skill. Training includes courses to promote functional excellence as well as leadership skill. His goal (based on Motorola): a six-sigma improvement in quality throughout the organization.[11]

Nineteenth-century steel magnate Andrew Carnegie hired Henry Clay Frick as one of his right-hand men, a Prime Mover in his own right in the field of coke ovens. He wanted Frick's ovens to help vertically integrate his steel business, and he wanted Frick because of his managerial genius. (Frick was not so able in union relations and helped precipitate the infamous Homestead Strike in Carnegie's absence. He and Carnegie also had other disagreements that led eventually to their complete alienation.) He hired steel expert William Jones to run his first great steel plant, the Edgar Thompson Works. He helped develop Charles Schwab, later to become famous as president of Bethlehem Steel Co. Carnegie wrote, "I am sure I never could have [been successful] without my partners, of whom I had thirty-two, the brightest and cleverest young fellows in the world."[12] In this he was no doubt correct. Louis Hacker quotes one witness before a congressional committee who said, "Carnegie . . . exceeded any man I ever knew in his ability to pick a man from one place and put him in another for maximum effect."[13]

John Chambers, the CEO of the very successful Cisco Systems, aims to get the top 10 percent to 15 percent of people in the industry. Cisco actively seeks to reach potential applicants through unusual venues such as fairs, festivals, and home and garden shows. Current employees are linked up with prospects and given a bonus if the prospect is hired. It also recruits through its sophisticated Web site and is constantly coming up with innovative recruiting ideas.[14]

Michael Dell, a brilliant visionary but inexperienced in many facets of business, had the good judgment to hire Mort Topfer from Motorola to run operations (especially purchasing and manufacturing), Kevin Rollins to manage American operations, and several Apple executives to fix his power notebooks. Over the past several years, Dell stock has soared at a rate that makes other dynamic companies look anemic. (Naturally, the company is now under attack by rivals, who want to use direct marketing and cost reduction to take away Dell's market share.)

Walt Disney depended heavily on the brilliant animation skills of Ub Iwerks, who was a better animator than Disney himself. Iwerks was once hired away from Disney until Disney hired him back again. He also hired hundreds of other talented animators. Walt depended heavily on his brother Roy to manage the business side of the company.

Chrysler was originally saved by Lee Iacocca, but his own weakness as a CEO began to hurt the company. Robert Eaton revived it again with the help of Bob Lutz, who no one thought would stay when Eaton became CEO. Lutz was especially skillful at combining intuition with market data when designing new cars. The two men's talents complemented each other perfectly.

One of Michael Eisner's first steps when he became CEO of Disney was to bring in top-notch talent. He acknowledged that "One of the keys to success is having people who are all better than you."[15] His team of sixty new executives included superstars Jeff Katzenberg, Frank Wells, and Gary Wilson. Getting talent and keeping it, however, are two different things. Wells died in a tragic accident. Katzenberg left in a huff when he did not get Wells's job and took some top executives with him. The talented finance-wizard Steve Bollenbach did not stay long. Recently, Disney has experienced an accelerated exodus of talent that may or may not be a sign of problems to come, though it is ominous that Disney has been in the doldrums in recent years. Executive turnover is not necessarily fatal; it all depends on whether departing talent can be replaced by equal talent. Sam Walton was able to do it after several of his top executives quit. It remains to be seen if Eisner can also do it.

Pierre DuPont was such a determined talent collector that he bought entire companies solely for the purpose of getting outstanding people. (Note the difference between DuPont's philosophy and that of many contemporary acquisitors who want the acquired company's technology and customer list but show little interest in the talents of its employees.) DuPont's most brilliant decision with respect to love for ability occurred after he was named president of General Motors by J. P. Morgan in 1920. He knew that he was not very knowledgeable about the automobile industry, so he appointed Alfred P. Sloan to the post of operations vice president. In 1923, DuPont resigned from GM and Sloan was appointed president—and the rest is history. Sloan far surpassed Henry Ford in his ability to manage and soon made GM the number one automobile company in the world.

Henry Ford hired many able people to work for him—James Couzens, George Holly, Ernest Kanzler, William Knudsen, Charles Sorenson, John Wandersee, and others—and they made enormous contributions to the success of the company, especially in its early years. However, in the long term, Ford failed to fully utilize his managerial talent because he could not tolerate disagreement. As the years passed, consumed with the desire to run things the way he wanted, Ford managed more and more on the basis of personal whim and became less and less open to the ideas of others. Most shocking was his decision to let Knudsen depart. Ford admitted that Knudsen was "the best production man in the United States."[16] Ford said, "I let him go, not because he wasn't good, but because he was too good—for me."[17] This disastrous decision was symbolic of Ford's downfall, and also a cause of it. Knudsen went to General Motors and played a critical role in its resurgence—at Ford's expense.

Few Prime Movers are more respected (and envied) for their ability to attract talent than Bill Gates. Gates observed early in his career that many of the programmers IBM hired were not highly capable. Microsoft's philosophy was: If you're not good, you don't stick around. Gates loaded the company with brilliant people: Paul Allen was his early partner; Steve Ballmer was his right-hand man and now runs the company; Charles Simonyi and Gordon Letwin were gifted programmers. Gates acknowledges "that in terms of IQ, you've got to be very elitist in picking the people who deserve to write software."[18] The supersmart, according to Gates, can evaluate a long printed code at a glance, learn very rapidly, ask acute questions, concentrate intensely, and possess photographic recall. Microsoft does not wait for people to come to it (although it gets 120,000 résumés each year); it drains the brains of other companies at every opportunity. Like Pierre DuPont, it acquires other companies specifically to acquire their talent. Gates admits, "Take our 20 best people away, and I will tell you that Microsoft would become an unimportant company."[19] Note the explicit recognition here that some people are more critical to the company's success than others.

Gates is now raiding other companies and universities to build a whole new brain trust, which will staff an enormous research and development effort. It includes 245 of the brightest people in the world in fields such as lasers, minicomputers, graphics, software technology, and even statistical physics.[20] Microsoft's technology chief, Nathan Myhrvold, expects the lab to create enough revolutionary new products to more than pay for itself for decades to come.

Microsoft recently has been suffering a brain drain of its own (including Myhrvold). Most of the leavers are 40-something multimillionaires who no longer have the drive to put in the long hours and/or who want to start their own companies. Microsoft, however, probably has the talent pool to replace them.

The ability of Gates to attract talent brings up an important principle: Successful growth companies more readily attract talent than those that are unsuccessful or declining—not only because of the stock options that are offered but because people like to work in companies that are efficacious (i.e., companies that know what they are doing and where they are going). Talented people also like to work with other talented people, and they like the chance to get ahead. The reverse side of this coin is that companies that are declining or struggling tend to bleed talent (as occurred during the dark days at IBM and AT&T). Able people do not want to work either for CEOs who do not seem to know what they are doing or where their abilities are not appreciated. Turning around a company in a downward spiral often requires hiring a highly regarded outside CEO, who has enough of a reputation to bring other talented people on board.

When IBM Chief Lou Gerstner agreed to save IBM, he brought several top executives with him. His right-hand man is Larry Ricciardi. One of his key roles is challenging Gerstner's thinking. Ricciardi is described as extremely bright and quite willing to express his opinion, which Gerstner appreciates. "I do not want people around me who tell me . . . what they think I want to hear."[21]

Roberto Goizueta of Coca-Cola was widely praised for his ability to develop a deep pool of managerial talent and his ability to delegate responsibility as one means of doing it. Board member Susan King says, "For years, Coke has been identifying, maintaining and developing the best young talent. It's not something that happens overnight."[22] His first right-hand man was Don Keough, who had been a rival for the CEO job. His second, and eventual successor, was M. Douglas Ivester, whom he hired away from Ernst & Whinney. Ivester himself, however, was reputed to have been less successful in developing his managers, which may have contributed to the loss of his own job.

Intel, which was started by founders Robert Noyce and Gordon Moore and continued by Andy Grove, takes enormous pains to find and hire the best. Professors at engineering schools and professional friends are asked to name the brightest students they know. Promising candidates are interviewed as many as six times. These interviews are considered so important that even the CEO cannot interrupt them. All employees are given annual ratings and even rated against each other. Employees who leave may be given exit interviews by Grove himself, so that he can learn if company policies need improvement.

The multitalented Wayne Huizenga relies heavily on right-hand man Steven Berrard. Berrard honed his skills at Blockbuster and ran Republic Industries and AutoNation. His special skill is implementing the strategy that Huizenga has laid out. Huizenga also has outstanding executives running his other businesses such as his hotel chain, Extended Stay America.

Ken Iverson and his colleagues at Nucor, Dave Aycock and Sam Siegal, hired very talented managers—"smart, down-to-earth, and ambitious" (John Correnti, Keith Busse)—but not very many of them because they fervently believed in a very lean management structure.[23] In contrast to many companies, Iverson steered clear of MBAs from top-rated schools because they tended to be too arrogant. (When he was CEO, Iverson had a temper and was not averse to having shouting matches to resolve disagreements.) Steelworkers were hired, based not on their experience at steelmaking but on their willingness to learn and take responsibility. Plant manager Keith Busse, who was in charge of building a plant containing a machine that had never been used before, related that "No one [here] has ever built a steel plant before. . . . Most of 'em have never done construction of any kind. What better way is there to learn? The mind's a powerful thing."[24] Busse was right. They built the plant and made it into a tremendous success. (Busse got passed over in favor of Correnti for CEO when Iverson became board chairman, so he quit and started his own steel company. Recently Nucor itself had a palace revolt in which Iverson and Correnti were pushed out. It remains to be seen if the remaining managers can sustain Nucor's enviable record of growth.)

Steve Job's early alter ego at Apple was Steve Wozniak, who was the technical genius behind the Apple computer. He also hired many brilliant programmers and technicians, who under his leadership made the Apple and Macintosh personal computers the foundation of a multibillion-dollar business. Unfortunately, Jobs was never able to find a COO who was capable of both managing and dealing with Jobs's mercurial style of management—in fact, Apple has yet to find a CEO who can succeed long term. Now that Jobs is back and doing well, it remains to be seen whether or not Apple will prosper in the long run.

Mark McCormack, CEO of International Management Group, originally found and negotiated with all his clients himself. He soon realized, however, that this limited his ability to expand, so he deliberately set out to hire people smarter than he was and let them develop their own ability to serve clients. He even hired people who had beaten him out in competition for a client, concluding that this showed they had ability. A former vice president commented that McCormack "demands that his people be aggressive, smart and imaginative. . . . He will accept ideas rapidly, and if you do well, he will leave you alone."[25]

With respect to the selection process, few Prime Movers besides Gates put more emphasis on it than Ross Perot. When he ran EDS, applicants initially had to start by filling out a twenty-page questionnaire. The applicant was then interviewed by everyone in the company—at the same time. Perot then talked to the applicant's wife to make sure she did not object to the outrageous hours the employee sometimes would be expected to work (e.g., eighty hours a week), and the fact that he might sleep at the office some nights or even spend weeks away from home. Later, the questionnaire was shortened and interviewing was conducted by a three-person team; it was still a grueling process. At one point, only one out of every seventy applicants was hired. One of the things EDS wanted to know was whether the person had the potential to manage. When one candidate complained that EDS screened as though it was hiring vice presidents, the reply was, "We are." Perot did not always wait for applicants to come to him. A favorite target of his raids for ability was IBM, from which he stole salesmen, programmers, and engineers. EDS became famous for its capable, dedicated workforce, which helped make Perot a billionaire.

John D. Rockefeller, the world's first business billionaire, chose a very able right-hand man in Henry Flagler, who had been a successful shipper in Cleveland. (After leaving Rockefeller, Flagler developed railroads and resort hotels in Florida.) It was said of Rockefeller: "All he wanted to know about a man was whether he was honest and able."[26] He did not object to disagreement if the person could back it up. At meetings, he often just listened to others exchange ideas without saying a word, but at the end he could tie all the points together and come to a firm decision.

The hiring procedures at Cypress Semiconductor would not embarrass Perot. Like EDS under Perot, Cypress raids other companies for talent, but even more aggressively. President T. J. Rodgers sends out raiding parties with the deliberate aim of hiring top talent in some technical specialty away from specific companies. Hiring is a critical part of top managers' jobs, rather than being delegated to the HR department or lower-level personnel. Potential employees are evaluated at great length. There is a specific set of hiring procedures that every recruiter must follow. In-depth reference checks are made. Every candidate is subjected to at least four interviews; the interviews are tough and technically demanding. All candidates are rated numerically. Wavering recruits are even visited at home by senior managers. Furthermore, when an employee does not work out as planned, the hiring file is examined in detail to see if anything was missed or if the employment procedure needs improvement. This rigorous procedure enables Cypress to amass top-flight talent and is a major reason for its rapid growth. Great efforts are also made to retain talent when other companies try to raid Cypress, which is now approaching the $1 billion sales mark.

Starbucks CEO Howard Schultz attributes his success in considerable part to surrounding himself with outstanding executive talent. One of his hit products, Frappuccino, was invented by the manager of a California store, who served it to customers without Schultz's knowledge. He personally did not like the iced coffee blend, but there was enough evidence from people who did like it to convince him to test and refine it further before rolling it out in 1995. In three years, it generated $100 million in revenue.

James Sims, CEO of Cambridge Technology Partners, invests a staggering $10,000 per employee per year on employee training—more than ten times the average of other high-tech companies. Sims claims that this helps the company retain employees because they can develop their skills without having to look for growth opportunities elsewhere. His highly skilled workforce has a competitive advantage over rivals, especially in terms of the speed with which they can complete projects.

Sam Walton spent endless hours nosing around competitors' stores for merchandising ideas. At the same time, he prospected for talent. He would not always require experience as long as the person was highly motivated. His first manager, Willard Walker, was hired away from a five-and-dime store. Walker was a capable manager, but he was no dummy when it came to investing. He bought stock in Wal-Mart when even Walton wasn't sure it was going to succeed. One thing that Walton looked for in his managers was love of retailing. Walton hired many able executives, including Bob Thornton, Ron Mayer (who later left the company), Ferold Arend, and Jack Shewmaker. When Walton first tried to hire David Glass, the current CEO, Glass would not come. But Walton was relentless, and eventually Glass accepted. It took him twenty years to convince Don Soderquist to join. Walton was smart enough to hire people with the skills that he lacked (e.g., distribution). He had some rough times when disgruntled managers left and took others with them, but he always managed to hire new talent to replace those who quit.

GE is another company that is known for its deep pool of talent. Critical to GE's success, aside from Jack Welch, is Gary Wendt, who for twelve years directed the fastest-growing and most profitable part of the company, GE Capital Services, which encompasses twenty-seven different businesses. Under Wendt, GE Capital averaged 18 percent profit growth over his last five years. If this part of the company were to stand alone, it would rank twentieth on the Fortune 500 list. Wendt, who like Welch was a visionary leader, relied heavily on Denis Nayden to execute his plans. Wendt pushed relentlessly for growth; thus, only people with enormous ability and great self-confidence were hired and retained. It is noteworthy that Welch and Wendt did not get along particularly well, but Welch respected Wendt's ability enough to want to keep him for twelve years.

Welch is known to accumulate volumes of data from many different sources on his executives. "We spend all our time on people," he says.[27] Depending on the individual, regular assessment leads to promotion, further development, or, in some cases, termination.

Falls from Grace

Business leaders fail for many reasons. Some are just not smart enough to do the job. Some are inflated egoists who want to play the role of a CEO but not actually do the necessary work. Some lack moral principles; others do not have to drive to succeed. A common reason for failure, however, is the inability or unwillingness to hire, use, and retain people of ability. I noted above that this flaw helped cause Henry Ford's downfall and almost destroyed the company. Ford's was a mixed case because he was initially extraordinarily successful, but his attitude, along with his judgment, seemed to get worse with age. Some of his later executives (e.g., Harry Bennett) were more like thugs than managers.

Bob Nourse, former CEO of Bombay Co., a specialty furniture dealer, is a similar case, though on a smaller scale.[28] Nourse was considered a brilliant entrepreneur after his initial success, which lasted several years; then for seven years, the company's stock lagged due to lackluster performance. In 1990, Nourse hired Michael Glazer, an experienced retailer, to run the company. Glazer did an outstanding job for five years, generating substantial increases in sales and operating income. The stock price rose from the $2 to $5 range to $32 by the end of 1993. In mid-1994, however, just when the company had achieved record sales, Nourse choked off Glazer's strategy, which had depended heavily on sales promotions. It seems that Nourse had resented Glazer's success. At this point, the company started on a long downward slide that led to Glazer's resignation in early 1995. This was followed by an exodus of key managers. Nourse took over the helm himself but could not stem the slide, and the company went into the red. The stock price plummeted until the board fired Nourse. Without Glazer and his key managers, the talent was simply not there.

The lack of a good right-hand man harmed Oxford Health Plans founder Stephen Wiggins. He grew the company brilliantly but was unable to manage the growth and was fired as CEO. He describes himself as "an entrepreneur first, a professional manager second.[29] There is nothing wrong with this except that he should have hired a top-notch professional manager to compensate for his own lack of managerial expertise.

The inability to tolerate men of ability may also have contributed to the downfall of AT&T CEO Robert Allen.[30] Although he had some successes, he made many disastrous decisions, and AT&T's performance consistently lagged the market. Notably, Allen was never able to develop or retain a competent right-hand man or anyone who might succeed him. Most executives with high potential eventually quit the company. Allen even opposed the hiring of his successor, C. Michael Armstrong, forcing the board to do it over his head and push him into early retirement.

Stories like this are not uncommon in business, but few stories are more tragic than that of William Agee. Agee was a very bright financial expert who previously had been with Bendix until a failed takeover of another company backfired. He was given control of an old-line international construction firm, Morrison Knudsen, even though he had no previous experience in the construction business (other than having been on the company's board). According to insiders, Agee, despite his own lack of knowledge, continually downplayed the talents of his best managers and ended up getting rid of them. One director observed that "he'd move people up, but then when they got to where we could see them, he'd move them back down. . . . As soon as we liked someone, Bill would say he wasn't a performer. . . . All of sudden, we started hearing horror stories about him, and then he was out. . . . He was afraid to have talent around."[31] Finally, Agee was left with only young, inexperienced managers who were afraid to argue with him. After making a series of disastrous business decisions and withholding key information from the board, he was fired. The company eventually went bankrupt.

Some brilliant leaders can get by for a time, when the organization is not too large, without exceptional managerial talent simply on the force of their own energy and knowledge. But when the leader does not have all the needed expertise and fires everyone who does have it, the company has no chance. As a board member put it, Agee did not have enough confidence in himself to be able to tolerate highly competent people. Instead of being an ability magnet, he was an ability repeller. Conventionally, such a problem is attributed to a big ego, but as I noted in the previous chapter, it is really a sign of a small ego that the individual is trying desperately to cover up. The man with a genuinely strong ego thrives in the light emitted by the ability of others; he is not afraid of being partly in their shadow.

The Role of the Individual in an Age of Groupism

Given the importance of able individuals to the success of organizations in general and the success of Prime Movers in particular, what are we to make of the modern emphasis on groups and teams? There is no doubt that this is the age of groupism.[32] Groups and teams are everywhere: There are cross-functional teams, product teams, new product teams, project teams, customer teams, service teams, sales teams, task teams, process-improvement teams, quality-control teams, natural-work teams, cost-reduction teams, financial teams, and self-managed teams. Some MBA programs are even focused around student teams.

But in recent years, the emphasis on groups and teams has gone far beyond any rational assessment of their practical usefulness. We are in the age of "groupomania." Teams have become endowed with almost mystical qualities. It is as though putting people into a team endows them with superhuman capacities and makes them virtually omnipotent. Teams, it is implied, will cure almost any organizational disease, solve any problem, achieve any goal. But, of course, they will not. Somewhere along the way, two important principles have been forgotten.

The first principle is: *Teams are composed of individuals.* I am not entering into a sociological debate concerning whether teams are more than the sum of their members; my point is more fundamental. It is a metaphysical fact that groups and teams are composed of separate, sovereign individuals whose brains are not interconnected. This is the meaning of the concept of individualism at the metaphysical level. There is no superorganism called a group apart from its individual members. Take away the parts and the whole is gone. Although group members may teach and inspire one another, they do not automatically endow each other with the knowledge or intelligence that none of them possess, skills that none of them have, or moral virtues that all of them lack.

But you would never know this from reading recent articles on this subject. As a case in point, consider an article in *Fortune* magazine that glorifies teams.[33] Seven high-performing teams are described: the Navy Seals, the Dallas Cowboys offensive line, the Tokyo String Quartet, the University of North Carolina women's soccer team, the Massachusetts General Hospital emergency-trauma team, the Boots and Coots international firefighting team (hellfighters), and the Childress stockcar racing team. I quote in full the author's conclusions about what makes them all successful:

> We are talking here about teamwork at a rarefied level, a swarm of people acting as one. These folks have checked their self-interest back in the garage somewhere and moved to another zone. It's a state in which team members—be they musicians, commandos, or athletes—create a collective ego, one that gets results unattainable by people merely working side by side. It's all about humility, of course. Is that why it's such a scarce thing in the business world?[34]

In sum, the author is saying that effective teams are not composed of individuals with skills, values, minds, and egos but of egoless, humble ciphers, who, by some unnamed process, merge into a superorganism with an ego of its own.

The article is striking for the way this conclusion ignores the story's own content. Let us take a look at the facts the author mentions in the very same article. First, the team members in question are brilliantly talented. The Navy Seals are initially selected based on extremely rigorous criteria and then put through a hellish training regimen that only 30 percent of this elite group gets through. The Dallas Cowboys line in question consisted of five huge (300 pounds or more), hardworking, and highly trained individuals, who their coach claims are the best he has ever had (several were all-pros). The members of the Tokyo

String Quartet are all skilled enough to be virtuoso soloists. The North Carolina women's soccer coach puts the team members through ferocious practices and each week posts the performance of individual players in every practice drill. The Massachusetts General team consists of experts in several medical specialties. The Boots and Coots hellfighter team is so selective that they refuse to hire anyone they have not known for years and trained extensively. Only the Childress team denigrates skill, seemingly because most of the team activities do not require a high skill level.

Does the author expect us to believe that these teams would still be highly effective if their members were not incredibly able, hardworking, and trained to an extraordinary high level of skill? Does he think an offensive line consisting of untrained, 200-pound, lazy wimps who worked very smoothly together could carry the Cowboys to a Super Bowl victory? Michael Schrage, the author of an article in another business publication, got it right when he observed that "a collaboration of incompetents, no matter how diligent or well-meaning, cannot be successful."[35] Consider, for example, the ambitious reengineering plan at team-oriented Levi-Strauss that came in very late and way over budget. Business writer Stratford Sherman writes, "When a bunch of highly aspirational pants experts try to envision the inventory forecasting software of the future, their openness, honesty and respect for one another's opinions cannot alter the fact that none of them really know what they are talking about."[36]

The inadequacy of team spirit or team cohesion alone in fostering good performance was revealed in an article on the 1994 Olympic Games. U.S. team coaches stressed team cohesion more than ever before, but some of the most cohesive teams did very poorly (e.g., men's soccer, women's volleyball). The men's soccer coach explicitly rejected the concept of the hotshot superstar in favor of players who could lift team spirits. Apparently, they failed to also lift team scoring. Ability aside, psychologist Roberta Kraus, who worked with several Olympic teams, argues that too much team focus can be damaging motivationally. "Players who have lost their individuality inside the team become weaker because they don't have a sense of their unique role. That means they tend to hesitate and not assert themselves when their particular abilities are called for."[37]

Group success depends on the heroic efforts of individual members. Effective groups are composed of individuals with a high degree of task-relevant knowledge and ability, strong values and goals, and the willingness and courage to think for themselves. These individuals are most able to stand up to group conformity pressures, champion organizational change, and contribute to goal attainment.

My emphasis on the individual is not idle chatter. Recently the CEO of Honda had to rid the company of excess "consensus management which he found slow and unfocused, [and under which] no hard decisions were made."[38] He began by stressing the need for more individual initiative.

Consider the following story recently told to me in confidence:

> As a consultant to an airline manufacturer, I was helping to troubleshoot a system that would test part of the avionics [i.e., electronics] for their new aircraft. The test system was not working, and for two weeks they had had a large team studying the test system, but they could not figure out what was wrong with it. I spent three days analyzing how the system was built, and then told the committee chairman that in two hours I could test the system performance, because I now understand where the system would fail first. He laughed and said, "You mean to tell me that all these engineers have been studying this problem for two weeks and all by yourself you are going to characterize the system performance in two hours?" I said, "Yes," and I did.

> The problem was that each engineer saw a small part of the problem, but no single mind had studied the problem as a whole (i.e., the total system). They had thirty-two channels of information, but, because of a faulty design, no more than two could work at the same time. This meant that some of the avionics could not be fully tested by the system. [In an actual airplane, if the

avionics were to malfunction, it would lead to disaster.]
Well, this discovery started a panic. So what did they
do? They made another team of these same engineers,
and they brainstormed ideas at random and then *voted*
on how to fix the system! In disgust and horror, I said
to the team leader, "You don't really think this is going
to work, do you?" He admitted that they had no clue
as to what to do, but said at least everyone felt they
had participated! Finally, one member of the team, who
seemed to have some real understanding of what the
problem was, took over the project, selected his own
small team of knowledgeable people, and fixed it. Who
knows what went on in other units? I know that once
the whole avionics system and all backups went dead
during a test flight, and they never could explain it. If
this is the way they characteristically analyze problems,
I don't ever want to fly in this airplane.

This striking example illustrates an important principle: A
team working on a complex problem is helpless unless one or
more individual members grasp the system (i.e., nature of the
problem) as a whole. Simply throwing a large number of minds
at the problem will not necessarily produce effective results. It
reminds one of the oft-told tale of the team of blindfolded men
feeling the different parts of an elephant: Each man thought the
part that he perceived was the whole. The proper resolution is
that at least one member has to remove his blindfold and perceive the entire animal. On complex tasks, this has to be a person
of exceptional ability and knowledge.

The existence of a group adds only one fundamentally new
(albeit important) element to what is present with individuals:
coordination (communication is critical in groups, of course, but
it is the means by which coordination is achieved.) Group members have to cooperate or coordinate their activities if they want
to reach their goal. In basketball, for example, a disorganized
bunch of freelancers do not have a chance (other things such as
ability being equal) against a disciplined team where each member knows his role and fulfills it.

This brings me to another important principle: *The motive*

for group cooperation is egoistic. Cooperation does not involve self-sacrifice unless the individual has no interest in the success of the group. Consider the following example: Imagine a basketball player, Pete, who is a very good ball handler and passer, plays defense well, and rebounds effectively. But he is not a very good shooter, averaging only about six points a game. If Pete is rational, which means that he recognizes his limitations yet wants to take the actions needed to win, he will play within his ability, using his strengths and avoiding his weaknesses. Rather than taking a lot of shots, he will set up plays for others and pass the ball to them so that they can score. Conventionally, Pete would be called an "unselfish" player because he does not try to score a lot of points, but the truth is exactly the opposite. Pete's attempt to score a lot would, in fact, be egoless and irrational because he would risk losing the game and thereby undermine his own goal. It would be a contradiction to claim that he wants to win and then take actions that make it impossible. By passing, playing tough defense, and rebounding, Pete is being selfish in relation to his goal. Only if he truly wanted to sacrifice himself should he take as many shots as possible; this would guarantee that the team would lose.

What, then, are we to make of the humility that was praised so highly in the earlier quote on teams? Are the Dallas Cowboys linemen really humble, simply because they do not boast and seek the limelight? Quoting the author, who once again ignores his own data, "[One lineman] says he and his colleagues are especially proud that opponents have been able to penetrate their protective curtain and dump quarterback Troy Aikman on his fanny only about once per game this season."[39] Does the author of the *Fortune* magazine article believe that these linemen would be just as effective if they were not proud of their achievement, that is, if they did not personally care how well they performed? Does he expect us to believe that the Navy Seals are not personally proud of being good enough to be accepted into one of the most elite military units in the world? Does he think that it is not in the self-interest of each member of the North Carolina women's soccer team to work hard and cooperate so that they can win the national championship?

Groups do not become effective by destroying the egos of

their individual members. An individual with no ego (i.e., no motive power) will not be of any use to anyone. An individual with no ego will not be motivated to contribute to group performance. Therefore, what the group needs to do is to harness the egos of its members in order to achieve a common goal that is personally valued by each member. To be motivated, each member must be convinced that the group goal has personal significance. For example, in a sports team this goal is winning, which leads to personal satisfaction. In a work team, it is success in solving some problem, which contributes to company success, which in turn aids job security and future opportunity. Therefore, a key task of team and organizational leaders is to show members why working for a group or organizational goal is in their self-interest. The leader can start by giving a convincing rational explanation for the important goal in question.

Linking rewards to performance is also crucial (see the next chapter). In every team, there are apt to be members who contribute more than others and those who contribute less. Naturally, members resent free riders who get the same rewards as everyone else. In the case of team-based incentives, this is usually handled by group members pressuring any recalcitrant members to do their proper share or, as a last resort, asking them to leave. This procedure has been very effective at Nucor.[40]

Of course, teams whose members are both motivated and able do not inevitably succeed. There can be many reasons for this: The problem, as given, may be unsolvable; there may not be adequate support (e.g., resources) from outside the group; the time allowed may be too short; the means for implementing the solution may not be provided; the team goal may be unclear; or there may be personality conflicts among the members. Furthermore, team members may not possess the needed team management skills to effectively coordinate individual efforts. For example, they may not have developed a viable method for settling disputes. However, this type of problem is usually resolved through training.

There are certain individuals, however, who are incapable of working in peer groups because they have no peers. I am not referring here to individuals who are neurotic or totally blind to the basic requirements of group functioning (e.g., taking turns when speaking), although such people do exist. Rather, there are some people whose knowledge, ability, confidence, ambition, energy, and passion are so overwhelming—so much greater than anyone else's—that they cannot function as a member of a group of equals. Groups would destroy them, or vice versa. Prime Movers, men like Harold Geneen, Bill Gates, Jack Welch, and Michael Milken, have to be leaders.

We do need to use some teams and groups in the management of organizations. But we should not forget that they are composed of individuals and that, at root, organizations rise (and fall) as a result of the thinking (or nonthinking) of individual minds. Love for ability in others means loving, nurturing, and respecting those individual minds.

Modern intellectuals who attempt to deride the importance of the individual typically do so by caricaturing individualism. As noted earlier, they portray the individualist leader or executive as an isolated figure who claims to know it all, acts like a petty tyrant toward subordinates, refuses to accept good suggestions, micromanages everything, and takes all the credit for any successes. Such a leader is an irrationalist (and an inflated egoist), not an individualist.

The antidote to such irrationality is not distributing leadership around the organization—at least not in the sense of giving up the CEO's critical role in setting the basic course for the organization as a whole. The antidote is rational leadership: formulating a viable vision, hiring the best people possible, and making it clear what has to be accomplished. Given that these people are competent and accept the CEO's vision, they can and should be allowed to lead in their own divisions, departments, and domains.

Conclusion

Organizations rise and fall on their brainpower: how much they have and how well they use it. Only individual minds exist. Prime Movers are especially adept at finding, using, and keeping talented individuals. To properly use and keep good people (and to succeed in general), business leaders must be virtuous—

that's right, I said virtuous. In the next chapter, I shall discuss what virtue consists of.

Notes

1. A. Rand, *Atlas Shrugged* (New York: Signet, 1992), p. 537.
2. Ibid., p. 670.
3. H. Lancaster, "Joseph Goodell Knows About All the Pitfalls of the Corporate Life," *The Wall Street Journal,* November 12, 1996, p. B-1.
4. A. Grove, *Only the Paranoid Survive* (New York: Doubleday [Currency], 1996).
5. J. Weber, "Mr. Nice Guy with a Mission," *Business Week,* November 25, 1996, pp. 135, 137.
6. R. Charan and G. Colvin, "Why CEOs Fail," *Fortune,* June 21, 1999, pp. 69ff.
7. J. Huey, "In Search of Roberto's Secret Formula," *Fortune,* December 29, 1997, p. 234.
8. N. Deogun, "Roberto Goizueta Led Coca-Cola Stock Surge, and Its Home Prospers," *The Wall Street Journal,* November 20, 1997, pp. 1ff.
9. See A. Rand, *The Virtue of Selfishness* (New York: Signet, 1964), and Rand, op. cit.
10. "What Should You Say When an Employee Quits?" *Inc.,* March 1998, p. 59.
11. Interview with Lawrence A. Bossidy, *PW Review,* June 1997, pp. 41–53.
12. Quoted in L. Hacker, *The World of Andrew Carnegie: 1865–1901* (New York: Lippincott, 1968), p. 358.
13. Ibid., p. 358.
14. P. Nakache, "Cisco's Recruiting Edge," *Fortune,* September 29, 1997, pp. 275ff.
15. Quoted in J. Flower, *Prince of the Magic Kingdom* (New York: Wiley, 1991), p. 163.
16. R. Lacey, *Ford: The Men and the Machine* (Boston: Little Brown, 1986), p. 274.
17. Ibid., p. 274.
18. R. Stross, "Microsoft's Big Advantage—Hiring Only the Supersmart," *Fortune,* November 25, 1996, p. 160.
19. Ibid., p. 162.

144The Prime Movers

20. R. Stross, "Mr. Gates Builds His Brain Trust," *Fortune,* December 8, 1997, pp. 84ff.
21. Quoted in "Big Blue's Blunt Bohemian," *Business Week,* June 14, 1999, p. 107.
22. D. Greising, "What Other CEOs Can Learn from Goizueta." *Business Week,* November 3, 1997, p. 38.
23. K. Iverson, *Plain Talk* (New York: Wiley, 1998).
24. R. Preston, *American Steel* (New York: Prentice Hall, 1991), p. 16.
25. E. Swift, "The Most Powerful Man in Sports: Mark McCormack," *Sports Illustrated,* May 21, 1990, p. 102.
26. A. Nevins, *John D. Rockefeller: The Heroic Age of American Enterprise* (New York: Charles Scribner's Sons, vol. 1, 1990), p. 395.
27. Quoted in R. Charan and G. Colvin, op. cit., p. 74.
28. E. Welles, "The Fall of Bombay," *Inc.,* January 1996, pp. 48ff.
29. S. Jackson, "Not Everything Oxford Did Needs Repair," *Business Week,* March 9, 1998, p. 38.
30. J. Keller, "How AT&T Directors Decided It Was Time for Change at the Top," *The Wall Street Journal,* November 20, 1997, pp. 1ff.
31. B. O'Reilly, "Agee in Exile," *Fortune,* May 29, 1995, p. 59.
32. Portions of this section of the chapter were based on E. Locke, "The Importance of the Individual in an Age of Groupism," in M. Turner, ed., *Groups at Work: Advances in Theory and Research* (Mahwah, N.J.: Lawrence Erlbaum, in press).
33. K. Labich, "Elite Teams Get the Job Done," *Fortune,* February 19, 1996, pp. 90ff.
34. Ibid., p. 99.
35. M. Schrage, "The Rules of Collaboration," *Forbes ASAP,* June 5, 1995, p. 88.
36. S. Sherman, "Levi's As Ye Sew, So Shall Ye Reap," *Fortune,* May 12, 1997, p. 116.
37. J. Schrof, "Team Chemistry Set," *U.S. News & World Report,* August 5, 1995, p. 54.
38. A. Taylor, "The Man Who Put Honda Back on Track," *Fortune,* September 9, 1996, p. 96.
39. K. Labich, op. cit., p. 94.
40. K. Iverson, op. cit., pp. 109ff.

8

Virtue

Virtue is not an end in itself. Virtue is not its own reward or sacrificial fodder for the reward of evil. Life is the reward of virtue—and happiness is the goal and the reward of life.[1]

—John Galt in *Atlas Shrugged*

The reader may be asking two questions in reaction to the title of this chapter:

1. Why put virtue at the end of the book?
2. What on earth does virtue have to do with making money?

This chapter will answer both questions.

To answer the first: I have actually been discussing virtue all along, although I have not exhausted the topic. In order to answer the second question, we must first understand what virtue is. By virtue, I do not mean the traits of character that are conventionally called virtuous: piety, humility, faith, self-sacrifice. I do not consider these to be virtues.

Nor do I agree with the *Harvard Business Review*'s attempt to deal with the issue of virtue. Consider its oft-cited article (first published in 1983 and reprinted in 1997) entitled "The Parable of the Sadhu," which is supposed to provide insights into business ethics.[2] The story involves a foolish Indian holy man, a Sadhu, who evidently, due to his own lack of foresight and planning, was found half-naked, suffering from starvation and hypothermia, near a mountain pass. The moral issue was: What obligation did the various hikers who came along have to the Sadhu? The article provided no answer but declared that the issue was too complex for one person to solve and that a solution required a shared group consensus. This, of course, is no answer at all. Group subjectivism is not a code of ethics.

Furthermore, the Sadhu case has nothing to do with business and is irrelevant even to ethics. The topic of ethics cannot be properly addressed by discussing "lifeboat" situations. Man's need for ethics does not derive from the necessity for dealing with emergencies that he will probably never encounter, but from his need to live successfully on an everyday basis. As for the Sadhu, he acted irrationally by exposing himself to extreme risk without proper preparation. As a result of failing to use his rational judgment, he placed his life at the mercy of the hikers who, unlike him, had rationally planned their trip by dressing warmly and carrying food. The hikers' decision to leave him food and clothing was more than generous and does not merit the hand-wringing exhibited by the author of the article.

With respect to business and to life, what is needed is an objective approach to the subject of ethics. This is made even more urgent by recent polls that show business students to be cynical about the whole subject of morality. This is undoubtedly the result of the widely held view that moral principles are nothing more than arbitrary subjective preferences. I disagree.[3]

Values

To understand virtue, we must understand the nature of values. A value, to quote Ayn Rand, is "that which one acts to gain and/or keep."[4] Value presupposes an answer to the question, "Of value to *whom* and for *what*?"[5] Value presupposes the existence of an entity capable of goal-directed action. Goal-directed action is possible only to entities faced with a fundamental alternative, that is, entities to whom the outcome of an action makes a difference. It is only to living entities that action can make a difference because only living entities face the fundamental alternative of life or death. It is only because a living entity's existence is conditional upon specific courses of action that we can describe its action as goal-directed. The ultimate aim of goal-directed action is the preservation of the organism's life. It is only to living organisms that something can be desirable or undesirable, valuable or harmful. Thus, "It is only the concept of 'Life' that makes the concept of 'Value' possible."[6]

Given that life is the ultimate standard of value, we must address this question: How does man survive? In the case of the lower organisms, goal-directed action is automatic. For plants, such actions are regulated by built-in physiological mechanisms (e.g., root growth, turning leaves toward the sun). In the case of the lower animals, the faculty of consciousness guides motion through the environment, but such actions are not volitionally chosen. Physiology, memory, and the pleasure-pain mechanism automatically promote life-enhancing actions, within the limits of the animal's capacity to adapt.

In man, however, innate physiological mechanisms and feelings of pleasure and pain, though present, are not sufficient for survival. Man's consciousness is conceptual (rational) and volitional. Man is not automatically preprogrammed to switch on (i.e., to focus on the facts and integrate them), and he is not automatically endowed with knowledge. To learn how to survive, man has to choose to think, to discover how to sustain his life, and to act consistently on his knowledge. Man's fundamental guide to action is his code of morality. "A code of values accepted by choice is a code of morality."[7] The purpose of a code of morality, a code of values, is to promote and protect man's life.

Egoism

A proper (pro-life) moral code is necessarily egoistic.[8] Egoism is implicit in the fact that the purpose of a moral code is to guide one's actions so as to further one's survival. The concept of egoism identifies the proper beneficiary of one's moral code: oneself. A moral code that demands self-sacrifice or self-immolation would be a flagrant contradiction of the whole purpose of such a code. Advocating a code of self-sacrifice in response to the fact

that man needs a moral code would be the equivalent of recom-
mending poison in response to the fact that man needs food.

Although a moral code that fulfills its proper, life-preserv-
ing function is necessarily egoistic, the concept of egoism itself
does not identify *what* is in one's self-interest (i.e., what actions
are pro-life). The next question to address, then, is, What is required for man to act in his own interest? Mindless hedonism—
indulging the pleasures of the moment—will not work to
preserve life long-term. Emotional indulgence may give the temporary illusion of pleasure to drugged hippies, but it is not
man's tool of survival. To survive, man has to acquire and practice virtue; a virtue is the action required to gain or keep a value.

Rationality

Survival for man means long-range survival. He cannot survive
for long by considering only the situation of the moment and
acting on impulse. He must consider the implications of his
every choice and action across the range of a lifetime. Man's
primary tool for long-range survival is his mind, his rational faculty. Through thinking, he must identify facts and principles
(general truths) that can guide his long-range actions with respect to the thousands of concrete choices and situations he will
encounter. It is his mind that discovers how to find, produce,
and store food. It is his mind that discovers how to build shelter
and make clothing. It is his mind that discovers philosophy,
identifies scientific truths, invents tools, creates technology, for-
mulates the principles of government, designs cities, and produces wealth.

If man's chief tool of survival is his mind, it follows that
his highest virtue must entail the proper use of his mind. Since
thinking is a volitional process, the proper use of his mind is not
automatic. The basic alternatives are to use reason as his means
of gaining knowledge and making choices or to use some other
method. By default, the only other method is using feelings
(emotions)—either his own or the feelings of others. But feelings, as critical as they are for motivation and joy in living, are
not tools of knowledge. Reason, which integrates and identifies

the material provided by the senses, is man's tool of knowledge. Because man's survival depends fundamentally upon gaining knowledge and using that knowledge to guide action, rationality is the highest virtue.

Reason is not, at root, antithetical to emotion. Emotions are the consequences of automatic, subconscious value judgments or appraisals and are, therefore, the product of ideas. If one has an emotion that conflicts with one's conscious, rational judgment, it means that one holds one or more subconscious ideas that conflict with one's conscious ideas. Consider, for example, an unmarried CEO who is strongly attracted to an applicant of the opposite sex who has very little knowledge or ability of the type needed in his company. His reason says: Do not hire her. His emotion says: I want her working here. Why does he want her? Probably because he is attracted to characteristics that she possesses (e.g., charm, beauty, intelligence, other types of ability) and that he values, but which have nothing to do with her company-relevant abilities. Since reason is volitional, he has the power to identify the reasons behind the conflict and take the appropriate action (e.g., do not hire her, but ask her for a date).

In the realm of work, it is fully appropriate to act on egoistic passion of the type described in Chapter 6, if such action is consistent with one's rational judgment. For example, if one passionately loves the real estate business, then it is proper to go into it provided one acquires the knowledge and skill needed to be successful. On the other hand, it is not proper to burn down a competitor's office no matter how much one loves to win at competition. (I will show below why such actions are not in one's self-interest.)

Prime Movers are neither blind emotionalists nor emotionless rationalists. They are passionate lovers of their work and of success, who use reason to guide their choices and actions. Reason comes first, emotion second. If and when Prime Movers run into trouble (other than for reasons of lack of ability), it is often because they have subconsciously reversed this order (e.g., Henry Ford in his later years).

Rationality means taking reality seriously and not trying to evade it simply because it makes one feel temporarily unhappy. GE CEO Jack Welch is an excellent example of this virtue in action. One of his six rules of business (which I quoted in Chapter 3) is: "Face reality as it is, not as it was or as you wish . . . facing reality is crucial in life, not just in business. You have to see the world in the purest, clearest way possible, or you can't make decisions on a rational basis."[9]

The number of ambitious businesspeople who have foundered because they indulged in wishful thinking at the expense of reality are legion. The active mind, which I discussed in Chapter 3, is an expression of the virtue of rationality. Reason is an active and not a passive process and, in business, requires a never-ending determination to understand one's business, technology, strengths, weaknesses, potentialities, competitive threats, future needs, and opportunities.

Hewlett-Packard's Carly Fiorina regards humility before (i.e., acceptance of) reality as a virtual axiom of management. Part of being reality-centered, she asserts, is being aware that you do not know everything and admitting errors when you make them. Errors cannot be corrected unless they are first acknowledged.

Harold Geneen of ITT is another example of a reality orientation. Geneen was adamant about the need for managers to make decisions on the basis of unshakable facts—as distinguished from apparent, presumed, reported, accepted, and hoped-for facts.[10] He insisted on "a discipline of adhering to factual objectivity in dealing with the realities of our business problems."[11]

Similarly, Ken Iverson insists on objective information, especially with respect to performance, which Nucor measures with numbers in order to eliminate the subjective.[12] Of course, there is always uncertainty in business, but that does not eliminate the necessity to be sure that you know what you know.

Legendary investor Warren Buffett identifies the principle explicitly. Asked to explain the key to his success, he denies that IQ is sufficient: "The big thing is rationality. I always look at IQ and talent as representing the horsepower of the motor, but the output—the efficiency with which that motor works—depends on rationality."[13]

Love of ability in others (see Chapter 7) is also an expression of rationality. A rational man knows that unless he is running a one-person business, he cannot do the thinking of 100, 1,000, or 10,000 other people, and that his success will depend heavily on the talents of the people who work for him. The greater the scope and size of his business, the more talent he needs.

Rationality means thinking in principles in the realm of business management. The range-of-the-moment pragmatist who decides to do whatever seems to work today, without regard for tomorrow, will not succeed for long. The quick fixers who postpone maintenance, lower quality, record future orders as sales, undermine merit pay, engage in little deceptions, ignore customers, or mistreat employees in order to jack up the next quarterly statement, while ignoring the underlying problems, will be the ones who eventually get "fixed" when the consequences of their actions come home to roost.

Let us now consider other virtues, all of which are implied by the virtue of rationality.

Independence

The virtue of independence refers to one's acceptance of the responsibility of using one's own judgment for the purpose of sustaining one's own life. The need for this virtue stems from the fact that every mind and every body is individual. Anyone who defaults on this responsibility can only live as a parasite on the thinking and effort of other people. This undermines one's capacity to live.

Consider the man who replaces his perception of reality with the opinions, feelings, whims, or assertions of other people. The first question he must confront is: Which other people? People differ in their opinions about every imaginable subject, so how does he know whom to trust? If he asks two (or a hundred) people and they disagree, how is he to decide between them? If he asks another person whom to trust about judging trustworthiness, he is twice removed from reality. And if his mind is unfit to perceive or grasp reality, how can it be fit to pick some other person to do it for him? In judging others' opinions, how will he be able to distinguish between the arbitrary or the evil and the rational? Abnegating his mind reduces man to helplessness. He might get lucky temporarily and follow a herd that happens, for the moment, to know where it is going, but eventually he is bound to run off a cliff. Survival then becomes a matter of chance.

The concept of independence has been deliberately misconstrued by collectivists who insist that individuality is an illusion because men live in a society where they depend on others for knowledge and goods. True independence for the collectivist would mean living alone on a desert island using only the knowledge one discovered by oneself and producing all the goods needed to survive. This, of course, is absurd.

It is not a breach of independence to seek and use the knowledge of others, including experts. Using knowledge discovered by others is critical to survival. But an independent man will judge the experts for himself. He will listen to their arguments, examine the facts they cite, study their past performance, check out their reputation, and evaluate their decisions on a continual basis. He will not conform mindlessly just because a majority believes something. In the end, he may accept the experts' or majority's decisions or reject them, in accordance with his best judgment of the evidence and arguments.

In Chapter 2, I noted that Prime Movers were men of independent vision. Because they were breaking new ground, they consistently rejected the status quo and conceived of a product, service, technology, or industry that no one had thought of before, or that others had thought of and rejected as impossible or impractical.

Although Prime Movers are leaders, not followers, they do not reject the virtue of independence when they take account of what their competitors are doing. Business is by its nature competitive, and knowing your competition is part of holding the full context of knowledge relevant to your business. However, there is a big difference between blindly copying competitors' visions (because they must know what they are doing) and understanding what they are up to and its potential value. Sometimes the basic concept of a competitor (e.g., discount retailing by Kmart) is taken over by someone else (e.g., Wal-Mart) but put into practice far more effectively.

Independence applies to the realm of action as well as to the realm of thought. It does not involve producing all the goods one consumes but rather taking responsibility for earning a living through voluntary trade with others. Dependence means living secondhand solely on the efforts of others. Parasites are counting on others to exert the effort that they choose not to exert and hoping that not too many others will get in on the game so that they will not starve. They favor independent action by others to sustain their life. Parasites want to survive on the generosity of others who have exerted effort, or to force others to support them (through government coercion). If everyone in society were a parasite, all would starve. Although some Prime Movers have been inconsistent, the best of them (e.g., Commodore Vanderbilt and James J. Hill) did not want and did not seek government favors (e.g., crippling their competitors) or subsidies (i.e., money taken from taxpayers) to help their businesses. What they wanted above all was freedom: the freedom to trade, to take risks, and to take the consequences, penalties, and rewards of their own decisions. Such men are the opposite of Folsom's political entrepreneurs who want to get rich through government favors that protect them from the vicissitudes of the free market.

It must be stressed that independence does not mean an emotionalist defiance of authority—defiance for the sake of defiance. Doing the opposite of what other people are doing is simply another form of dependence. If a businessman goes against the crowd, it should be because he rationally judges the crowd to be wrong, not because he wants to be different from them. For example, Nucor's Ken Iverson told stock analysts that his company would not accept the conventional emphasis on short-term results, insisting that the company would function better following a long-term (three- to five-year) perspective.[14]

Productiveness

The virtue of productiveness is the process of using one's mind to create material values. Man is neither a ghost nor a machine (nor a ghost in a machine), but an integrated entity, a unity of mind and body. It is his rational mind that identifies the values—and the means to achieve them—which make possible his physical survival, comfort, and well-being. Knowledge is not an end in itself but a means to the end of living successfully on earth. This means that knowledge must be used to guide action. The virtue of productiveness was implicit in my previous discussions of drive, the need for action, and egoistic passion.

Productiveness, as I noted previously, is not an expression of man's lower nature but of his true spiritual nature. By spiritual, I mean based on the best within him. Man's highest faculty is his rational faculty, his capacity to think and to reason. This is the source of his ability to discover and pursue great values, especially the values that make life and happiness possible. *Wealth creation is not a necessary evil as some have claimed, but a moral achievement.* It requires the consistent use of man's highest mental faculties and consistent effortful action. Without production, life on earth would be impossible. Hunting and gathering gifts provided by nature (e.g., wild animals, nuts and berries) would only support a few people and not for very long. It is man's creative capacity applied to action that has enabled mankind to rise from the swamps to the stars.

Great scientists and inventors (and rational intellectuals) are producers in their own way; they provide the knowledge and technology that others can use. But it is the industrialists and their helpers (e.g., engineers, bankers) who directly produce the goods and services that sustain our lives.

Prime Movers stand out from others in their extraordinary capacity for production, for producing far beyond what they consume. Others might be able to build a house or run a shop, but Prime Movers create, enlarge, or change entire industries. Others might employ a few helpers; Prime Movers employ thousands. Others might create thousands of dollars in wealth, but Prime Movers create millions or billions. Others accept the course of history; Prime Movers make history.

*   *   *   *

The previous three virtues (rationality, independence, productiveness) have been addressed, at least implicitly, in other chapters. It is now necessary to deal with three virtues that have not been discussed yet: honesty, integrity, and justice.

Honesty

Few virtues have been more misunderstood than that of honesty, and not only in the realm of business.[15] On the one hand, it is universally (though incorrectly) conceded that dishonesty is motivated by and a reflection of egoism. People lie or cheat, it is said, because they are selfish, that is, because they *want* to get away with something. For example, a businessman deceives a customer so that he can make a sale or cheats a partner so that he can make a bigger profit. Such actions are allegedly in his self-interest because, after all, he *wants* the money.

The solution to such moral corruption, it is claimed, is to sacrifice one's self-interest out of duty (e.g., to God, to society). Thus, the choice that is offered to the businessman (or anyone else) is: Do what you really want—succeed and be immoral—or give up what you really want—sacrifice yourself and be moral. This means either sacrifice others to yourself or sacrifice yourself to others. In other words, you can be either practical or moral but not both.

Everything is wrong with this ghastly dichotomy, not the least of which is the separation of morality from living successfully. Let us scrutinize honesty in more detail. Honesty means "the refusal to fake reality"[16]; therefore, it includes but is wider in meaning than lying or cheating. Honesty requires an active mind and a ruthlessly objective focus on, and evaluation of, all the facts relevant to a decision. Suppose, for example, a businessman is confronted with two seemingly contradictory facts: His best product is selling at record levels, but customers are complaining in record numbers about its inadequacies. An honest CEO will focus on resolving rather than evading this paradox by gathering more evidence. Consider Thomas B. Watson, Jr., who observed that IBM's mechanical sorters were selling in record numbers while customers were complaining that they did not have enough storage space for all the cards. This helped him to see the potential value of electronic computers. A lesser man would have faked reality by focusing only on present sales (which gave him good feelings) and evaded the evidence that future sales were threatened (which gave him bad feelings).

Honesty also means honesty in one's motivation. An honest man seeks knowledge because he intends, when appropriate, to act on it. A dishonest man seeks to evade or rationalize his knowledge so that he does not have to act on it. For example, when Lou Gerstner first became CEO at IBM, he asked its customers what IBM was doing wrong so that he could improve customer service. He did not ask for the negative information and then ignore it or proceed to tell customers that they were mistaken. He used the information to improve the company. Similarly, in 1976 Sam Walton invited a group of noncompeting retail experts to critique his Wal-Mart stores. Their critique was devastating, but Walton did not dismiss the critics. Instead he made the episode a turning point in the company's history. The company made massive changes as a result of the critique and made the company much stronger as a result.

When dealing with others, an honest man appeals to others' intelligence and knowledge, not to their stupidity, gullibility, and ignorance. When he appeals to ignorance, then reality, facts, and logic become his enemy, and his rational faculty is twisted into a tool for distorting rather than perceiving reality. Consider, for example, cigarette manufacturers. As a former smoker, I concluded in the late 1950s (long before government warnings were required) that smoking was a risk factor in lung cancer, based on findings reported in many newspapers and magazines at that time. Wouldn't it have been better for the manufacturers at this time, who were privy to the same data, to simply say, "There is some evidence that smoking may be a risk factor in lung cancer. Choose your own risk," rather than denying the whole issue until the evidence became too overwhelming to evade (and the government stepped in)? This tactic would also have put full and clear responsibility for smoking and its consequences squarely where it belonged: on the consumers who, if they voluntarily chose to smoke, knew the risks involved.

Now consider the temptation that a businessperson might have to lie or cheat openly. Even though one might feel the *desire* to take such an action, *it is not, in fact, in one's self-interest to do so.* Consider the following fictional, but realistic, example.

Businessman A takes out a loan to manufacture a new product that his company has never made before. He has been unable to make the product according to specifications and is running out of cash. The bank will not lend more money for this product. The customers will be angry if the product is late. What should Businessman A do? Here are some dishonest options:

1. Ship the faulty product, demand payment, and hope the customer will not figure it out for a while.
2. Get another bank loan on the pretense that it is for some other project.
3. Take money from your children's college savings accounts, but do not tell your wife or kids because it would upset them.
4. Take the money from the employees' pension account, but do not tell them because they would not agree to this.

If Businessman A chooses option 1, the customers will eventually discover that the product does not work and either refuse payment (if they discover the problem in time) or demand immediate repayment. They might even take him to court for fraud. Furthermore, they will no longer trust him to make products for them and will probably withdraw future business. They are also likely to let the word out to other companies that he is not to be trusted. If he chooses option 2, he is breaching the trust of his bankers. When they discover his deception, they will demand repayment or threaten court action on the grounds that he has committed fraud. Furthermore, they will be disinclined to lend him any more money, and his reputation within the local business community will be undermined or destroyed. If he takes option 3, he will have breached the trust of his wife and his children, perhaps irrevocably, and undermined his children's educational opportunities. If he selects option 4, he has cheated his employees, undermined their retirement plans, and set himself up for accusations of theft.

Thus, in practical terms, his dishonesty will not only threaten the long-term viability of his business and breach or severely undermine the trust of everyone he does business with and of his loved ones. It may also lead to the loss of key employees, which will further threaten his business. (And if certain employees find out that he has been dishonest and do not care, that is even worse. The next step could be that *they* will do things to deceive *him*.)

But the damage is not only practical. Consider what his dishonesty will do to his thinking process. Instead of focusing on the actual problem he is faced with and how to really solve it, he will be focusing on how to fake reality so that the problem will appear to be solved. Even a short-term infusion of cash will not do anything to address the real issue: What is he going to do about that product? Furthermore, once he starts lying, he must use other lies to cover up the first lie and then will have to keep track of which lie he has told each person so that he will not give himself away. For example, if he lies to his banker, he will also have to lie to his comptroller about how he got the money and to his legal staff regarding its legality. His whole focus will not be on seeing reality but on the management of unreality. He will not be appealing to the intelligence of others, but to their ignorance. His goal will be to ensure that they do not perceive what is true. His enemy will become anyone who does perceive the truth, who wants to understand the facts, or who is curious or mentally alert. *The result will be the destruction of his own capacity to think—the very action he must rely on to succeed in business.*

It must be stressed that virtue in this example does not consist primarily of resisting temptation. Rather, it means taking reality seriously, thinking long-range, and acting accordingly.

It is important to understand that virtues cannot be isolated from each other. The individual or businessperson who seeks to fake reality automatically undermines the virtue of rationality. By relinquishing judgment in order to delude victims, he gives up independent judgment. By destroying his mind's capacity to think about reality, he undermines the ability to be productive.

The better type of businessperson has always said that "Honesty pays." This is true, but in a much deeper sense than people realize. It is a matter of not only being honest with customers, which is the context in which the homily is usually expressed, but also being true to facts, to evidence, to reality. Honesty pays because it entails the mind being true to its proper function.

Contrary to the duty view of morality, honesty is not self-

sacrificial but profoundly egoistic, that is, pro-life and pro-suc-
cess. It is both moral and practical. To quote Ayn Rand, "Honesty is not a social duty, a sacrifice for the sake of others, but the
most profoundly selfish virtue man can practice: his refusal to
sacrifice the reality of his own existence to the deluded consciousness of others."[17]

The temptation to be dishonest is most frequently a result
of the desire for a short-range benefit motivated by the impulse
of the moment (e.g., taking money from the cash drawer when
nobody is looking, jacking up the bottom line using a gimmick
just this once). In the lower type of person, there is a deliberate
decision to reject all moral principles in favor of personal desires
(e.g., petty criminals). In the very lowest type, there is actual
enjoyment (of a perverse kind) at the idea of deceiving others
and evading reality in principle (e.g., the professional con man).

Dishonesty almost always works to a degree in the short
run. Otherwise, people would not be so prone to try it. Any idiot
can lie and deceive other people—temporarily. But the bottom
line is that no one can make money in the long run (in the absence of a government subsidy or monopoly) without being essentially honest. All Prime Movers have not been totally honest
in everything they did. For example, John Paul Getty tricked his
mother out of part of her estate, but he had to produce when it
came to oil. As Andrew Carnegie put it, "I have never known a
concern to make a decided success that did not do good, honest
work."[18] Wendy's founder Dave Thomas considers honesty to be
the number one ingredient for success. This is literally true in
that no one could even produce, much less sell, anything at all if
they *consistently* evaded reality. Consider one simple illustration:
If the producer does not deliver what the customer wants at the
agreed-upon price, the producer will not get any more business.

Based on my own research, the accusation, now accepted
as gospel, that the great nineteenth-century industrialists were
robber barons who gained their wealth dishonestly is essentially
false. (There were some crooks, as there are in every country and
period.) The purpose of such accusations is to pretend that no
one can be that much better than the rest—that no one can be a
Prime Mover. But the facts of history show otherwise. The great
tycoons may have been ruthless, in the sense that they relent-

lessly sought market dominance and put less able competitors out of business, but a determination to succeed is not dishonesty. John D. Rockefeller, for example, put many small refineries out of business (including one run by one of his brothers), but that was because he was better at the oil business than they were, especially with respect to cost control. He typically offered smaller refiners whose plants he wanted to purchase the choice of cash or stock in Standard Oil. Those who chose the stock were very happy in the long run. Those who chose the cash often were not. Rockefeller also used his market clout to get rebates (e.g., volume discounts) from the railroads—a practice that has been condemned and even outlawed, but which, in fact, is a perfectly valid competitive practice.

There were lawless confrontations among nineteenth-century business factions upon occasion (e.g., railroads versus pipeline companies vying for rights-of-way), but these were typically the result of the failure of the government to make clear legal rulings and to enforce existing laws. Henry Ford, during his period of decline, wrongly used "thuggery" to oppose unions but failed to stop them. Such actions, however, did not and could never have made a success of the Model T, which was built during Ford's most rational and profitable period.

Commodore Vanderbilt tried to bribe the New York state legislature, but political corruption was so rampant at the time, and the legislatures held such total power, that no other course was possible if one wanted to stay in business. Vanderbilt's opponents beat him on one occasion because their bribes were bigger than his bribes. Vanderbilt's goal was not to get favors but to get freedom. He made money because he managed his railroad efficiently. The way to eliminate such bribery and the buying of political favors (and to promote campaign reform today) is to take away the government's power to interfere in the economy except to prevent fraud or physical force.

In the business world, as in every other realm of society, there are degrees of honesty. Small doses of dishonesty are like small doses of poison. They do not kill you right away, but they make you less healthy. Fred Smith almost destroyed his career in the early years of FedEx by forging a bank document but managed to escape punishment and went on to make the company immensely successful by giving his customers honest value for their money.

Contrast Smith with the unfortunate Daniel Gill, former CEO of Bausch & Lomb, who failed to mend his ways. For years, Gill tried to make up for not developing products that sold well by pressuring managers to increase the sales of existing products at any cost and by apparently tolerating deceptive accounting practices. Finally, *Business Week* blew the whistle, and the board of directors fired Gill in the wake of the ensuing scandal and plummeting earnings.[19]

Being consistently honest when others are not can bring competitive advantage. John Bogle's insistence that mutual fund managers tell investors the full costs of joining the fund and reporting the fund performance compared to the market earned him many admirers and new investors. Mark McCormack's sports marketing reputation was greatly enhanced by consistently acting in a trustworthy manner. This, in turn, attracted more clients.

Another aspect of honesty is openly acknowledging problems and poor performance. Such acknowledgment is a prerequisite to future improvement. An inspiring example here is CEO Ken Iverson of Nucor. In the early days of the company, when it was called Nuclear Corporation of America, an irate stockholder demanded to know why the feckless company was doing so badly. Iverson replied, "It's a rotten company, what can I say?"[20] Such candor is extremely rare among CEOs who prefer to blame failure on such factors as difficult market conditions, a slumping economy, or unforeseen circumstances. Iverson, of course, unburdened by any desire to fake reality, went on to make Nucor the most valuable steel company in the United States and its stockholders rich.

I will end this discussion with my own favorite example of the importance of honesty in business. In 1912, America's greatest financier, J. P. Morgan, was called before the House Banking and Currency Committee, which was investigating the role of money trusts in the economy. At one of the Pujo hearings (as they came to be called), the committee's counsel, Samuel Untermeyer, asked Morgan whether commercial credit was based primarily upon money or property:

Morgan:	No sir, the first thing is character.
Untermeyer:	Before money or property?
Morgan:	Before money or anything else. Money cannot buy it. . . . Because a man I do not trust could not get money from me on all the bonds in Christendom.[21]

Now let us consider briefly the relationship of honesty to loyalty. Although the days of mutual loyalty based on lifetime employment are now gone, employee loyalty is still valued. A disastrous error that mediocre business leaders (and, unfortunately, even some Prime Movers on occasion) make is placing loyalty to the company above loyalty to the truth. Loyalty to the company is proper if it signifies honesty and not betraying company secrets; but all too often, it is taken to mean agreement with company policies and strategies regardless of their merit or moral worth (i.e., my company, right or wrong). Consider the plight of engineer Roger Boisjoly, who blew the whistle on the O-ring problem after the *Challenger* space shuttle disaster and who also had warned about it before the disaster. He had objective data on the O-ring danger, which he attempted to show to relevant company and NASA officials before the launch, but they refused to look at it. His reward for his disloyalty in telling the truth after the tragedy was the destruction of his career as an engineer. (He now lectures on ethics.) Had his knowledge been taken seriously at the outset, there would have been no *Challenger* disaster. Carly Fiorina gives some good advice here: "Never sell your soul—so that you can be proud of yourself in the end."

Integrity

Integrity means loyalty to one's rational convictions in action. Loyalty to the irrational is not integrity. The Ku Klux Klan member is not showing integrity, but rather its lack, when he attacks nonwhites. His entire philosophy is based on evasion of facts.

Consistently following whims that contradict reason and reality is an expression of irrationalism, not integrity.

As an integrated being of mind and body, it is not sufficient for a man to claim that he has good convictions or intentions. Anyone can talk the talk. But to *really* hold convictions means to consistently act on them. A man who professes the virtue of honesty and then lies when it is convenient is not honest. A man who claims to value independence and then renounces his judgment when he is told to obey an authority figure without reason is not independent. A man who claims to value productiveness and then demands that the government (i.e., taxpayers) be forced to support him does not value productiveness.

Integrity is often hard to practice because it requires that when one acts, one hold one's convictions firmly in mind. One can lose sight of one's values due to mental passivity—by not bothering to ask oneself if a planned action is consistent with what one believes to be right. Or one can let oneself be overwhelmed by emotion, without bothering to understand or question the source of the emotion (i.e., the ideas behind it). Or one can surrender one's judgment when confronted by opposition from others, fearing their disapproval.

It is not a moral compromise if there is disagreement about a practical matter (e.g., the price one will pay for a good or service). If no moral principle is at stake, each party can properly modify its original asking or selling price. Nor is it a breach of integrity to give in to a holdup man or obey a government edict. Moral choices are impossible when one is confronted by the threat of physical force. Force negates man's ability to use his rational judgment. Finally, it is not immoral to change one's convictions if one is rationally convinced that one's previous view was wrong. In such a case, integrity demands that one change one's viewpoint in accord with the facts.

But to compromise one's moral principles means to give them up—in principle. To put a breach between one's perception of reality and one's actions means to negate one's mind altogether. It is, in effect, saying, "This is what I believe to be right—so what?"

To compromise with evil (i.e., the irrational, the anti-life) benefits only the evil. Consider, for example, a businessman who makes a deal with Mafia hoodlums: He agrees to launder some drug money for the hoods if they will blow up his competitor's store. This clearly benefits the criminals. They get respectable money that they can use to commit more crimes. What does the businessman get? A short-run benefit, in return for which he sells his self-respect, destroys all his virtues, and puts his body and soul in permanent hock. The hoods can use him however they please in the future. The benefits the criminals got were made possible only by the businessman's compromise.

Of course, the compromising businessman does not breach his integrity in this fashion. He is more likely to sell out in less flagrantly crooked ways. Consider a manager, Mr. B, who fully supports his company's policy on promotion by merit, who has to choose one of three candidates for promotion. The manager considers one to be clearly superior, in terms of ability, knowledge, character, and effort, to the other two. There is clear objective evidence about performance to support this choice. When the word gets out about this decision, however, all hell breaks loose. One of the two who were not selected has the most seniority and complains bitterly. The other is a minority and claims discrimination. Mr. B's boss claims that he does not like conflict but nevertheless tells him to make his own decision. Mr. B's peers claim he is asking for trouble. So Mr. B rescinds his original decision and promotes both of the other two candidates instead ("just this one time"). He then tells the jilted employee that his boss made him do it.

Observe what Mr. B has done. He has breached the virtue of integrity by acting against his own merit principle. He has also breached the virtue of rationality by ignoring the facts. Further, he has breached the virtue of honesty by lying to the jilted employee. He has breached the virtue of independence as well, by negating his own judgment in favor of the feelings and pressures of others. He has also undermined the future productivity of the company, and himself, by promoting the less able employees. (The jilted employee will undoubtedly look elsewhere for work.) He has destroyed his own self-respect by selling out his virtues. And, finally, Mr. B has lost the respect of all the able employees by demonstrating that he stands for nothing and cannot be trusted.

The damage will not stop there, however. Consider what the decision will do to the future motivation of the remaining employees when they conclude that promotion has nothing to do with merit. The better ones will also look around for more promising jobs elsewhere. When the word gets out that the company is political, it will begin to attract political manipulators instead of hardworking, competent people. And Mr. B himself will become a cynic, crying that truth, fairness, and justice are an illusion, thereby further undermining his ability to manage effectively.

Compare Mr. B to Cyrus McCormick, about whom it was said, "When publicly criticized he replied sharply and moved ahead along the course that he had determined upon. Popularity and applause were dear to him, but he believed that the sacrifice of his own convictions was too high a price to pay for acclaim."[22]

No, a single bad personnel decision might not destroy a company, but to the degree that lack of integrity becomes a pattern, it will undermine the CEO's and the company's effectiveness. However, sometimes a single action can be so shocking that it undermines trust for good. Consider a CEO who preaches trust and openness and then sells part of the company to a competitor without telling the employees (who learn of it through the grapevine). Such a CEO may never be trusted again.

It is a truism that integrity starts at the top—in that the CEO serves as a role model for others and conveys, through his words and actions, what types of employee actions are expected and prohibited. Study after study shows that integrity is critical to leadership effectiveness.[23] A CEO without integrity most fundamentally loses trust (i.e., credibility). This has ramifications throughout the organization and undermines him from the start. A rotten apple inevitably rots other apples or makes the good apples leave. Nonintegrity breeds cynicism in followers, which undermines their commitment to the organization and its goals. Like honesty, integrity is not a social duty but a profoundly egoistic virtue.

James Casey of UPS said, "We have become known to all who deal with us as people of integrity, and that priceless asset is more valuable than anything else we possess."[24] This was especially true of customers: When UPS promised to deliver, it delivered.

Coca-Cola's Robert Woodruff showed that he was true to his word in 1933 when he threatened to move the company out of Georgia if the state passed an exploitative tax on Coke's intangible assets (e.g., stocks and bonds). The governor of Georgia thought Woodruff was bluffing and approved the tax anyway. So Woodruff packed up the company and moved it to Delaware, where they stayed for ten years until the tax was repealed. Apparently, the state has not tried such a move since.

The most disgraceful lack of integrity is shown by those CEOs who, out of one side of their mouth, scream (justifiably) for freedom from government controls and beg, out of the other side of their mouth, for government subsidies and protection from competitors (e.g., tariffs).[25] In contrast, there are others like T. J. Rodgers of Cypress Semiconductor who think in principles and oppose corporate welfare for everyone.

Justice

The virtue of justice means rationality applied to other men. This means perceiving them objectively, according to their actual characteristics—ability, knowledge, expertise, reliability, effort, performance, honesty, integrity—and evaluating them according to a rational standard. Knowing whether another person is for or against you and your values can be a matter of life or death. Electing to office or taking a joyride with the wrong person can be fatal. The failure to judge employees objectively and treat them as they deserve can destroy a business.

Persons of justice operate on the trader principle. Ayn Rand wrote:

> A trader is a man who earns what he gets and does not give or take the undeserved. He does not treat men as masters or slaves but as independent equals. He deals with men by means of a free, voluntary, unforced, uncoerced exchange—an exchange which benefits both parties by their own independent judgment. A trader

does not expect to be paid for his defaults, only for his achievements.[26]

Similarly, a trader pays others according to their achievements.

There are at least three fatal errors that people can make with respect to the virtue of justice:

1. *Refusing to judge others at all.* After all, the saying goes, there is some good in everybody. The refusal to judge others means that you do not distinguish between good and evil. This benefits the evil and undermines the good. Imagine the consequences of treating an employee who stole from your business the same as one who helped you make a profit. It is not a big step from refusing to judge to "loving thine enemy." Loving the antivirtuous means loving the anti-life. A quicker road than this to self-immolation is hard to imagine.

2. *Judging others arbitrarily (subjectively).* To reject all principles and to declare that "I'll judge people on the basis of whatever I feel like at the moment" means to reject facts, reason, and morality in favor of whim. Bias in judging others means evaluating them according to emotion rather than reason. Racial bias is an example. It means judging people on the basis of how their skin color makes you feel rather than on their actual competence and character. Being subjective means that whether you support good or evil, competence or incompetence, is a matter of chance.

3. *Judging others according to the facts and professing proper standards but not acting on this knowledge (hypocrisy).* This last is the most common in business. The virtue of justice requires that one act on the trader principle; this means giving people what they deserve. The businessperson who flouts this principle (e.g., by giving big raises to cronies regardless of performance) is courting disaster. In the last chapter, I noted the importance for business success of hiring and developing people with ability. However, to get the full benefit of such people, one has to keep them. The more able the individuals, the more jobs they can find elsewhere and the more they will be sought after. If they are not rewarded fairly, they will be quick to leave. If, for some special

reason, they have to stay, their full passion will no longer be engaged.

Let us see how Prime Movers have practiced the virtue of justice.

Few CEOs in history have been more explicitly concerned with justice than Mary Kay Ash. As a victim of injustice in her previous jobs, she was determined to treat her own employees better than she had been treated. Mary Kay knew from her work experience that employees who are badly treated become demoralized. Thus, she decided to treat people with respect and give them individual attention. In addition, she was determined to reward people consistently for good performance. One could call justice the core value—or virtue—of her company. This virtue is manifested in many ways. For example, sales directors continue to get a percentage of the sales of trainees they have recruited and trained, even when the directors move to a new location. Income is based on sales performance, not politics. Commissions are generous, but not irrational. Those who achieve exceptionally high sales are awarded various prizes including public praise, pink Cadillacs, and gold bumblebee pins adorned with diamonds. Mary Kay's philosophy has yielded a very dedicated workforce.

UPS's James Casey solved the problem of reward in a non-publicly held company by awarding stock bonuses to managers with private stock shares that are given a fair market value by the board of directors. Managers can buy additional shares as well. UPS received criticism over its treatment of hourly workers, mainly because of its use of part-time workers who received less compensation than the rest of the workforce. It is not unjust, however, for a company to pay what the market will bear. If it could not recruit enough part-timers for the wage it is offering, it would be forced to up its offer. The other side of the justice coin is not paying people more than they are worth. Unless one is getting extra skill or better performance for the extra pay, paying above market can be suicidal.

Andrew Carnegie surrounded himself with forty or so partners who were extraordinarily able (e.g., Charles Schwab). He rewarded them handsomely, and when he sold the company in

1901, they became millionaires. He paid his mill workers above industry rates in order to motivate them and to forestall unionization. On the other hand, he did not tolerate people who could not produce. (Carnegie did commit a seeming injustice to Henry Clay Frick. After a number of conflicts with Frick, Carnegie and his stockholders enforced an agreement that stockholders could be forced to sell their shares back to the company. However, the stock price Frick was offered, though technically consistent with the original agreement, was far below the real value of the stock. So Frick initiated an ugly and public court battle, which he won. Carnegie also paid the price in bad publicity.)

Pierre DuPont practiced justice in many ways. He used objective measures (e.g., return on investment) to assess performance. He promoted non-DuPonts to important positions in accordance with their proven competence. He allowed key executives to buy GM stock on generous terms. Division managers received salaries equal to his own. All this made for tremendous loyalty and helped make GM a success.

Henry Ford doubled the hourly pay (to five dollars) of production employees at his Highland Park assembly plant. (A little over half of this had to be earned through performance.) This bonus markedly increased the number of applicants for jobs, decreased turnover, and allowed Ford to run a third shift.

Bill Gates's sense of justice was expressed early when he protested the injustice of Altair hackers copying his and Paul Allen's BASIC software program. They correctly pointed out that software, like hardware, is the product of someone's effort. True to his own principle, Gates makes wide use of stock options to compensate outstanding work at Microsoft. Given the company's rigorous hiring procedure, there is much outstanding work to reward. Thousands of Microsoft employees are now millionaires and fiercely loyal to the company. A recent article claims that Microsoft has two constituencies: its employees and its customers.[27] This is true in spirit, if not in fact. Employees are the means, not the end. CEOs need competent, happy employees who take the actions necessary to make customers happy. (Practical problems can arise when so many stock options are given that the stock value gets watered down, or when the company buys so much stock back to prevent watering that profits get eroded.)

Intel's Andy Grove also uses stock options to reward employees and employs a large number of people who have become millionaires. Intel's brilliant successes have been made possible by the many talented people it has been able to retain. As in every large company, however, conflicts do arise and a number of able people have left the company over the years. Tim Jackson's book, which (considering the brilliant success of the company is inappropriately focused more on negatives than positives) reveals that in a few cases employees were not treated justly.[28] But such treament cannot be the norm in a successful company because if it were, not enough able people would stay and work to develop and market successful products.

Under Iverson, Nucor's compensation system is totally focused on pay for performance—from everyone at the plant level all the way up to the CEO level. Plant workers are grouped into teams, and incentive pay aligns their interests with those of management. Department managers' pay is based on how well their subordinates perform. Company officers are paid below market but can make large bonuses if the company achieves sufficient return on stockholders' equity. There is no bonus if this figure goes below 8 percent. Iverson has nothing but contempt for executives who get huge salaries even as their companies lose money.[29]

The late Roberto Goizueta totally revamped the appraisal and incentive systems when he came to Coca-Cola. No more rewards for attendance, only for performance. Rewards came in the form of bonuses, stock options, and stock grants that came to maturity at retirement. Many managers became millionaires under Goizueta; as with Gates at Microsoft, this enabled him to retain a large number of highly talented managers.

Michael Milken's employees at Drexel Burnham loved him because he made them rich when they performed well themselves. A couple of them (2 out of about 400) betrayed him when they feared the government would turn on them if they did not provide dirt on Milken, although their information proved nothing. Many who worked for Milken went on to become very successful after Drexel Burnham closed down, but the company could not survive without his genius. Similarly, ITT never really prospered after Geneen's retirement. If there is too large a gap between a Prime Mover and the next level down, even accumulating and retaining talent may not be enough to keep the company moving after the Prime Mover departs. This is not always an issue of poor succession planning; it can be a reflection of the fact that genius is a rare commodity.

Mark McCormack of IMG rewards people in part by putting them in "hot" areas of the business. He does not evaluate performance just on annual net sales but also on taking risks and on taking steps to attain profits in future years. He also considers the difficulty of the tasks they have undertaken.

Ross Perot did not have enough money when he started EDS, so he paid low salaries but offered stock in the company, even though it had not gone public. New employees had to stay seven years to cash in. It worked; many became millionaires. Quite a few other companies have successfully used the same tactic.

T. J. Rodgers uses a rigorous procedure to evaluate employees for raises at Cypress. They are divided into focal groups of five to twenty-five people, and every member of each group is compared to every other member and ranked on the basis of total contribution to the company. Many checks are made to eliminate bias. Only the best performers get big raises. A similar method is used to grant stock options.

Howard Schultz at Starbucks grants stock options to all employees. Sam Walton also did this—eventually. At first, only the managers got a stake in the stores, and the sales clerks got as low wages as they would work for (though not out of line for the discount retail business). Later Walton realized that highly motivated employees would help increase profits if they saw a benefit for themselves. So he initiated a profit-sharing plan for all employees, along with incentive bonuses and discount stock purchase plans. Some employees have accumulated several hundred thousand dollars in their profit-sharing accounts over the course of their work careers at Wal-Mart. Not surprisingly, these people love the company.

It must be stressed that justice is not only a matter of pay and bonuses. It is also reflected in giving recognition for accomplishment, giving credit where credit is due, and promoting the most deserving subordinates.

Justice is not only appropriate with respect to employees. Cyrus McCormick stressed justice vis-à-vis his customers buying the reaper by offering a written, money-back guarantee. If customers did not think they were getting fair value for their money, they could return the reaper for a full refund within six months. This money-back guarantee policy has been imitated by many great businesspeople.

Virtues as Guiding Corporate Principles: BB&T

It is rare when a company explicitly uses virtues as its guiding principles, but John Allison, CEO of BB&T Corp. (a fast-growing, highly profitable, $30 billion banking company headquartered in North Carolina) does just that. BB&T lists the following in its value statement:

1. Fact-based decision making (reality)
2. Reason (objectivity)
3. Independent thinking
4. Productivity
5. Honesty
6. Integrity
7. Justice
8. Pride
9. Teamwork
10. Self-esteem

Furthermore, the company selects new employees using several carefully structured interviews, specifically with the above virtues and values in mind. The logical connection between these virtues and values, which the evidence indicates are consistently practiced, and the company's success is obvious.

The Evil of Initiating Force

The one evil that businesspeople (and all people of virtue) must avoid is the initiation of physical force or fraud against others—

whether they be suppliers, bankers, customers, employees, or stockholders. To use force means to deal with others in such a manner that the principle of voluntary trade is abrogated.

Taking money from others without their consent means to reduce oneself to the level of a wild animal; a wild animal's only means of survival is forcibly devouring other animals. For animals this is proper, as it is the only means of survival possible to them.

This is not man's mode of survival. Using physical force as a means of dealing with others leads to Hobbes's war of all against all and the destruction of civilized society. The only way for man to survive long-range in society is through reason and voluntary trade with other men. The initiation of force destroys man's ability to think; it negates his mind at the root. To tell a man "Do what I say or die (or go to jail)" is to tell him "Don't think and don't act on your judgment. What you have concluded on the basis of reason is totally irrelevant to your life." No wealth can be created when men function on such a principle. This is why communist and socialist countries cannot produce wealth on more than a minimal scale. Note also in Figure 1-1 of Chapter 1 the progressive decline in the rate of growth of the U.S. economy since 1900—a consequence of steadily increasing government controls.

Fraud is an indirect form of force. If a man signs a check to buy a shipment of steel and the shipment he ordered does not exist, it is the same as if the seller held a gun to his head. The buyer would not have signed the check if he had known there was no steel; thus, the deal was not made with his consent.

What the criminal is counting on, of course, is that some people will do the thinking and production, and he will take it over by force. He is counting on other people to use reason so that his use of force will pay off. If his victims were brutes like himself, there would be nothing to steal. (Observe again, as Ayn Rand has argued, that evil functions only as a parasite on the good.[30])

Capitalism—wealth creation—is only possible when men are free to think and to trade value for value by voluntary consent. It takes two to make a trade. Free trade does not guarantee that both parties will get what they want; nor does it mean that the two parties will be equal in their economic power. Microsoft properly has the power to insist that if PC makers want to install Windows 95 or 98 in their computers, then they have to install other Microsoft programs, too. Apple does not have this power.

The whiners who go to Washington for protection against powerful competitors want the government to use force to stop those who think better and act more successfully than they do. They want to substitute political power for the economic power that they did not earn.

Conclusion

It is *not* the case that the amount of money one earns is a measure of one's virtue. The amount one earns depends on many factors, including one's ability, the profession one has chosen, and market conditions. It *is* the case, however, that it requires virtue to make money. Wealth creation requires these virtues: rationality, independence, productiveness, honesty, integrity, and justice. If a businessperson fails to practice these virtues, he or she will either go bankrupt or be "forced" into the role of criminal in order to seize the wealth he cannot earn. Those who earn wealth deserve to feel proud of what they have done. To repeat a point I have made before: *Earning money is a moral achievement*, not the product of some lower faculty.

It is a colossal injustice that men who earn great wealth are condemned for it on the grounds that they are robber barons or monopolists or greedy materialists—and then praised if they give it all away. How can it be good to give money away if it was earned through evil actions? The moral evaluation should be reversed. It is the creation of wealth that is morally good. What one chooses to do with it afterward is secondary. Those who make enormous fortunes cannot spend it all on themselves even if they wanted to, so they have to do something with it. Those fortunate enough to be the recipients of such largesse should not fail to ask this question: What made it possible? The answer is: virtue—combined with ability. Nor should they fail to thank the producer for being so genuinely selfish.

Notes

1. A. Rand, *Atlas Shrugged* (New York: Signet, 1992), p. 939.
2. B. McCoy, "The Parable of the Sadhu," *Harvard Business Review*, May/June 1997, pp. 55ff.
3. For a detailed discussion of a rational approach to the subject of ethics, see L. Piekoff, *Objectivism: The Philosophy of Ayn Rand* (New York: Dutton [Penguin], 1991). My discussion of virtue is based on chapters 7 and 8 of this book.
4. A. Rand, *The Virtue of Selfishness* (New York: Signet, 1964), p. 15.
5. Ibid., p. 15.
6. Ibid., p. 17.
7. Ibid., p. 23.
8. Ibid., p. 31.
9. N. Tichy and S. Sherman, *Control Your Destiny or Someone Else Will* (New York: Doubleday, 1993), pp. 12–13.
10. H. Geneen, *Managing* (New York: Avon, 1984), p. 101.
11. Ibid., p. 103.
12. K. Iverson, *Plain Talk* (New York: Wiley, 1998), p. 18.
13. "The Bill & Warren Show," *Fortune*, July 20, 1998.
14. K. Iverson, op. cit., p. 18.
15. For a detailed discussion of the virtue of honesty in business, see E. Locke and J. Woiceshyn, "Why Businessmen Should Be Honest: The Argument from Rational Egoism," in A. Rand, *Why Businessmen Need Philosophy* (Marina Del Ray, Calif.: Ayn Rand Institute Press, 1999).
16. L. Peikoff, op. cit., p. 267.
17. A. Rand, *Atlas Shrugged*, p. 937.
18. L. Hacker, *The World of Andrew Carnegie* (New York: Lippincott, 1968), p. 354.
19. M. Maremount, "Judgment Day and Bausch & Lomb," *Business Week*, December 25, 1995, p. 39.
20. R. Preston, *American Steel* (New York: Prentice Hall, 1991), p. 73.
21. Quoted in D. Chernow, *The House of Morgan* (New York: Simon & Schuster [Touchstone], 1990), p. 154.
22. W. Hutchinson, *Cyrus Hall McCormick* (New York: Appleton-Century-Crofts, 1930), p. 753.
23. See E. Locke and associates, *The Essence of Leadership* (New York: Lexington, 1991).
24. J. Casey, "Our Partnership Legacy," *United Parcel Service* (UPS: 1985), p. 7.

25. Andrew Carnegie himself benefited from a steel tariff, but he was a man of genuine productive ability.

26. A. Rand, *The Virtue of Selfishness* (New York: Signet, 1964), pp. 34–35.

27. R. Lowenstein, "Microsoft and Its Two Constituencies," *The Wall Street Journal*, December 4, 1997, p. C–1.

28. T. Jackson, *Inside Intel* (New York: Dutton, 1997). Jackson is the preeminent modern in his approach to his subject. The modern writer is primarily concerned with flaws (clay feet) and only secondarily with virtues, even if virtues predominate. For example, rather than giving Grove credit for the brilliant success of Intel's chips and strategic reorientations, he stresses that the chips were not that good, that other companies' chips were better, and that the strategic decisions should have been started sooner and completed faster. Similarly, in relation to the issue of justice, he focuses only on a few of Intel's 15,000 or more employees and only on injustices.

29. K. Iverson, op. cit., pp. 112–113.

30. This is discussed at length in L. Peikoff, op. cit.

9

How to Make a Billion Dollars

[M]oney is the root of all good. . . . When men live by trade with reason, not force, as their final arbiter—it is the best product that wins, the best performance, the man of best judgment and highest ability.[1]

—Francisco d'Anconia in *Atlas Shrugged*

Why a billion and not a million? Because making a million is not that hard today in this country. I do not mean that it is a cinch, but if you have two working spouses (or even one) with good jobs and not too many children, if you save and invest a decent percentage of your income and do not indulge in excessive conspicuous consumption, developing a net worth of a million dollars is a reachable goal. In fact, assuming a 10 percent compounded annual return (from the stock market) and no taxes, it only requires an annual investment of $2,259 in a retirement account to reach $1 million after forty years. Millions have done it and millions more could.

I am not saying that your whole life should be focused around saving for the future at the expense of the present. It would be foolish to live in misery so that you could have lots of money when you are age 65 and then die. A rational person lives both short- and long-range, enjoying the present in every way possible and also planning for the future.

Most people (including myself) are not capable of making a billion, but many are. In the late nineteenth and early twentieth centuries, only one person did it: John D. Rockefeller. Now, with a much bigger economy, there are scores of billionaires, with the number growing all the time. (For a summary of the wealth created by leading Prime Movers in this book, see Appendix A.)

What it takes is what I have discussed in the previous chapters. In summary, here are seven points:

1. *Know and use your ability.* Not everyone has enough ability. Intelligence, especially mathematical ability, is important in most businesses. It is critical that your innate ability be used to gain practical knowledge about the business you are in. Furthermore, this knowledge must be upgraded continually. How do you know what you can learn? Do not take an IQ test because no one knows the minimum IQ you need for any particular business. Rather, undertake challenging jobs and tasks and see how far you can go before you have to say, "Even when I try very hard, I cannot get this." General confidence is very beneficial, but it cannot be divorced from confidence in being able to do the specific tasks you are confronted with; that comes from skill building. It is critical to be objective about your knowledge, skill, and ability because those whose reach is beyond their grasp will not make money; they will only lose what they have. If your job or your business outgrows your cognitive capacity, get out.

Note also that you can often outperform smarter people, especially if they are arrogant because they think that ability alone will carry them. Ability is only one factor in the equation. Following are six more.

2. *Follow your passion.* Make money doing something you love doing. The ideal attitude is: This is the greatest job (career) in the world; I can't believe I get paid to do this. The point is not that making money without loving the work is too selfish; rather, it is too unselfish. It is not a very happy life to work fifty to a hundred hours a week doing something that bores you to death for the pleasure of a paycheck that comes once or twice a month. Nor will you be able to sustain the enormous effort required to succeed over the long term unless you love the work itself. Working for money alone, which usually means wanting it in order to show off, is also unselfish in another way. Wanting to be rich just to be a big shot shows a lack of independence. It means other people are controlling your life and your soul.

Furthermore, doing work you hate for money you claim to love will put you in a perpetual state of conflict that will sap your energy and undermine your mental and physical health. Burnout is often caused by such conflicts. If you do not like what you are doing, try something else. (If there has to be a trade-off—between doing work you love for less money or work you do not love for more money—go for the work.) Of course, if you do not yet have a passion, try things until you find out what you like.

3. *Keep an active mind.* Under capitalism, to make money means to think continually. It means constantly trying to improve every facet of your business. It means upgrading your products and inventing new ones, increasing quality, decreasing costs, improving speed, upgrading skills, bettering customer service, revising strategy, solving problems, discovering new opportunities, creating new markets, questioning assumptions, making new causal connections. To stop thinking is to regress. Imagine a roller coaster that has lost its power at the top of a run. It will coast down the next segment, but eventually it will stall as its remaining momentum takes it only partway up the next rise; then it will fall back. In a competitive market, there is no rest for the passive, especially in today's dynamic, global business climate.

4. *Develop an independent vision.* Figure out a product, market, strategy, or technology that has future promise—something you can do that no one else has done and yet has appeal to customers, or something that others are doing successfully but which you can do better than they can. Listen to the experts; they can tell you about what is now known. But remember, they cannot tell you what is not known. In the end, after you have considered the relevant evidence, make up your own mind, using your best rational judgment; then go for it. If it becomes clear that your initial vision cannot work, develop a new one.

5. *Take tenacious action.* Do not live in a world of dreams. Put your ideas into action; take a never-ending series of actions. Set ambitious goals, but not so ambitious that you reach beyond your means. Many companies have been destroyed by not being able to manage growth. Steady growth that you are in control of

can get you to a billion faster than whipsawed gyrations caused by poor planning. It is critical that you never be stopped by failure; use failure as a learning experience. If the whole business fails, start another one, but never repeat past mistakes. Do not pretend that you can lead a balanced life like all the psychologists tell you. If you want to make it big, you must put your whole heart and soul and all or most of your spare time into the business, especially at the beginning. Either do not get married at this stage, find a wife who does not mind not seeing you very much, or prepare to get divorced. Make sure you have the energy, stamina, and health to travel frequently and to tolerate nights without much sleep. It is ideal if you can get by on four hours (but needing six hours is not disqualifying).

6. *Hire great people.* Hire the most able people you can find. These should be people with the particular skills your business needs. They may know more than you about their specialties. (If they are more able than you across the board, you had better go to work for them.) If they reject your vision and cannot convince you to change, fire them. Also fire them if they are dishonest. Do not compromise on the issue of honesty, no matter what their ability. Nothing is more dangerous to a business than a smart person who is dishonest. That person can do a hundred times more damage than someone who is dumb and dishonest.

If they are able and honest but cannot get along with people (and cannot learn to do so), instead of firing them, consider creating a job where they can work alone. (Sam Walton had David Glass and Jack Shewmaker swap jobs when he discovered that the very able Shewmaker was not very good at handling people.) Do not cripple brilliant minds by forcing them to work too much in groups. Bring their knowledge to bear when it is needed, and use buffer people to insulate them from others. Remember that the needs of the company with respect to ability may change over time. Any person whose job outgrows him or her must be replaced.

7. *Practice virtue as a means of success.* Never accept the disastrous dichotomy of the practical versus the moral. Pro-life virtues are a means to success in business and in every other area of life. The virtue of rationality means that you take reality seri-

ously and do not substitute emotions for thought. It also means that you think long-range (e.g., by considering the consequences of your actions).

The virtue of independence means that when you have considered all the facts and the opinions of others, you make your own judgment as to the right course of action. If you want to be a follower, go to work for someone else. Do the same if your judgment is always wrong. (It means you have the wrong job.) Further, do not go whining to the government when your competitors threaten you because they are competent. Fight back by being smarter or more tenacious than they are, or hire or merge with someone who can help you.

The virtue of productiveness is what you practice when you create goods and services. This requires the setting of challenging goals and the exertion of the thought and effort needed to achieve them.

The virtue of honesty means not faking reality in any way. Do not evade facts, contradictions, failures, or unpleasant information and do not try to deceive others; this would only make you the slave of their delusions.

The virtue of integrity means walking your talk. It also means respecting your inner, rational convictions. Integrity breeds both respect and trust and prevents cynicism.

The virtue of justice means rewarding merit inside the company and trading value for value with customers. People are eager to trade with a person of justice and they shun anyone who is unjust.

Some of those who like the concept of virtue will be asking, "This is all very well in theory, but what about the disreputable so-and-so's I have to do business with or compete with?"

Let me first list three types of disreputable characters. The first type tries to get special government favors at your expense. In a mixed economy, every businessperson is at risk from such types. Your only short-range defense, unfortunately, is to hire your own lobbyist to protect your interests. (The long-term solution is to get the government out of the economy altogether.) The second type routinely commits fraud. Take that person to court, where he or she belongs. The third type is the most common. This person is the CEO of a company you deal with or compete with and is virtuous some of the time, but not all the time, and does not go so far as to commit outright fraud. This type is the most frustrating. Often the best action is patience: If a company is *fundamentally* lacking in virtue, it will eventually lose its best employees and its customer base, and you will be able to get back any business it took from you. You will also be able to use your own company's reputation for trustworthiness as a competitive advantage. In the case of an untrustworthy supplier, you can work to establish a relationship with a new company and eventually switch all your business there. However, being trustworthy will not compensate for lack of competence (e.g., poor products or noncompetitive prices).

Virtue does not always pay immediately. Other people can get away with the irrational temporarily, especially if they are smooth talkers. But reality is inexorable; eventually, the anti-virtuous, which means the irrational, must fail because it is anti-reality. (The Asian banking crisis is a recent example.)

Is it the case, then, that anyone who has ability and follows the above principles is guaranteed to make a billion dollars? No. You can make an honest error in judgment about an issue that no one could have known about in advance (e.g., a new discovery that undermines your technology). You can be strangled by new or old government regualtions, or you can encounter one or more competitors who are even more able than you are. These principles are best viewed as prerequisites or preconditions for creating great wealth.

Those who lack the ability or stamina to make $1 billion need not despair. The principles still apply if you are only able to make $100 million or $10 million or $2 million. Only the scope or scale of action is different.

Other Traits

In the course of my research, I observed that some Prime Movers possessed traits other than the ones I have mentioned so far. The question is: How fundamental are these other traits? I will discuss five of them: competitiveness, charisma, communication, frugality, and patience.

Competitiveness

Capitalism is, by its nature, competitive. Customers are constantly choosing whether to spend their money on one product or service versus another. If, with respect to a given product or service, the producer of X gets the money, the producer of Y (who is in the same market) will not. Competitiveness, as a trait, is related to drive, but it is drive focused specifically around beating other people. Many Prime Movers are extremely competitive. Former Coca-Cola CEO Douglas Ivester recounted the following saying of McDonald's founder Ray Kroc at an employee meeting: "What do you do when your competitor's drowning? Get a . . . hose and stick it in his mouth."[2] Sam Walton once said, "Competition is actually the reason I love retailing so much."[3] Bill Gates is a relentless competitor and hires people who are like him. When Microsoft personnel see a weakness in a competitor, they take as much of its business as they can— before the competitor does the same to them. John D. Rockefeller put refiner after refiner out of the oil business. It is no accident that many (though not all) Prime Movers were avid members of sports teams and that the war slogan "Crush the enemy" is so popular in discussions of strategy.

One can call this ruthlessness, but ruthlessness—an unswerving determination to take away your competitor's customers—is perfectly appropriate in business so long as no one uses force or fraud. Many industries, such as the oil industry and the car industry, begin with scores or hundreds of competing companies. It is not unusual for most of them to lose money until one, driven by a Prime Mover, emerges from the pack and consolidates or dominates the industry. The resulting efficiencies of scale replace a hundred or a thousand small, inefficient businesses with one or more world-class competitors.

The Wal-Marts and the Starbucks are greatly resented by the competitors they put out of business, but it must be recognized that these competitors are put out of business because the bigger companies answer customers' needs better than the smaller ones. The customers are not forced to patronize the big outfits; they voluntarily choose to do so because of better prices, service, or product choice. The real reason that people oppose free competition between the big and the small, other than hatred for the good, is that they want to succeed through stagnation.

Although all businesses must take into account their competitors and even learn from them, there is an enormous danger involved in being focused solely on what one's competitors are doing. A company that is always responding and never leading will end up being led from the outside rather than from within. It will end up having no central purpose other than to do what everyone else is doing. Since most businesses have many competitors with overlapping products and services, trying to copy everyone can lead to a total loss of focus. A follower will never have the first-move advantage. And if it copies the wrong competitor, it can self-destruct if the competitor fails. Many businesses have gone the way of the lemmings. Sometimes it is better *not* to compete with a given competitor but, rather, to go one's own way. Independent judgment is required to decide which market or market segment one wants to compete in, and on what terms. For all these reasons, I did not make competitiveness a primary trait, even while acknowledging its relevance. Perhaps the best way to summarize my view is to say that competitiveness is important within the context of an independent vision.

Charisma

In recent years, the concept of charismatic leadership has been studied extensively by management researchers. To understand what is known, we first must understand what the concept means. Charisma has two different aspects: style and content. With respect to style, charisma refers to a personality style that features speaking in a captivating voice, making eye contact, using animated facial expressions, and projecting a dynamic, confident presence. Such people are very effective in politics (at least in terms of getting elected), but there is little evidence that such a style is required for business success. Unlike many writers on leadership, I see almost nothing in common between the traits required for political versus business success. (For example, success in politics—in today's pragmatic, anti-principles culture—seems to require having a *lack* of integrity, which may explain the political mess our country is in, and the contempt with which people view most contemporary politicians.) Many Prime Movers were and are notoriously uncharismatic in their personalities (e.g., John D. Rockefeller, Eckhard Pfeiffer). The key to business success does not lie in getting a crowd emotionally aroused. Warren Bennis has pointed out, quite correctly I believe, that a charismatic aura, rather than being a cause of success, may be attributed to great business leaders as a *consequence* of their success.

Content, however, is another matter. The content side of charisma centers around vision.[4] This, as we have already seen (Chapter 2), is critical. Vision alone, of course, does not lead to success; it has to be combined with the other factors we have discussed (including strategy and good management techniques).

Communication

It is axiomatic that business leaders must communicate with their employees, customers, and others in some fashion. But it does not follow that they must be great public speakers. Most are not, nor are most of them great writers. Some contemporary Prime Movers will not even use e-mail. What I think is essential is that they do whatever it takes to get their message across. This is as much a matter of tenacity as of skill and technique. Getting an idea across means getting people to understand what you want and why. Sam Walton, for example, tried to visit every store in person as often as he could; he also led company cheers. He would relentlessly push a pet idea, such as store greeters, until he had worn down all opposition. He made TV broadcasts by satellite. He called frequent meetings of managers; he also made sure managers got frequent quantitative feedback about their performance.

Ken Iverson requires managers to hold regular meetings with employees and also insists that they talk informally with employees on a regular basis. Furthermore, the company conducts formal employee surveys every three years. Managers who cannot learn to communicate with employees are terminated. Observe the difference between the actions described above and the actions typical of self-important CEOs or managers who sit in their office and send out memos, which are usually ignored.

There is no one best way to communicate; what works best depends on context and purpose, although most businesspeople I have talked to strongly believe that, in addition to e-mail, some face-to-face contact (which should include listening as well as talking) is critical to building and sustaining morale.

One could put forth a very good argument for making communication a core trait, but I think its importance is implicit in the traits I have already discussed. For example, communication is implicit in the idea of a drive to action. Taking action onself is a form of communication because every CEO is a role model for his or her employees. People with drive also work hard to get other people to act, and that necessitates communication. Probably communication is best viewed as a learned skill.

Prime Movers also need information. They get information by directly observing the facts (e.g., reading sales reports, observing competitors' products) and by listening. Their goal in listening is not to defend the status quo but to get information that will help them make good decisions. If they have hired people of ability, their employees will provide them with a lot of useful data and many creative ideas. Getting information, however, is implicit both in the concept of an active mind and in the concept of hiring and utilizing able people. It is critical to listen to negative as well as positive information. This helps prevent the leader from getting too cocky and too divorced from what is happening in the real world.

Frugality

Profit is the difference between revenue and costs. Thus, all successful businesspeople (who do not have a government subsidy) must be cost-conscious. This is obvious if one's market strategy is to sell goods at the lowest possible cost (e.g., Wal-Mart). But it is even true if one's market niche is in high-priced, quality goods or services. For example, when Toyota first built the Lexus, it provided more luxury for the dollar than did Mercedes, so Mercedes was forced to come out with cheaper models in order to try to protect its market share. Businesspeople who waste money on unnecessary luxuries or who fail to constantly look for ways to reduce costs will always be vulnerable to competitors who discover ways to undersell them, unless they have a product or service that cannot be duplicated. Cost-consciousness, which is an aspect of strategy, is narrower in scope than the traits I have discussed in this book. However, businesspeople with active minds, competence, and drive are those most likely to discover cost-saving strategies.

Patience

To say that Prime Movers need patience seems paradoxical, especially when I specifically noted in Chapter 5 that they are impatient to take action. Both claims are true, but in different respects. They are driven to take an endless stream of actions as they move toward their goals, but they are patient about the process of building their businesses. They do not try to take shortcuts that entail foolish risks in order to make the big kill. They build incrementally, through a series of hundreds of thousands of decisions, often spanning a period of ten to twenty years or more. Each success leads them to set their sights higher and enlarge their businesses through vertical integration, geographic expansion, product innovation, industry consolidation, or technological improvements. They are more like a combination of marathon runner and hurdler than a sprinter. The sprinter goes all-out but cannot last very long and may run so fast in the wrong direction as to be unable to change course when needed. The marathon runner is always in motion, ready to accelerate to overcome obstacles and threats or decelerate temporarily to prepare the next move, and the hurdler is never resting, always quickly moving toward a new goal and ready to master the next hurdle. It is true that large fortunes can be made much more rapidly today than in the nineteenth century, since the economies of most semi-free countries are larger and technological or market changes occur more rapidly. By the same token, fortunes can be lost much faster if the wrong action is taken or the right action is taken too slowly. Today's marathon runners-hurdlers must go at a much faster pace and be far more agile than in the past. Patience does not mean passivity or indecisiveness; rather it is recognition of the fact that business empires cannot be built overnight. In this respect, patience is implicit in the virtue of rationality.

Male and Female

Despite having identified several females as Prime Movers in this book (e.g., Mary Kay Ash, Darla Moore, Carly Fiorina), I have used the male pronoun for the purpose of literary convenience. However, I am convinced, especially from talking to Carly Fiorina, that the requirements for successful wealth creation and business leadership are identical for men and women. It is debatable whether men and women use different styles of management, but style is not substance. The tasks that must be performed by a business leader do not change just because the CEO is a woman (or a minority or a person from another country). Success under (real) capitalism requires certain traits and qualities; the gender, race, or nationality of the leader is irrelevant. Of course, in cultures in which women are viewed as second-class citizens, such as Japan and many parts of the Middle East, women would have a terribly difficult time even becoming CEOs, but if they made it, they would still need the qualities discussed in this book.

Strategy

It must also be stressed that there are many aspects of management I have not discussed in this book. For example, every business must have a viable competitive strategy. (There are also specialized strategies within functional specialties such as marketing and finance.) Hundreds of books and articles have been written on this subject, and I will not repeat any of that material here. I believe that people of ability who follow the above principles are the ones most likely to develop effective strategies and to successfully modify strategies that are not working.

There are certain business strategies that are timeless and universal. Five key ones are:

1. Quality
2. Innovation (new products, services, and technologies)
3. Customer service
4. Speed
5. Cost (low)

I do not know of any time period or country in which these were not important; however, these are very broad principles. The form in which they are defined and implemented changes continually. The Model T was considered a high-quality car in 1920; it would not be today. The lightbulb was an innovation in 1879; it is not now. Once, a money-back guarantee was all you needed to demonstrate good customer service; that does not suffice anymore. A two- to four-week time lag in filling an order was once considered speedy service, but not in this decade. A good price for a pocket calculator was once a hundred dollars, but not in 1999. As long as there are still people who think creatively, there will be changes and improvements in the applications of these principles. Those who are most skillful, tenacious, and virtuous are the ones most likely to envision and implement such improvements.

Management

Similarly, I have not discussed management techniques in this book. Thousands of books have been written about this topic. Prime Movers must learn and use good management techniques to make their businesses successful. Techniques, of course, change over time due to changes in technology, competition, and the economy, but there are certain timeless principles (e.g., planning, budgeting, setting goals, measuring performance, giving feedback, communicating, inspiring, coordinating through teamwork, using an organizational structure that fits your strategy). There are many different ways in which these principles can be applied, and creative managers are constantly discovering improved applications (as well as new principles). Computers, for example, have revolutionized and are still revolutionizing management. Prime Movers who are not themselves exceptionally skilled at management usually have the good sense to hire people who are (e.g., a right-hand man or woman).

The Success Quartet

I will mention here a four-part management formula, which involves several elements discussed earlier, that Prime Movers have used time after time to make money:

1. Hire extraordinarily able people, and train them if necessary.
2. Give them, or urge them to set, outrageous goals.
3. Give them full responsibility—within the bounds of their ability, ethics, the company's strategy, and your vision—as to how to achieve them.
4. Reward them generously but fairly for performance, and do not require that goals be fully met if they are extremely difficult.

Naturally, this quartet must be used in conjunction with all the other factors.

Business and Religion

Conservatives like to argue that there is a strong tie between business and religion. It is certainly true that a number of Prime Movers (e.g., John D. Rockefeller, John Pierpont Morgan, Mary Kay Ash) have had strong religious convictions. But it does not follow from this, as Burton Folsom and others seem to imply, that their religious convictions contributed to their business success.[5] Let us begin by considering the three *essential* attributes of the religious view. In metaphysics, religion advocates supernaturalism, the doctrine that God can and does intervene in natural and human affairs at will to bring about certain ends. In epistemology, religion endorses faith as the means of knowledge. Faith means belief in something in the absence of evidence, reason, or logic. In ethics, religion advocates altruism (i.e., self-sacrifice) as the highest virtue and condemns selfishness.

In my studies of Prime Movers, I do not know a single case in which a businessman created wealth through the consistent utilization of these religious principles in his business affairs. First, praying for miracles in order to create wealth is not and has never been the path to business success. (Observe the current state of Iran for the consequences of that policy.) In fact, the evidence reveals quite the opposite. Successful wealth creators are focused first and foremost on reality and on understanding or discovering the laws of nature and the laws of the marketplace (e.g., customer satisfaction). Even though some of them do pray, their wealth was created through their own actions. The failure to focus on the relevant facts will eventually spell the doom of any business enterprise.

Second, wealth creators use reason, not faith, as their means of discovering facts. Consider, for example, Thomas Edison, who was successful (despite numerous setbacks and errors) both as an inventor and as a businessman. When he was inventing, he would conduct thousands of experiments until he was able to figure out what actually worked. When an experiment failed, he would try another one until he solved the problem. It is true that successful wealth creators sometimes use intuition, but intuition is not the same as faith. As noted earlier, intuition (i.e., gut feel) is a subconscious judgment that one makes based on conclusions reached from past experiences. Such judgments may or may not be correct and have to be validated by further study and data gathering. No businessperson can operate solely on gut feel. In fact, it is precisely when Prime Movers rely too much on gut feel and persistently ignore the judgment of reason that they get into trouble. Henry Ford, for example, almost bankrupted his company because he was too much in love with the Model T and refused to recognize the need to develop new models and, as a result, let General Motors take the dominant market position.

Third, the motive power of Prime Movers is not selfless service to humanity but, as I noted, egoistic love of their work, of the process of earning wealth, and of the rewards they could earn. To illustrate, consider the following mental experiment: Could Mother Teresa, the epitome of selfless service to others, have conceived, created, or run a major (or even a minor) profitable business enterprise? Obviously not. Even her charity work would have been impossible were it not for alms given to her by people who created the wealth that she gave away.

Folsom agrees with George Gilder that great entrepreneurs suppress their own desires in order to be of service to others, but this is grossly misleading.[6] Entrepreneurs are not in the business of service but in the business of trade with others. In a voluntary trade, neither party sacrifices to the other, both get what they want for themselves by trading value for value (e.g., money for goods). The soup kitchen volunteer is not a valid model for what wealth creators do.

It is not that Prime Movers are indifferent to the benefits of their work. They love it when their customers take joy in their products (e.g., the Model T, Windows 95). The more joy customers experience, the more of the product Prime Movers are likely to sell. But to create, one must love the doing, the process of creation. The work of creation—the effort, the long hours, the setbacks, the conflicts, the threats of competitors, the struggle—is much too difficult to be sustained by anything less than a grand passion. As I noted earlier, passion alone is not enough; the passion must be tied to reality and guided by reason—but the passion must be there.

A number of businesspeople have claimed that they do explicitly follow one Biblical principle when conducting their business affairs: the Golden Rule (Do unto others as you would have them do unto you). This principle is sound, however, only when the principles you are following are rational. Imagine, for example, a con man whose guiding doctrine was con and be prepared to be conned, or a hood who lived by the code of kill and be prepared to be killed, or a ruthless Machiavellian pragmatist whose philosophy was manipulate and be prepared to be manipulated. The Golden Rule is not a sound doctrine divorced from the content of the moral principle involved. Fundamentally, the Golden Rule implies the need for consistency in one's actions, that is, not acting on one rule for yourself (e.g., dishonesty) and expecting others to follow a different rule when they deal with you (e.g., honesty). The Golden Rule is applicable when it comes to honesty because honesty is a rational moral principle, both in business and in life.

One last point about business and religion. There have been some business leaders who seemed to view the primary function of religion not as a guide to everyday action but as a means of saving their souls from perdition. John Pierpont Morgan was a case in point. Evidently such men did not view their business achievements as sufficient evidence of their virtue—which means that within their own souls, Plato had won: Wealth creation was somehow tied to the ignoble. I hope that I have shown in this book that wealth creation is a moral and noble activity. The ultimate moral sanction of business is man's right to his own life, which includes the right to trade freely with others and to reap the benefits of that trade. Those who make an honest profit should not feel guilt for their sins but rather pride in their achievements.

Giving Back

One frequently hears successful businesspeople say, "Now that I have made my fortune, it is time to give back to the community." I have always wanted to ask these people, "Well, what was it you took that did not belong to you? Didn't you earn your money honestly?" The implication of the term "give back" is that you did not really earn what you made. The modern arch villain here is Andrew Carnegie, who tried to justify wealth creation by arguing that wealthy business leaders were just holding the money "in trust" for society—thus implying that society had the right to take it back whenever it wanted. Such a cowardly principle puts every wealth creator on the defensive and induces guilt instead of pride. I recently saw a TV talk program in which the host asked a very famous and successful Prime Mover if he accepted Carnegie's thesis. The CEO had no answer. Years later, this same CEO caved in and accepted Carnegie's gospel. The proper principle, which Prime Movers should assert proudly, is: *I earned my wealth through my own, honest efforts; therefore, it belongs to me by right.* Observe that this principle endorses (rational) egoism as moral and rejects the notion of man as a selfless servant of others (altruism).

It is not that I am opposed to generosity. Businesspeople who have made tens of millions or tens of billions of dollars would find it very hard, even if dissolute, to spend all their money on houses and toys. Furthermore, many do not want to turn their children into playboys or spoiled heiresses by leaving them so much money that they never have to work for a living. So they have to do something with their money, and giving it away to various causes is their only real choice unless they want to be buried with it. But how should they choose? There are many options, but one thing is for sure: They should not give it to their enemies (e.g., those intellectuals and educational institutions that oppose capitalism).

Antitrust

The single factor most likely to arrest the progress of Prime Movers in the process of creating wealth is the government. Only the government has a monopoly over the use of physical force. It is proper for the government to use such force in retaliation against criminals (e.g., those who have initiated force against innocent victims). However, in the case of antitrust, government coercion is used against the innocent—specifically, against those who are so competent and aggressive in the marketplace that they earn market dominance. The government, along with the whiners among those who are outcompeted, claims that the dominant Prime Movers are engaging in unfair competition. Look closely at any type of so-called unfair competition, however, and you will find that what is really involved is competition that no one else can match.

Those who support antitrust legislation often defend it with the following scenario: What if a company attains market dominance, raises prices, beats back new competitors by selling below cost, and then stifles all further innovation? Of course, a company has the right to try to do this, since it has the right to set the terms under which it is willing to trade with others. However, such actions can only be temporary. Raising prices encourages consumers to buy less, thus undercutting sales. Thus, it is in a Prime Mover's self-interest to keep prices low, like Henry Ford did. High prices also tempt more competitors, including foreign competitors, to enter the market. If a dominant company sells below cost for very long, this eats into its own profits. Finally, if a dominant company fails to innovate, other companies will take away the dominant company's business. IBM found this out; so did GM, Kodak, and Xerox.

The flawed rationale behind the concept of unfair competition is the premise that economic power is something that the government must limit in the same way and for the same reason that it limits political power (police power). This view is wrong, because economic power and political power are fundamentally different. Economic power is the power of voluntary trade, the power of incentive.[7] For example, if Producer A says to a merchandiser, "If you want to market my product, you have to sell it with attachments X and Y at price Z," this is not coercion. The merchandiser does not have to agree to the terms but has no moral right to the products of Producer A except on the terms the producer offers. The fact that Producer A has more clout (i.e., more ability to bargain) than the merchandiser reflects the market power it has earned due to past success. Producer A has no power to prevent the merchandiser from growing or combining with others or finding other manufacturers. The merchandiser is still free to think, to invent, to act, to function, to try to succeed.

Political power is the power of physical force. When the government says to obey its edict or go to jail, it is saying to stop thinking, to ignore the judgment of your own mind—you are no longer free to function. *Antitrust law is nothing more than the attempt to crush the creative capacity of great wealth creators through coercion.* As long as Prime Movers do not use force or fraud or receive government favors, they should be left free to function.

If they are good enough to dominate the market, they should be allowed to reap the fruits of that achievement. If they are not good enough to sustain their advantage (as GM, Kodak, Xerox, IBM, and others were not), in a free market there will be plenty of competitors ready to take away their market share.

The motive behind antitrust, however, goes deeper.

Inequality

Most human traits (e.g., intelligence, ambition, tenacity) are distributed (for reasons we do not know) in the form of a normal or bell curve. Most people fall in the middle range, with progressively fewer people at the extremes. This implies that human achievement, if people are free to function, will be distributed somewhat similarly. There are very few people as brilliantly talented as Michael Jordan, Chopin, Michelangelo, Vermeer, Einstein, or Rockefeller. In the realm of business, it follows that a few will create enormous wealth, others will generate very little, and most will fall in the middle. (In the case of wealth, the bell curve is distorted because there is a lower limit on wealth but, theoretically, no upper limit.)

In Table 9-1, I show distribution statistics for seven countries, all mixed economies. It is quite striking to note that, in all seven countries, the top 10 percent of the population earns about 25 percent of the wealth, and the highest 20 percent earns about

Table 9-1. International comparisons of income distribution.

	Year	Lowest Fifth	Second Fifth	Third Fifth	Fourth Fifth	Highest Fifth	Top 10 Percent
Canada	1987	5.7	11.8	17.7	24.6	40.2	24.1
France	1989	5.6	11.8	17.2	23.5	41.9	26.1
Germany	1988	7	11.8	17.1	23.9	40.3	24.4
Italy	1986	6.8	12	16.7	23.5	41	25.3
Japan	1979	8.7	13.2	17.5	23.1	37.5	22.4
U.K.	1968	4.6	10	16.8	24.3	44.3	27.8
U.S.	1965	4.7	11	17.4	25	41.9	25

Source: World Development Report 1997.

40 percent of the wealth. In the United States, the top 5 percent now earns about 20 percent of the wealth (not shown in the table). In sum, people are not equal in their capacity for earning money.

This, according to Marxists and various sociologists, is immoral. But why? Because, to them, it is an axiom that everyone should get the same amount. The name of this ugly principle is egalitarianism—the doctrine that everyone is entitled to the same rewards whether they earned them or not.[8] This is more serious than a revolt against the principle of justice; it is a revolt against reality. It is a fact that some people are more able than others, that some people work harder than others, that some people are able to create or earn more wealth than others. The egalitarian whines that reality is unfair for not providing the impossible—that is, endowing everyone with the same genes and environment and character—and demands that society (i.e., government) make up for it by forcibly taking from those who produce and giving to those who do not.[9] The most consistent application of this policy is communism; the results of this philosophy in action are well known.

It is not the case that communism is a noble ideal and that men are not good enough to practice it. Rather, it is that communism, by negating man's right to his own life, embodies an evil ideal—an ideal that flies in the face of man's nature and the requirements of production and of life. The evil results are the inevitable consequence of the anti-mind, anti-life ideal. It must be noted that the intellectuals who warn us about the perils of social unrest as a consequence of income inequality *are the same intellectuals who cause that unrest in the first place* by screaming that some people are not getting what they are entitled to: other people's money.

The deepest root of egalitarianism is the motive I pointed out in Chapter 1: hatred of the good for being the good, which means hatred of the competent for being competent, hatred of the productive for being productive.

A good indicator of a country's moral stature is the degree to which people are allowed to create wealth unhampered by government coercion. America is still the country of Prime Movers because it is still the country where wealth creators have the most opportunity. But considering the torrent of abuse heaped on them, the persecution by antitrust laws, and the mountains of regulations that businesspeople must obey (regulations so numerous that no one could function for five mintues if they were all enforced), not to mention attacks by doom-preaching environmentalists, the opportunity for wealth creation cannot last—unless our country changes its moral code and declares that every person has an inalienable right to their own life, which means to use the judgment of their own mind to create their own wealth. (See Appendix B.)

Greed

The final insult of the wealth haters is the accusation that Prime Movers are greedy. What do they mean by this pejorative term? The dictionary defines greed as an excessive desire to acquire more than what one needs or deserves, especially with respect to material wealth.[10] Defined this way, I submit that greed is an anti-concept. Ayn Rand defines an anti-concept as "an unnecessary and rationally unusable term designed to replace and obliterate some legitimate concept."[11] The use of the phrase "needs or deserves" in the definition is meant to imply that one does not deserve more than one needs. If we take need to mean (conventionally) enough to survive, then the implication is that no one deserves to earn more than, let us say, $25,000 a year. Anything above that persumably would be, by the above definition, excessive.

At root, the concept of greed, when used to describe Prime Movers, is meant to obliterate the concepts of ambition and justice by implying that any desire to earn great wealth is inherently immoral and irrational and that to succeed in earning it is unjust—to those who haven't earned it. It is undeniable that if all men acted on the principle that they should earn no more than what they needed to survive, our society would revert to the economic level of the Dark Ages in very short order. It is obvious that those who accuse Prime Movers of greed (e.g., the environmentalists, the intellectuals) are simply haters of the good who want such men to feel unearned guilt as a punishment for their ability and achievement. Ultimately, they want men of ability to stagnate so that others will not feel inferior. The proper answer to the wealth haters is to assert proudly that as long as someone engages in voluntary trade with others, that person has the moral right, as an aspect of the inalienable right to his or her own life, to earn as much wealth as possible. Civilization moves forward on the shoulders of such people—and the more of them there are, the better.

It is proper, then, to end this chapter with a quote from the same speech I quoted at the beginning:

> *Money is made possible only by the men who produce . . . man's mind is the root of all the goods produced and of all the wealth that has ever existed on earth. . . . Wealth is the product of man's capacity to think. . . . Money [therefore] is the product of virtue. . . . To love money is to know and love the fact that money is the creation of the best power within you. . . . The words "to make money" hold the essence of human morality.*[12]
>
> —Francisco d'Anconia in *Atlas Shrugged*

Hatred of the Good[13]

Edwin A. Locke

Multibillionaire Andrew Grant was delighted. Since the year 2000, he and his staff of engineers and computer technicians had struggled desperately to successfully produce a revolutionary hovercraft car. Millions of man-hours of creative effort across a span of twenty years had at last come to fruition.

The car was a technological marvel. Its air-cushion drive meant that it could travel safely over any type of terrain. It was light in weight and thus very fuel-efficient. Its patented spherical design supported by interlocking ribs composed of a new metal Grant had invented made the car exceptionally strong. This, plus a computerized laser detection system that automatically moved the car up, down, or sideways if a collision were imminent, had cut by 90 percent the injury rate of people using his car.

Grant's car proved to be a brilliant success and enabled Grant Motors to gain a 60 percent, and growing, market share. Grant never sought publicity or acclaim, but he expected that his achievement would be appreciated. He was wrong.

His Big Three domestic competitors, Titanic, Reliable, and Safe Motor Companies, had reacted with fury. They demanded an anti-trust investigation, claiming that, through a series of interlocking patents, technological innovations, and high-pressure sales tactics, Grant Motors had achieved an unfair stranglehold on the automobile market. An international consortium of foreign car companies demanded a monopoly ruling by the World Court. None of these companies mentioned that the reason Grant Motors was taking away their business was that people liked its cars better than theirs.

The U.S. Automobile Dealers Association protested that Grant Motors was coercing them by requiring them to order Grant's own anti-collision system with every car rather than installing a competing model. They failed to note that it takes two to trade, and that neither party is required to make a deal if they do not like the terms.

The automobile unions screamed that Grant was causing unemployment as factory after factory owned by the Big Three was closed and union membership evaporated. They did not mention that for every Big Three factory that had closed, a new, non-unionized Grant Motor factory had opened.

The Green Earth Society warned that the air turbulence caused by Grant's cars could conceivably cause global warming, global cooling, global flooding, and global drought. These predictions were backed up by computer models based on "reasonable" assumptions. The society did not mention that there was no actual evidence for any of their claims.

Automotive Magazine screamed that Grant's patents were a public trust and therefore the patents should be given away to anyone who wanted them. It did not suggest that the copyrights to its magazine's articles should also be given away.

Professor Gerald Spookin, chairman of the Economics Department at Peoples University, wrote that Andrew Grant was another in a long line of "robber barons," who made his fortune by destroying the little guy and holding the common man in the vice-like grip of his monopolistic power. He did not explain how America could have become the wealthiest country in the world if its businessmen simply stole rather than created wealth.

Senator Oswald Lunt, chairman of the Joint Committee on Anti-Trust and Monopoly, went to TV to announce, "We will immediately begin hearings on the anti-competitive implications of the fact that Grant Motors is so successful, er, that is dominant."

Fantasy you say. But was our fictional Andrew Grant treated any better than John D. Rockefeller or Andrew Carnegie or Bill Gates? There is only one fundamental reason why great businessmen or great companies are hated, and it has nothing to do with so-called monopolies. They are hated, as Senator Lunt let slip, because they are good, that is, smarter, more visionary, more creative, more tenacious, more action-focused, more ambitious, and more successful than everyone else. Haters of the good do not want the less able to be raised up to the level of the great producers. They want to use government coercion to cripple the greatest minds so that lesser minds will not feel inferior.

Government coercion against the productive is a clear violation of their moral right to trade freely with others. Furthermore, depriving great minds, such as that of Bill Gates, of their right to economic freedom also deprives the rest of us of what they could produce. The freer such people are to function, the richer we all will be.[13]

Notes

1. A. Rand, *Atlas Shrugged* (New York: Signet, 1992), pp. 383, 387.
2. N. Deogun, "Can His Successor, Douglas Ivester, Refresh Coca-Cola?" *The Wall Street Journal*, November 20, 1997, p. B-1.
3. S. Walton and J. Huey, *Made in America* (New York: Doubleday, 1992), p. 204.
4. For example, see J. Conger and R. Kanungo, eds., *Charismatic Leadership: The Elusive Factor in Organizational Effectiveness* (San Francisco: Jossey-Bass, 1988). See especially the chapter by Robert House et al. See also S. Kirkpatrick and E. Locke, "Direct and Indirect Effects of Three Core Charismatic Leadership Components on

Performance and Attitudes," *Journal of Applied Psychology*, 1996, vol. 81, pp. 36–51.

5. B. W. Folsom, *The Myth of the Robber Barons* (Herndon, Va.: Young America's Foundation, 1991).

6. B. Folsom, *Empire Builders: How Michigan Entrepreneurs Helped Make America Great* (Traverse City, Mich.: Rhodes and Easton, 1998), pp. 169–70.

7. H. Binswanger, "The Dollar and the Gun," *The Objectivist Forum*, June 1983, vol. 4, no. 3, p. 1.

8. Some Prime Movers use the term *egalitarian* to mean something quite different from forced distribution of wealth. For example, Nucor's Ken Iverson (*Plain Talk,* New York: Wiley, 1998, p. 55) believes that executives should not view employees as inherently inferior beings but should treat them with respect, both intellectually and morally. He is contemptuous of corporate perks that serve to emphasize visible status differences. When it comes to rewards, however, Iverson is strictly pro-merit.

9. Egalitarianism or equality of results should be sharply distinguished from political equality, that is, equality before the law. These two principles, in fact, are contradictory. The only way to make people equal in results is to use the law to penalize the more successful.

10. *American Heritage Dictionary of the English Language*, 3rd ed. (Boston: Houghton-Miflin, 1992).

11. Defined in H. Binswanger, *The Ayn Rand Lexicon* (New York: New American Library, 1986), p. 23.

12. A. Rand, op. cit., pp. 382, 383, 384, 386.

13. Retitled "Many Want to Bring Down a Bill Gates So They Will Not Feel Inferior," *Los Angeles Daily News*, March 8, 1998, Viewpoint, p. 3.

Appendix A

Amounts of Wealth Created by (Selected) Prime Movers Mentioned in This Book

Creation of Real Market Value per year* (through 1997 only)

Company Name	CEO	Year Start	Market Value	Year End	Market Value	Creation of Market Value	Per Annum
IBM	Lou Gersiner	1993	$19,934,444,159	1997	$ 53,782,734,375	$ 33,846,290,216	8,462,072,554
General Electric	Jack Welch	1981	$15,143,502,750	1997	$126,727,734,375	$111,584,231,625	6,974,014,477
Coca-Cola	Roberto Goizeuta	1981	$ 4,400,440,044	1996	$ 92,415,551,307	$ 88,015,111,263	5,867,674,084
IBM	Tom Watson	1956	$20,174,332,721	1971	$ 92,569,828,960	$ 72,395,496,240	4,826,366,416
Intel	Andy Grove	1979	$ 1,417,943,526	1997	$ 84,292,343,750	$ 82,874,400,224	4,604,133,346
Microsoft	William Gates	1981	Founder	1997	$ 66,362,166,788	$ 66,362,166,788	4,147,635,424
AlliedSignal, Inc.	Lawrence Bossidy	1991	$ 3,594,479,614	1997	$ 13,879,687,500	$ 10,285,207,886	1,714,201,314
Wal-Mart	Sam Walton	1962	Founder	1991	$ 36,849,497,338	$ 36,849,497,338	1,270,672,322
Blockbuster	Wayne Huizenga	1967	$ 28,169,014	1994	$ 5,128,205,128	$ 5,100,036,114	728,576,588
Dell Computer	Michael Dell	1967	Founder	1997	$ 5,761,416,558	$ 5,761,416,558	576,141,656
Chrysler	Lee Iacocca	1978	$ 1,067,484,765	1992	$ 4,784,911,796	$ 3,717,427,011	265,530,501
ITT Corp.	Harold Geneen	1959	$ 1,961,241,419	1976	$ 6,110,738,137	$ 4,149,496,716	244,068,042
Federal Express	Fred Smith	1971	Founder	1997	$ 4,124,036,467	$ 4,124,036,467	158,616,787
Apple Computer	Steve Jobs	1976	Founder	1985	$ 1,296,924,373	$ 1,296,924,373	144,102,708
Getty Oil	J. Paul Getty	1926	Founder	1983	$ 5,417,158,735	$ 5,417,158,735	96,493,795
Nucor	F. Kenneth Iverson	1965	$ 59,786,816	1996	$ 3,045,817,081	$ 2,986,030,265	96,323,557
EDS	Ross Perot	1962	Founder	1984	$ 2,067,026,162	$ 2,067,026,162	93,955,826
Starbucks	Howard Schultz	1971	Founder	1997	$ 1,954,132,131	$ 1,954,132,131	75,158,928
Wendy's International	Dave Thomas	1969	Founder	1997	$ 1,396,470,000	$ 1,396,470,000	49,873,929
Cypress Semiconductor	T. J. Rogers	1982	Founder	1997	$ 694,651,386	$ 694,851,386	46,323,526
Pixar	Steve Jobs	1985	Founder	1997	$ 522,465,388	$ 522,465,388	43,538,782
Nike	Phil Knight	1968	Founder	1997	$ 1,033,792,948	$ 1,033,792,948	35,648,033
Mary Kay	Mary Kay Ash	1963	Founder	1985	$ 339,377,898	$ 339,377,898	15,426,268
Disney	Walt Disney	1938	Founder	1966	$ 377,634,935	$ 377,634,935	13,486,962

*Adjusted using Consumers Price Index (1982–1984 = 100).
Please note that the above table does not include adjustments for industry life cycles, business cycles, or possible lags in market value creation due to re-structuring efforts.

Appendix B

"Why Businessmen Need Philosophy"

by Leonard Peikoff

from a book by the same title by
Ayn Rand
(Ayn Rand Institute, 1999)

"Three seconds remain, the ball is on the one-yard line, here it is—the final play—a touchdown for Dallas! The Cowboys defeat the Jets 24–23!" The crowd roars, the cheering swells. Suddenly, silence.

Everyone remembers that today is the start of a new policy: morality in sports. The policy was conceived at Harvard, championed by *The New York Times*, and enacted into law by a bipartisan majority in Washington.

The announcer's voice booms out again: "Today's game is a big win for New York! Yes, you heard me. It's wrong for athletes to be obsessed with competition, money, personal gratification. No more dog-eat-dog on the field, no more materialism—no more selfishness! The new law of the game is self-sacrifice: place the other team above yourself, it is better to give than to receive!

Dallas therefore loses. As a condition of playing today it had to agree to surrender its victory to the Jets. As we all know, the Jets need a victory badly, and so do their fans. Need is what counts now. Need, not quarterbacking skill; weakness, not strength; help to the unfortunate, not rewards to the already powerful."

Nobody boos—it certainly sounds like what you hear in church—but nobody cheers, either. "Football will never be the same," mutters a man to his son. The two look down at the ground and shrug. "What's wrong with the world?" the boy asks.

The basic idea of this fantasy, the idea that self-sacrifice is the essence of virtue, is no fantasy. It is all around us, though not yet in football. Nobody defends selfishness any more: not conservatives, not liberals; not religious people, not atheists; not Republicans, not Democrats.

White males, for instance, should not be so "greedy," we hear regularly; they should sacrifice more for women and the minorities. Both employers and employees are callous, we hear; they spend their energy worrying about their own futures, trying to become even richer, when they should be concerned with serving their customers. Americans are far too affluent, we hear; they should be transferring some of their abundance to the poor, both at home and abroad.

If a poor man finds a job and rises to the level of buying his own health insurance, for instance, that is not a moral achievement, we are told; he is being selfish, merely looking out for his own or his family's welfare. But if the same man receives his health care free from Washington, using a credit card or a law made by Bill Clinton, that is idealistic and noble. Why? Because sacrifice is involved: sacrifice extorted from employers, by the employers' mandate, and from doctors through a noose of new regulations around their necks.

If America fights a war in which we have a national interest, such as oil in the Persian Gulf, we hear that the war is wrong because it is selfish. But if we invade some foreign pesthole for no selfish reason, with no national interest involved, as in Bosnia, Somalia or Haiti, we hear praise from the intellectuals. Why? Because we are being selfless.

The Declaration of Independence states that all men have an inalienable right to "life, liberty, and the pursuit of happiness." What does the "pursuit of happiness" mean? Jefferson does not say that you have a duty to pursue your neighbor's pleasure or the collective American well-being, let alone the aspirations of the Bosnians. He upholds a selfish principle: each man has the right to live for his own sake, his own personal interests, his own happiness. He does not say: run roughshod over others, or: violate their rights. But he does say: pursue your own goals independently, by your own work, and respect every other individual's right to do the same for himself.

In essence, America was conceived by egoists. The Founding Fathers envisioned a land of selfishness and profit-seeking—a nation of the self-made man, the individual, the ego, the "I." Today, however, we hear the opposite ideas everywhere.

Who are the greatest victims of today's attitude? Who are the most denounced and vilified men in the country? *You* are—you, the businessmen. And the bigger and better you are, the worse you are morally, according to today's consensus. You are denounced for one sin: You are the epitome of selfishness.

In fact, you really are selfish. You are selfish in the noblest sense, which is inherent in the very nature of business: You seek to make a profit, the greatest profit possible—by selling at the highest price the market will bear while buying at the lowest price. You seek to make money—gigantic amounts of it, the more the better—in small part to spend on personal luxury, but largely to put back into your business, so that it will grow still further and make even greater profits.

As a businessman, you make your profit by being the best you can be in your work, i.e., by creating goods or services that your customers want. You profit not by fraud or robbery, but by producing wealth and trading with others. You do benefit other people, or the so-called "community," but this is a secondary consequence of your action. It is not and cannot be your primary focus or motive.

The great businessman is like a great musician, or a great man in any field. The composer focuses on creating his music; his goal is to express his ideas in musical form, the particular form which most gratifies and fulfills him. If the audience enjoys his concerto, of course he is happy—there is no clash between him and his listeners—but his listeners are not his primary concern. His life is the exercise of his creative power to achieve his own selfish satisfaction. He could not funcion or compose otherwise. If he were not moved by a powerful, personal, selfish passion, he could not wring out of himself the necessary energy, effort, time, and labor; he could not endure the daily frustrations of the creative process. This is true of every creative man. It is also true of you in business, to the extent that you are great, i.e., to the extent that you are creative in organization, management, long-range planning, and their result: production.

Business to a creative man *is* his life. His life is not the social results of the work, but the work itself, the actual job—the thought, the blueprints, the decisions, the deals, the action. Creativity is inherently selfish; productivity is inherently selfish.

The opposite of selfishness is altruism. Altruism does not mean kindness to others, *nor* respect for their rights, both of which are perfectly possible to selfish men, and indeed widespread among them. Altruism is a term coined by the nineteenth-century French philosopher, Auguste Comte, who based it on the Latin "alter," meaning "other." Literally, the term means: "otherism." By Comte's definition and ever since, it means: "placing others above oneself as the basic rule of life." This means not helping another out occasionally, if he deserves it and you can afford it, but *living* for others unconditionally— living and, above all, sacrificing for them; sacrificing your own interests, your own pleasures, your own values.

What would happen to a business if it were actually run by an altruist? Such a person knows nothing about creativity or its requirements. What *his* creed tells him is only: "Give up. Give up and give away; give away to and for others." What should he give away? Whatever is there; whatever he has access to; whatever somebody else has created.

Either a man cares about the process of production, or he does not. If he cares about the process, it must be his primary concern; not the beneficiaries of the process, but the personal fulfillment inherent in his own productive activity. If he does not care about it, then he cannot produce.

If the welfare of others were your primary aim, then you would have to dismantle your business. For instance, you would have to hire needy workers, regardless of their competence—whether or not they lead you to a profit. Why do you care about profit, anyway? As an altruist, you seek to sacrifice yourself and your business, and these workers need the jobs. Further, why charge customers the highest price you can get—isn't that selfish? What if your customers need the product desperately? Why not simply give away goods and services as they are needed? An altruist running a business like a social work project would be a destroyer—but not for long, since he would soon go broke. Do you see Albert Schweitzer running General Motors? Would you have prospered with Mother Teresa as the CEO of your company?

Many businessmen recognize that they are selfish, but feel guilty about it and try to appease their critics. These businessmen, in their speeches and advertisements, regularly proclaim that they are really selfless, that their only concern is the welfare of their workers, their customers, and their stockholders, especially the widows and orphans among them. Their own profit, they say, is really not very big, and next year, they promise, they will give even more of it away. No one believes any of this, and these businessmen look like nothing but what they are: hypocrites. One way or another, everyone knows that these men are denying the essence and purpose of their work. This kind of PR destroys any positive image of business in the public mind. If you yourselves, by your own appeasement, damn your real motives and activity, why should anyone else evaluate you differently?

Some of you may reply: "But I really am an altruist. I do live for a higher purpose. I don't care excessively about myself or even my family. I really want primarily to serve the needy." This is a possible human motive—it is a shameful motive, but a possible one. If it *is* your motive, however, you will not be a successful businessman, not for long. Why is it shameful? Let me answer by asking the altruists among you: Why do you have such low self-esteem? Why don't you and those you love deserve to be the beneficiaries of *your* efforts. Are you excluded from the Declaration of Independence merely because you are a businessman? Does a producer have no right to happiness? Does success turn you into a slave?

You do not expect your workers to say, "We don't care about ourselves; we're only servants of the public and of our bosses." In fact, labor says the exact opposite. Your workers stand up proudly and say, "We work hard for a living. We deserve a reward, and we damn well expect to get it!" Observe that the country respects such workers and their attitude. Why then are businessmen supposed to be serfs? Aren't you as good as the rest of mankind? Why should you alone spend your precious time sweating selflessly for a reward that is to be given to someone else?

The best among you do not believe the altruist mumbo-jumbo. You have, however, long been disarmed by it. Because you are the victim of a crucial power, against which you are helpless. That power is philosophy.

This brings us to the question of why businessmen need philosophy.

The issue with which we began—selfishness vs. altruism—is a philosophic issue; specifically, it is a moral or ethical issue. One of the important questions of ethics is: should a man live for himself, or should he sacrifice for something beyond himself? In the medieval era, for example, philosophers held that selfishness was wicked, that men must sacrifice themselves for God. In such an era, there was no possibility of an institutionalized system of profit-seeking companies. To the medievals, business would represent sheer wickedness.

This philosophy gradually changed, across centuries, culminating in the view of Jefferson, who championed the selfish pursuit of one's own happiness. He took this idea from John Locke, who got it, ultimately, from Aristotle, the real father of selfishness in ethics. Jefferson's defense of the right to happiness made possible the founding of America and of a capitalist system. Since the eighteenth century, however, the philosophic pendulum has swung all the way back to the medieval period. Today, once again, self-sacrifice is extolled as the moral ideal.

Why should you care about this philosophic history? As a

practical man, you must care; because it is an issue of life and death. It is a simple syllogism. Premise one: Businessmen are selfish, which everyone knows, whatever denials or protestations they hear. Premise two: Selfishness is wicked; which almost everyone today, including the appeasers among you, thinks is self-evident. The inescapable conclusion: Businessmen are wicked. If so, you are the perfect scapegoats for intellectuals of every kind to blame for every evil or injustice that occurs, whether real or trumped up.

If you think that this is merely theory, look at reality—at today's culture—and observe what the country thinks of business these days. Popular movies provide a good indication. Do not bother with such obviously left-wing movies as *Wall Street*, the product of avowed radicals and business-haters. Consider rather the highly popular Tim Allen movie, *The Santa Clause*. It was a simple children's fantasy about Santa delivering gifts; it was seasonal family trivia that upheld no abstract ideas or philosophy, the kind of movie which expressed only safe, non-controversial, self-evident sentiments. In the middle of the movie, with no plot purpose of any kind, the story leaves Santa to show two "real businessmen": toy manufacturers scheming gleefully to swindle the country's children with inferior products (allegedly, to make greater profits thereby). After which, the characters vanish, never to be seen again. It was a sheer throwaway—and the audience snickers along with it approvingly, as though there is no controversy here. "Everybody knows that's the way businessmen are."

Imagine the national outcry if any other minority—and you are a very small minority—were treated like this. If a "quickie" scene were inserted into a movie to show that females are swindlers, or gays, or blacks—the movie would be denounced, re-edited, sanitized, apologized for, and pulled from the theaters. But businessmen? Money-makers and profit-seekers? In regard to them, anything goes, because they are wicked, i.e., selfish. They are "pigs," "robbers," "villains"—everyone knows that! Incidentally, to my knowledge, not one businessman or group of them protested against this movie.

There are hundreds of such movies, and many more books, TV shows, sermons, and college lectures, all expressing the same ideas. Are such ideas merely talk, with no practical conse-quences for you and your balance sheets? The principal conse-quence is this: Once you are deprived of moral standing, you are fair game. No matter what you do or how properly you act, you will be accused of the most outrageous evils. Whether the charges are true or false is irrelevant. If you are fundamentally evil, as the public has been taught to think, then any accusation against you is plausible—you are, people think, capable of any-thing.

If so, the politicians can then step in. They can blame you for anything, and pass laws to hogtie and expropriate you. After all, everyone feels, you must have obtained your money dishon-estly; you are in business! The anti-trust laws are an eloquent illustration of this process at work. If some official in Washing-ton decides that your prices are "too high," for instance, it must be due to your being a "monopolist": your business, therefore, must be broken up, and you should be fined or jailed. Or, if the official feels that your prices are "too low," you are probably an example of "cutthroat competition," and deserve to be pun-ished. Or, if you try to avoid both these paths by setting a com-mon price with your competitors—neither too high or too low, but just right—*that* is "conspiracy." Whatever you do, you are guilty.

Whatever happens anywhere today is your fault and guilt. Some critics point to the homeless and blame their poverty on greedy private businessmen who exploit the public. Others, such as John Kenneth Galbraith, say that Americans are too af-fluent and too materialistic, and blame greedy private business-men, who corrupt the masses by showering them with ads and goods. Ecologists claim that our resources are vanishing and blame it on businessmen, who squander natural resources for selfish profit. If a broker dares to take any financial advantage from a lifetime of study and contacts in his field, he is guilty of "insider trading." If racial discrimination is a problem, business-men must pay for it by hiring minority workers, whether quali-fied or not. If sexual harassment is a problem, businessmen are the villains; they must be fondling their downtrodden filing clerks, as they leave for the bank to swindle the poor widows and orphans. The litany is unmistakable: if anybody has any trouble of any kind, blame the businessman—even if a customer spills a cup of her coffee miles away from the seller's establishment. By definition, businessmen have unlimited liability. They are guilty of every conceivable crime because they are guilty of the worst, lowest crime: selfishness.

The result is an endless stream of political repercussions: more laws, more controls, more regulations, more alleged crimes, more fines, more lawsuits, more bureaus, more taxes, more need to bow down on your knees before Washington, Albany, or Giuliani, begging for favors, merely to survive. All of this means: the methodical and progressive enslavement of business.

No other group in the world would stand for or put up with such injustice—not plumbers or philosophers, not even Bosnians or Chechens. Any other group, in outrage, would assert its rights—real or alleged—and demand justice. Businessmen, however, do not. They are disarmed because they know that the charge of selfishness is true.

Instead of taking pride in your selfish motives and fighting back, you are ashamed, undercut, and silent. This is what philosophy—bad philosophy—and specifically a bad code of morality has done to you. Just as such a code would destroy football, so now it is destroying the United States.

Today, there is a vicious double-standard in the American justice sytem. Compare the treatment of accused criminals with that of accused businessmen. For example: if a man (like O.J. Simpson) commits a heinous double-murder, mobs everywhere chant that he is innocent until proven guilty. Millions rush to his defense, he buys half the legal profession and is acquitted of his crimes. Whereas, if a businessman invents a brilliant method of financing business ventures through so-called junk bonds, thereby becoming a meteoric success while violating not one man's rights, he is guilty—guilty by definition, guilty of being a businessman—and he must pay multi-million-dollar fines, perform years of community service, stop working in his chosen profession, and even spend many years in jail.

If, in the course of pursuing your selfish profits, you really did injure the public, then the attacks on you would have some justification. But the opposite is true. You make your profits by production and you trade freely with your customers, thereby showering wealth and benefits on everyone. (I refer here to businessmen who stand on their own and actually produce in a free market, not those who feed at the public trough for subsidies, bailouts, tariffs, and government-dispensed monopolies.)

Now consider the essential nature of running a business and the qualities of character it requires.

There is an important division of labor not taught in our colleges. Scientists discover the laws of nature. Engineers and inventors apply those laws to develop ideas for new products. Laborers will work to produce these goods if they are given a salary and a prescribed task, i.e., a plan of action and a productive purpose to guide their work. These people and professions are crucial to an economy. But they are not enough. If all we had was scientific knowledge, untried ideas for new products, and directionless physical labor, we would starve.

The indispensable element here—the crucial "spark plug," which ignites the best of every other group, transforming merely potential wealth into the abundance of a modern industrial society—is business.

Businessmen accumulate capital through production and savings. They decide in which future products to invest their savings. They have the crucial task of integrating natural resources, human discoveries, and physical labor. They must organize, finance, and manage the productive process, or choose, train, and oversee the men competent to do it. These are the demanding, risk-laden decisions and actions on which abundance and prosperity depend. Profit represents success in regard to these decisions and actions. Loss represents failure. Philosophically, therefore, profit is a payment earned by moral virtue—by the highest moral virtue. It is payment for the thought, the initiative, the long-range vision, the courage, and the efficacy of the economy's prime movers—the businessmen.

Your virtue confers blessings on every part of society. By creating mass markets, you make new products available to every income level. By organizing productive enterprises, you create employment for men in countless fields. By using machines, you increase the productivity of labor, thus raising the workingman's pay and rewards. The businessman, to quote Ayn Rand,

> is the great liberator who, in the short span of a century and a half, has released men from bondage to their physical needs, has released them from the terrible drudgery of an eighteen-hour workday of manual labor for their barest subsistence, has released them from famines, from pestilences, from the stagnant hopelessness and terror in which most of mankind had lived in all the pre-capitalist centuries—and in which most of it still lives, in non-capitalist countries.[1]

If businessmen are such great liberators, you can be sure that those who denounce you know this fact. The truth is that you are denounced partly because you *are* mankind's great providers and liberators, which raises another critical topic.

Selfishness is not the only virtue for which you are damned by today's intellectuals. They invoke two other philosophical issues as a club to condemn you with: reality and reason.

By "reality," I mean the universe around us; the material world in which we live and which we observe with our senses: the earth, the planets, the galaxies. As businessmen you are committed to this world, not to any other dimension alleged to transcend it. You are not in business to secure or offer supernatural rewards, other-worldly bliss, or the welfare of an ecological rose garden in the twenty-fifth century. You pursue real, this-worldly values, here and now. You produce physical goods and tangible services. You seek monetary profit, which you intend to invest or spend now. You do not offer your customers out-of-body experiences, UFO rides, or reincarnation as Shirley MacLaine. You offer real, earthly pleasures; you make possible physical products, rational services, and the actual enjoyment of this life.

This completely contradicts many major philosophical schools. It puts you into conflict with every type of supernaturalist, from the medieval-style theists on through today's "New Age" spiritualists and mystics. All these people like to demean this life and this world in favor of another, undefined existence in the beyond: to be found in heaven, in nirvana, or on LSD.

Whatever they call it, this other realm is beyond the reach of science and logic.

If these supernaturalists are right, then your priorities as businessmen—your philosophic priorities—are dead wrong. If the material world is, as they claim, "low, vulgar, crude, unreal," then so are you who cater to it. You are materialistic animals devoted to inferior physical concerns. By showering men with material values, you are corrupting and debasing them, as Galbraith says, rather than truly liberating them.

A businessman *must* be worldly and concerned with the physical. From the physical laws ruling your assembly line, to the cold, hard facts of your financial accounts, business is a materialistic enterprise. This is another reason why there could be no such thing as business in the medieval era: Not only selfishness, but *worldliness*, was considered a major sin. This same combination of charges—selfishness and materialism—is unleashed against you today by the modern equivalent of the medieval mentality. The conclusion they reach is the same: "Down with business!"

The third philosophic issue is the validity of reason. Reason is the human faculty which forms concepts by a process of logic based on the evidence of the senses; reason is our means of gaining knowledge of this world and guiding our actions in it. By the nature of their field, businessmen must be committed to reason, at least in their professional lives. You do not make business decisions by consulting tea leaves, the "Psychic Friends Network," the Book of Genesis, or any other kind of mystic revelation. If you tried to do it, then like all gamblers who bet on blind intuition, you would be ruined.

Successful businessmen have to be men of the intellect. Many people believe that wealth is a product of purely physical factors, such as natural resources and physical labor. But both of these have been abundant throughout history and are in poverty-stricken nations still today, such as India, Russia, and throughout Africa.

Wealth is primarily a product not of physical factors, but of the human mind—of the intellectual faculty—of the rational, thinking faculty. I mean here the mind not only of scientists and engineers, but also the mind of those men and women—the businessmen—who organize knowledge and resources into in-dustrial enterprises.

Primarily, it is the reason and intelligence of great industri-alists that make possible electric generators, computers, coro-nary-bypass surgical instruments, and spaceships.

If you are to succeed in business, you must make decisions using logic. You must deal with objective realities—like them or not. Your life is filled with numbers, balance sheets, cold effi-ciency, and rational organization. You have to make sense—to your employees, to your customers, and to yourself. You cannot run a business as a gambler plays the horses, or as a cipher wail-ing, "Who am I to know? My mind is helpless. I need a message from God, Nancy Reagan's astrologer, or Eleanor Roosevelt's soul." You have to *think*.

The advocates of a supernatural realm never try to prove its existence by reason. They claim that they have a means of knowledge superior to reason, such as intuition, hunch, faith, subjective feeling, or the "seat of their pants." Reason is their enemy, because it is the tool that will expose their racket: So they condemn it and its advocates as cold, analytic, unfeeling, straight-jacketed, narrow, limited. By their standard, anyone de-voted to reason and logic is a low mentality, fit only to be ruled by those with superior mystic insight. This argument originated with Plato in the ancient world, and it is still going strong today. It is another crucial element in the anti-business philosophy.

To summarize, there are three fundamental questions cen-tral to any philosophy, which every person has to answer in some way: What is there? How do you know it? And, what should you do?

The Founding Fathers had answers to these questions. What is there? "This world," they answered, "nature." (Although they believed in God, it was a pale deist shadow of the medieval pe-riod. For the Founding Fathers, God was a mere bystander, who had set the world in motion but no longer interfered.) How did they know? Reason was "the only oracle of man," they said. What should you do? "Pursue you own happiness," said Jeffer-son. The result of these answers—i.e., of their total philosophy—was capitalism, freedom, and individual rights. This brought about a century of international peace, and the rise of the business mentality, leading to the magnificent growth of industry and of prosperity.

For two centuries since, the enemies of the Founding Fathers have given the exact opposite answers to these three questions. What is there? "Another reality," they say. How do they know? "On faith." What should you do? "Sacrifice yourself for society." This is the basic philosophy of our culture, and it is responsible for the accelerating collapse of capitalism, and all of its symptoms: runaway government trampling on individual rights, growing economic dislocations, worldwide tribal warfare, and international terrorism—with business under constant, systematic attack.

Such is the philosophic choice you have to make. Such are the issues on which you will ultimately succeed or fail. If the anti-business philosophy with its three central ideas continues to dominate this country and to spread, then businessmen as such will become extinct, as they were in the Middle Ages and in Soviet Russia. They will be replaced by church authorities or government commissars. Your only hope for survival is to fight this philosophy by embracing a rational, worldly, selfish alternative.

We are all trained by today's colleges never to take a firm stand on any subject: to be pragmatists, ready to compromise with anyone on anything. Philosophy and morality, however, do not work by compromise. Just as a healthy body cannot compromise with poison, so too a good man cannot compromise with evil ideas. In such a setup, an evil philosophy, like poison, always wins. The good can win only by being consistent. If it is not, then the evil is given the means to win every time.

For example, if a burglar breaks into your house and demands your silverware, you have two possible courses of action. You might take a militant attitude: Shoot him or at least call the police. That is certainly uncompromising. You have taken the view, "What's mine is mine, and there is no bargaining about it." Or, you might "negotiate" with him, try to be conciliatory, and persuade him to take only half your silverware. Whereupon you relax, pleased with your seemingly successful compromise, until he returns next week demanding the rest of your silverware—and your money, your car, and your wife. Because you have agreed that his arbitrary, unjust demand gives him a right to *some* of your property, the only negotiable question thereafter is: How much? Sooner or later he will take everything. You compromised; he won.

The same principle applies if the government seeks to expropriate you or regulate your property. If the government floats a trial balloon to the effect that it will confiscate or control all industrial property over $10 million in the name of the public good, you have two possible methods of fighting back. You might stand on principle—in this case, the principle of private property and individual rights—and refuse to compromise, you might resolve to fight to the end for your rights and actually do so in your advertisements, speeches, and press releases. Given the better elements in the American people, it is possible for you by this means to win substantial support and defeat such a measure. The alternative course, and the one that business has unfortunately taken throughout the decades, is to compromise—for example, by making a deal conceding that the government can take over in New Jersey, but not in New York. This amounts to saying: "Washington, D.C., has no right to all our property, only some of it." As with the burglar, the government will soon take over everything. You have lost all you have as soon as you say the fatal words, "I compromise."

I do not advise you to break any law, but I do advise you to fight an *intellectual* battle against big government, as many medical doctors did, with real success, against Clinton's health plan. You may be surprised at how much a good philosophical fight will accomplish for your public image, and also for your pocketbook. For instance, an open public fight for a flat tax, for the end of the capital gains and estate taxes, and for the privatizing of welfare and the gradual phasing out of all government entitlements is urgent. More important than standing for these policies, however, is doing so righteously, not guiltily and timidly. If you understand the philosophic issues involved, you will have a chance to speak up in such a way that you can be heard.

This kind of fight is not easy, but it can be fought and won. Years ago, a well-known political writer, Isabel Paterson, was talking to a businessman outraged by some government action.

She urged him to speak up for his principles. "I agree with you totally," he said, "but I'm not in a position right now to do it."
"The only position required," she replied, "is vertical."

Note

1. Rand, A., *For the New Intellectual*, (New York: New American Library, 1961), p. 27.

Index of Company Names, Subjects, and Terms

Index of Names